Discordant Discourse
Revisiting Assam's Ethnic Issues

Discordant Discourse

Revisiting Assam's Ethnic Issues

Bitasta Das

KALPAZ

First Published, 2019

Published by

Kalpaz Publications
C-30, Satyawati Nagar,
Delhi – 110052
Ph.: 011-47034999, 9811692060
www.kalpazpublications.com
E-mail: kalpaz@hotmail.com

Printed at: G. Print Process, Delhi

Cataloging in Publication Data—DK
Courtesy: D.K. Agencies (P) Ltd. <docinfo@dkagencies.com>

Das, Bitasta, author.
Discordant discourse : revisiting Assam's ethnic issues / Bitasta Das.
pages cm
Revision of the author's dissertation (Ph. D.)—Centre for the Study of Culture and Society.
ISBN 9789353240615

1. Assam (India)—Ethnic relations. 2. Identity politics—India—Assam. 3. Ethnicity—Political aspects—India—Assam. 4. Ethnic conflict—India—Assam. 5. Assam (India)—History—Autonomy and independence movements. 6. Discourse analysis—Political aspects—India—Assam. 7. Assam (India)—Politics and government. 8. Assam (India)—Colonial influence. I. Title.

LCC DS485.A88D37 2019 | DDC 305.800954162 23

Contents

Acknowledgment

The present work owes to the endless encouragement and unflinching support of a number of people. This book is revised version of my Ph.D dissertation. The beginning of my research, at the outset, owes to the inspiration of my teachers at the Dept. of Cultural Studies of Tezpur University. The faculty of my Ph.D institute—Centre for the Study of Culture and Society (CSCS), Bangalore helped my rudimentary thoughts take shape into research questions. Subsequently, my association with the Centre for Contemporary Studies (CCS), Indian Institute of Science (IISc), Bangalore, made the completion of my research possible after much discussion and deliberation; changing the structure, organization of the manuscript to framing arguments in writing of this book. I am grateful to Prof. Raghavendra Gadagkar for providing a platform, in the form of CCS, for varied inquisitive minds to engage and share with each other. I am thankful to my esteemed colleagues Prof. Rajan Gurukkal, Dr. Uday Balakrishnan, Amrita Shah and Prof. Srinivasan Raghavendran for their invaluableadvice and support. I am indebted to Dr. Debjani Banerjee for being my sounding board and to Geetha ma'am for buffering my angst.

I thank my family for trusting me and for encouraging me to strive higher always. My sisters Bipasha, Bikalpa, Bidisha and Bidita, my brothers-in-law Tilak, Amar, Partha and Joutishman have patiently supported me as I turned my existential questions into academic questions. I thank Anthra, Rig and Jiyon for being my constant source of happiness. Lastly but not the least, I thank Vikram, my best friend and my partner for the affection and friendship and for holding me strong through thick and thin.

... for my parents

Preface

Contemporary nations are often viewed as beset by ethnic tensions. It has been widely argued that in recent times there has been an increase in intensity of ethnic conflict: that nearly half the independent countries of the world have been troubled by some degree of ethnically inspired dissonance. The word "ethnicity" is however only of recent origin. It was initially used to denote a minority group but now used to describe several wide-ranging affiliations—race, language, religion, kinship, sect, caste etc. The recent increase of use of the word "ethnicity" and the expansion of affiliations encompassed by the term "ethnic group" has come along with a rapid rise in "ethnic tensions". These developments necessitate a nuanced understanding of (a) whether the contemporary conditions have fostered a rise in ethnic tensions or (b) whether the term itself has been used to explain various tensions as ethnic tensions.

The objective of the present study, which proposes to culminate itself into a book, is to examine why tensions of the recent times often take on an ethnic dimension. It opens out the underpinning constituents of contemporary "ethnic" tensions. The study locates its inquiry on the ethnic situation in one of the Indian states—Assam. It foregrounds a need to probe beyond simplistic labeling of tensions and interrogate why the question of ethnicity has become apparently irrevocable in the case of Assam. The study argues that an overwhelming ethnic discourse exists in Assam, and that this discourse renders the imagination and expression of this region as fundamentally fragmented—ethnically.

In order to explore the discourse, the study examines three recent conflicts that have been named ethnic conflicts—the Assam Movement (1979-1985), the United Liberation Front of Assam or ULFA (1979-present) and the Bodo Movement (1987-present). All three movements had diversity: in participants, operational modality and goal. The Assam movement was an indigenous people's revolt against unchecked immigrants, the Bodo movement was a tribal uprising demanding autonomy, and the ULFA upsurge was an extremist movement aimed at secession. None of them were initiated as ethnic dissidence *per se*, and the content of ethnicity never remained the same. Examining why and how in the three instances the attempts to constitute broader identities failed and identities were reduced to specific ethnic units, the study forefronts the following argument: that while the presence and acknowledgment of diversity cannot be negated since earlier times, categorization of identities in Assam as essentially "ethnic" emerged at a specific junction—the British colonial period. Colonialism brought in a new dimension to the existing diversity; one of naturalizing the region as ethnically fragmented.

The study delves into the archival material and locates the processes that crystallized the identities of the people in ethnic terms. This work uses Michel Foucault's framework of discourse analysis to propose that colonial knowledge through various discursive strategies produced its subject. In the present study, the micro discourse of the macro British colonial knowledge is—the idea of ethnicity. It is my argument that colonial rule through the techniques of questioning and documenting every aspect of the life of the colonized masses naturalized the society of Assam in terms of ethnicity. The ethnic categories crystallized by the colonial ethnic discourse colours the imagination of the region, obstructing other modes of expression (indigenous people's identity attempted in the Assam movement, tribal identity attempted in the Bodo movement and dwellers of Assam identity attempted by the ULFA). The study claims that in this particular context ethnic expression arise from the nation's inability to emerge from the discordant colonial ethnic discourse about the region and the recurring ethnic tension is a corollary of the nation's inability to integrate all the sections of its people.

The study finally proposes that the tensions of the contemporary times need to be studied in their specific context—with respect to the dynamics that propel them to assume ethnic dimensions, in contrast to the existing parlance of unreflectively proclaiming the tensions as inherently ethnic malady.

Introduction:
Constituents of Ethnic Discourse

Contemporary nations are considered to have been beset by the rise of ethnic tensions. Studies propose that recent years have been marked by an increase in intensity of ethnic conflict and nearly half of the independent countries of the world have been troubled by some degree of "ethnically inspired dissonance"[1]. The word "ethnicity" is however of recent origin. Emergence of a new word reflects a new reality and a new usage reflects a change in that reality. The new word is "ethnicity" and the new usage is the steady expansion of the term "ethnic group". What was initially used to denote a minority group is now used to describe a wide ranging affiliation—race, language, religion, kinship, sect, caste etc. Conflicts of the present world, ranging from the ones in the Czech Republic after World War II to Hutu and Tutsi conflict in Rwanda, Catholic and Protestant in Northern Ireland, Walloon and Fleming in Belgium, Bengali and non-Bengali in (undivided) Pakistan, Chinese and Malay in Malaysia, Greek and Turk in Cyprus, Jews and other minorities on the one hand and Great Russians on the other in the Soviet Union, Ibo and Hausa and Yoruba in Nigeria as well as between the black and white in the United States have been termed as ethnic conflicts.

There is hardly any country in the world today which is not affected by ethnic concerns either socially or politically. Ethnic elements and nation building are often at odds with one another. Struggles that have been termed as ethnic are associated with nation building and state formation. Although Developmental theory, Marxist theory and general belief subscribed that with the advent of urbanization, ethnic ties would erode away but ethnicity has remained to be an extremely challenging factor in many societies and nation in the contemporary world. Subsequently, another line of belief conjectured that the forces of ethnicity may over take the national sentiment and the nation states may not long survive the ongoing outbreak of ethnic ramification. However, this too has not been proved correct. The unification of divided nations like Germany in 1990

(Federal Republic of Germany) and Vietnam in 1992 (Socialist Republic of Vietnam) have foregrounded that ethnic elements and nation building are in continuous dialogue with each other.

The recent global political scene has witnessed two types of ethnic tension: one, to form smaller units of state within the states and the other, to form larger union internationally. Europe and the break-up of the Tsarist, Ottoman and Austro-Hungarian empires saw a rampant of ethnic movement at the end of World War I. Another era that witnessed the upsurge of "ethnic" struggles in discrete parts of the world was just after decolonization, in the 1960s, like in Asia, Africa and successor states of European empires. Then again after the dissolution of Soviet Union and Yugoslav Federation in the 1990s, the conflicts that arose were termed as "ethnic". Among the more recent ones, the conflicts that have arisen in Sri Lanka, Bougainville and Balkans have been termed as "ethnic".

In the last few decades, a great deal has been written about the conflicts and the conflictual patterns and models. Ethno-national, ethno-communal, ethno-religious are some terms that have been used in the studies. Horowitz argues that all conflicts based on *ascriptive* group identities—race, language, religion, tribe, or caste—can be called ethnic (Horowitz:1985). In this usage, ethnic conflict can range from: i. Catholic-Protestant conflict in Northern Ireland and Godhra riot in India to ii. The Black-White conflict in United States and South Africato iii. The Tamil-Sinhala conflict in Sri Lanka, and iv. Shia-Sunni troubles in Pakistan can be all called "ethnic" conflicts.

The recent increase of use of the word "ethnicity" and the expansion of affiliations encompassed by the term "ethnic group" along with a record of rapid rise in "ethnic tensions" necessitates a nuanced understanding whether a) the contemporary conditions have fostered a rise in ethnic tensions or b) varied contemporary tensions have been explained as ethnic tensions. Old lines of division have been found in most of the groups who are now in tension— race, language, religion, kinship, sect, caste etc. What are the conditions then that enable to conflate them together under the label of "ethnic conflict"? What can be labelled as "ethnic" and what cannot be? Has the "labelling" facilitated or has obstructed better understanding of the tensions?

This book proposes to unravel the underpinnings that constitute contemporary tensions as "ethnic" tensions; what is the essence of the tensions that facilitate in framing them as "ethnic"? Has the deployment of the term to describe the present crisis aided or impeded our appreciation of the predicament of the contemporary times? What is the role of the nation state vis-à-vis the ethnic tensions? To explore these questions, the present book locates its study on the ethnic situation in one of the Indian states—Assam. India has engaged with ethnic contestations from various pockets at different times. Constitution Telangana from Andhra Pradesh in June 2014 and before that, three different states in November 2000—Jharkhand, Chattisgarh and Uttaranchal from Bihar, Madhya Pradesh and Uttar Pradesh respectively are recent examples of its ethnic quandary. The ongoing numerous movements[2] are more instances of the dissidence within the country. However, among all the states within the country Assam stands out in terms of its incessant assertions that have been called ethnic tensions.

Assam has broken up into five separate states even before India had completed three decade of its Independence. Present day, Assam continues to face pressing challenges of further such divisions. Demands for autonomous region within the state, claims for carving out exclusive states from the state or in extreme cases assertions for absolute secession from India are being raised consistently from various quarters. Assam was historically called a "melting pot" of diverse linguistic, religious, traditional cultures. But contemporary Assam is called an "ethnic cauldron" owing to the colossal mêlée which is largely termed as "ethnic" conflicts. The present work claims that in this particular context ethnic expression arise from the nation's inability to emerge from the discordant colonial ethnic discourse about the region and the recurring ethnic tension is a corollary of the nation's lag to integrate all the sections of its people. Thereby, the book proposes that the tensions of the contemporary times need to be studied in their specific context—with respect to the dynamics that propel them to assume ethnic dimensions, in contrast to the existing parlance of unreflectively proclaiming the tensions as inherently ethnic malady.

The approach to the present study comprises appropriate heuristic methods for the analysis of data relating to the three assertions—the Assam movement, United Liberation Front of Assam and the Bodoland movement, their socio-economic context and politico-cultural situation. A critical analysis of the data by means of conceptual tools enables us to reach out the complex synergy of the politico-cultural universe constituted by multiple ideas, institutions, relations, structures, systems and processes at the macro as well as micro levels. The socio-economic universe is not transparent. It is not visible as surface reality and therefore one has to access it through the analysis of the material basis of politico-cultural practices. The study of the socio-economic and cultural synergy of movements necessitates the use of social scientific methodology with its sophisticated heuristic techniques and social theoretical hermeneutics.

As regards the primary approach—heuristics, the present study has critically analysed the data from primary and secondary sources. The primary sources of the study consist of the original documents like slogans, songs, pamphlets, letters, diaries etc., and the data generated from the field through survey, select interviews and extended discussions. The secondary sources consist of the published and unpublished literature in the form of documents besides what is available by way of oral accounts of the participants in the movements.

As regards the secondary constituent of methodology, hermeneutics or the science of interpretation we have sought to depend on the theoretical framework of discourse analysis as enunciated by the French thinker, Michel Foucault.[3] Michel Foucault is evoked in the context of spelling out the methodology is for two reasons: the first and foremost is the suitability of his concept of discourse to comprehend the subject matter of the study, and the other is the dubiousness created by the non-technical use of the term 'discourse' by many ever since Foucault's technical coinage of it. Many social and culture studies researchers use the term in a sense neither lexical nor technical with the sad consequence of turning its semantics dubious. Discourse is a technical expression used by Foucault to mean the phenomenon of power – knowledge combine acting on people as its subjects. It involves a two way process namely objectification and subjectification, the first relating to the enunciation of new knowledge necessary for the transformation of individuals and the next relating to the constitution of subjects. It is an inseparable process in the sense that the objectification or knowledge creation is what realises the mental preparation of the individuals for being the subjects. According to Foucault meanings, passions and values are created as part of a discourse, the elements of which constitute people the subject who live in them unconsciously. Discourse as objectification of ideas and concepts or knowledge, turns people into the subject, who understand themselves as distinguished from others, and make sense of historical as well as the contemporary events around them. Circulation of ideas or the means of communication plays a crucial role in the process.

The discourse comes into being with the formation of discursive conditions that mould the thoughts of individuals who in their turn as subjects of the discourse translate their thoughts into actions as construed by the discourse. A discourse has its macro dimension with epistemic base of epochal range and myriads of discursive strategies that facilitate subjectification. It has a micro dimension of multiple minor discourses of short-term temporality. In the present study, the macro discourse of epochal range is British colonialism and the micro discourse is ethnicity. Ethnicity is conceivable as discourse in the technical sense, for the knowledge it generates and circulates leads to the transformation of people into its subjects who form part of the movement. Ethnic discourse is created and perpetuated by its subjects who acquire the resourcefulness to generate and circulate the ethnic knowledge, values, passions and morality. The whole is a process or phenomenon of power knowledge combine, too diffuse to precisely locate any conspiratorial agents behind, though those in control of the ethnic movement decide what the people do when and how.

The thrust of the present study is on the cultural dynamic rather than on the socio-economic. An attempt has been made at understanding the movements empirically and preparing a factual account of them in terms of time – space. The study part pertains to the discourse analysis of the phenomenon that encompasses all the movements under study. Taking discourse as its central framework of comprehension, the study proceeds with the identification of each movement as a discursive manifestation.

Studies on Ethnic Expressions around the World

Ethnic resurgence have been variously seen; as ways to preserve threatened cultural heritages; to soften class lines; to protect and win economic and political advantages for disadvantaged groups; and to restrict the state from attaining overwhelming power. Besides sociology, major research on ethnicity is also being carried out in such disciplines like Anthropology, Political Science, History, Economics and Social Psychology.[4] But serious study of ethnicity owes much to the works of Max Weber, who defines ethnic groups as mass status groups. Weber's perspective combines the subjective and objective aspects of ethnicity and balances their cultural and political bases. He considers primacy, political factors and historical memories in the shaping of a sense of common ethnicity and the prevailing preoccupation with cultural and biological differences in limiting ethnic affiliation. He writes:

> The belief in group affinity, regardless of whether it has any objective foundation, can have important consequences especially

> for the formation of a political community. We shall call 'ethnic groups' those human groups that entertain a subjective belief in their common descent because of similarities of physical type or of custom or both, or because of memories of colonization and migration; this belief must be important for the propagation of group formation; conversely, it does not matter whether or not an objective blood relationship exist. Ethnic membership (*Gemeinsamkeit*) differs from the kinship group precisely by being a presumed identity, not a group with concrete social action, like the latter. In our sense, ethnic membership does not constitute a group; it only facilitates group formation of any kind, particularly in the political sphere. On the other hand, it is primarily the political community, no matter how artificially organized, that inspires the belief in common ethnicity. (Weber 1975: 35)

The idea that Weber puts forward subscribes to our understanding that cohesive strength of ethnic groups arise from 'belief' which may or may not have objective foundation. According to some definitions, distinctions become "ethnicity" only when markers, such as language, religion, race etc, cease to be mere means of social distinctions but become the basis of political identity and claim to a specific role in the political process or power. No part of the world today is demographically homogenous. Migration, assimilation, intermarriage etc has enriched the world with heterogeneity. "Ethnicity", as a term, has its recorded history which is not even a century old. It was registered in the *Oxford English Dictionary* in the year1953. This was the first time it was recorded in any English dictionary (Hutchinson and Smith 1996:4). The meanings were assigned as "the essence of an ethnic group" or "the quality of belonging to an ethnic community or group" (Chapman et al., 1989:15).

"Ethnicity" is also used to refer to a distinct field of study: the classification of peoples and the relations between groups in a context of 'self-other' distinction (Eriksen, 1993:4). However, the adjective "ethnic" is believed to have originated much earlier, in the Middle Ages. "Ethnic" is considered to have its roots in the ancient Greek term *ethnos*. *Ethnos* was used to refer to non-Christian and non-Jewish pagan in New Testament Greek, as a synonym of *gentile*. *Ethnie*, is the noun form in French with an associate adjective *ethnique* which are also thought to have come from Greek roots. As the English language has no concrete noun for *ethnos* or *ethnie*, the French term is used here to denote an "ethnic community" or "ethnic group". However, it is generally agreed that ethnicity is a form of group allegiance. It denotes a kind of personal identification involving a set of symbols or traits which serve as the basis for this identification. Beyond this point, scholars are divided in opinion.

Large amount of work has been done on the concept and meanings of ethnicity and its resurgence, especially after World War II. This large quantity of material generated in the research centres, government agencies, book series, journal etc have been called "academic ethnicity industry" (Basham and DeGroot 1977:423). The immense interest in the ethnic subject not only denotes its magnitude of importance in contemporary world but also forefronts that it is rather a complex phenomenon to decipher.

The existing approaches towards the study of ethnicity can be broadly divided into two divisions: primordialists and instrumentalists. Edward Shil, Clifford Geertz and Max Weber can be reckoned as the earliest propounders to argue that ethnicity is essentially primordial in its essence. Edward Shils was the first to use the word "Primordialist" in 1957. He essentially distinguished personal, primordial, sacred and civil bonds. According to him, even in modern and civic societies, social ties, outside and apart from the civil ties still exists. Subsequently, Clifford Geertz (1963) explained that there exists some 'overpowering' and 'ineffable quality' attached to certain ties, which the participants tended to see as exterior, coercive, and 'given'. Explaining this from the perspective of tensions in peoples of new states for search of an identity and demand for progress, he affirms that this tension is due to the fact that people's sense of self remains bound to certain 'actualities'. These actualities are of blood, race, language, locality, religion or tradition. Likewise, Max Weber defines the "ethnic" groups as "those human groups that entertain subjective belief in their common descent because of similarities of physical type or of customs or both, or because of memories of colonization and migration; this belief must be important for the propagation of group formation; conversely, it does not matter whether or not an objective blood relationship exists". Strong criticisms towards the primordialist approach have come from the line of thought which rejects the discrete, unchanging character of ethnicity forwarded by the primordial stand. Eller and Coughan (1993) have attacked this line of enquiry as static and naturalistic, devoid of explanatory disposition. Other scholars maintain that in the modern world with colonialism, migration, intermarriage, assimilation etc "pure" nature of ethnic community as proposed by the primordialists stand is difficult to retain. Also, individuals attain various identities at different situations, so ethnic identities are often overlapping with other social identities and are malleable and not discrete as suggested by the stand.

The "Instrumentalist" stand proposes the opposite approach towards ethnicity. Here the role of interest and status groups is assigned utmost agency. Ethnicity is considered to be a social, political or cultural resource for these groups. In contrast to the "given, ineffable, exterior" quality of ethnicity as proposed by primordialists, ethnicity in instrumentalists' view is a social construct. One strand emphasize upon elite competition and manipulation of specific symbols for gaining support of the masses (Brass, 1991, Cohen, 1974) while other strand stresses on the strategies that elite groups apply to secure power. According to this belief, elite groups utilize certain symbols as 'rational choices' affiliating them to ethnic or national communities and generate consensus for political goals. The approach taken by Cohen, 1969, 1994; Hall, 1993 and Bhabha, 1990 is that individuals choose elements from the range of ethnic and cultural heritage to construct their group or individual identities. The instrumentalists stand has been criticized for assigning pure materialistic interest to the ethnies. Strong criticisms have come from Connor's subjectivist and Fishman's historical critiques. According to them, ethnies and nations have long aroused collective fervour that many other social identities have failed to do. Therefore, the significance of ethnies cannot be diluted as mere interest oriented collectivity. Recent studies have meanwhile forwarded radical primordial approach to the study of ethnicity. Sociobiologists have forwarded genetic reproduction theory to explain the solidarity of ethnies. According to them, the mechanism of "nepotism" and "inclusive fitness" bind the group together. The myths of descent correspond to this nepotism in comprising the ethnic groups. This line of belief is not void of criticism. Reynolds, 1980; Van de Berghe 1986 have attacked this line of thought for percolating the social realities to biological drives, also this theory fails to explain the solidarity within large ethnic groups and nations. Mc Kay 1982 and Scott 1990 have attempted to combine primordial and instrumentalist approaches together on a theoretical level. But the empirical accuracy of this theory is still not evident. Three other significant approaches towards the study of ethnicity have been that of Fredrick Barth's emphasis on the social boundaries. For him maintenance of ethnic boundaries, rather than the cultural content it encloses, is important for the perpetuation of the ethnic groups. According to him ethnic groups persists through specific 'border guard', like language, customs, dress etc. though transaction through these boundaries often take place. Donald Horowitz's "social psychological" and Armstrong and Smith's "ethno symbolic" are two other approaches that have been proposed in the recent times. Horowitz (1985) approach relates mainly to non-colonial context. For him ethnic groups' strength lies on their cultural and economic resources. These resources determine the strategies of the ethnic groups. According to this approach the base of the ethnic groups lie on kinship and is consolidated by the historical account.

However, it is unhelpful. Ethnicity is not a static or fixed entity. Like culture, ethnicity continuously renews, rebuilds, reformulates itself in accordance to external circumstances and structural changes in the society. For instance, the conventional ethnic divisions in Peninsular Malaysia are "Malay", "Chinese", "Indian" and "Other". According to the constitution of Malaysia, "Malay" is a person born locally, habitually speaks Malay, follows Malay custom and follows Islam. However, a group *Peranakan* who had been originally of Chinese origin have adopted much of Malay culture and including cuisine, dress, language and religion. Adoption of these features, typically have allowed them to qualify as Malay (Hirchman: 1987). The "cultural content" that most line of enquiry, especially the Primordialist, emphasizes upon had been historically "created" through a complex interaction of the social, economic and political aspects which became "natural" over the period of time. On the other hand, the "created" nature of ethnicity that Instrumentalist and few other perspectives hold also gets "naturalised" and get embedded in the ethnic life with time. Therefore, study of ethnicity in the precise compartmental purview does not adequately serve in understanding the dynamic attribute of ethnicity. Primordial and Instrumental aspects of ethnicity are ways in which ethnicity maintains and renews itself.

There has been a tendency to reduce a wide range of conflicts as "ethnic" conflict in the recent times. In contrast to this, the book proposes that such categorization is not helpful to understand and appreciate the crux of the problem and the reason why "ethnic" tensions have become endemic. Such categorization eventually reduces the complexities of the problem by placing them under a large rubric. Analysis of each tension in its own historical and political context provides us a lucid understanding of problem and why similar tensions have become rampant.

In the case of Assam, the colonial ethnic discourse has played a major role in defining the population strictly on "ethnic" terms. The "ethnic" tensions in this context are residues of the colonial practice of identifying the people of Assam according to their ethnic affiliation.

Mapping Assam's Ethnic identities

The state of Assam, situated at the geographic north-eastern region of India, lies between 89 degree 42 minutes E longitude to 96 degree E longitude and 24 degree 8 minutes N latitudes to 28 degree 2 minutes N latitudes. It is surrounded by Arunachal Pradesh, Nagaland, and Manipur in the east; Mizoram and Meghalaya in the south; and Tripura in the west. Assam shares international boundaries with Bhutan in the northwest and Bangladesh in the southwest. Except for a narrow corridor running through the foothills of the Himalayas connecting the state with West Bengal, Assam is almost entirely isolated from rest of India. It comprises a total land area of 78,438 square km. The river Brahmaputra flows along its east to west distributing many tributaries both in the northern and southern bank. The eastern high land is generally called the Upper Assam and the western low land the lower Assam. Brahmaputra along with its many tributaries creates the fertile Brahmaputra valley. While in the south, the Barak river forms the Barak valley. Assam consists of twenty three districts among which KarbiAnglong and North Cachar are two hill districts, situated between the two valleys. Assam is one of the richest biodiversity zones in the world. The dense forest consists of tropical rainforests, deciduous forests, riverine grasslands, bamboo orchards, Sal tree forest and numerous wetland ecosystems. Kaziranga and Manas are the two UNESCO World Heritage Sites in Assam. In addition to these there are three more National Parks and eleven Wildlife Sanctuaries in Assam. Besides the rare one horned rhinoceros, the forests homes numerous other endangered flora and fauna. Three hundred and fifty plants found in these forests have been recorded to have medicinal values together with a range of exquisite orchids. Golden Langur, White-winged Wood Duck, Bengal Florican, Black-breasted Parrotbill, Pygmy Hog, Greater Adjutant, Tiger, Elephant, Hoolock Gibbon, Jerdon's Babbler are few of the endangered fauna still surviving in these forests. Majuli island situated within Brahmaputra in the upper Assam is the largest river island of the world. Assam is endowed with petroleum, natural gas, coal, limestone natural resources and minerals such as magnetic quartzite, kaolin, sillimanites, clay and feldspar are also found here. It is among the highest tea producing regions of the world. Needless to add, Assam has very rich natural resources that can be the bone of contention between the state government and the Central government.

Assam was called Pragjyotispura in the ancient times. It is believed that in the Indian epic *Mahabharata* as well as in some principal Puranas, like the *KalikaPurana,* the region that is mentioned to as Pragjyotispura is (undivided) Assam. In other inscriptional and scriptural ancient documents the province has been referred to as Lauhitya and Kamrupa. Some scholars believe that the present name "Assam" is derived form of the word "Asom". "Asom" has its origin in Sanskrit which means peerless or unparalleled and Assam is its Anglicised version derieved from the British. According to another strand of beliefs this word originates and describes the might of the Ahom dynasty which ruled Assam for six hundred years in the medieval period. Assam became a part of British India in 1826 with the signing of the Treaty of Yandaboo with the Burmese. The Burmese had invaded Assam in the early 19th century. The British defeated them in three subsequent battles between 1824 to 1826 and were finally able to establish its domination in Assam, Manipur, Rakhine (Arakan) and Taninthayi (Tenasserim). British Assam consisted of a much larger region including present Arunachal Pradesh, Meghalaya, Mizoram and Nagaland. These states finally separated from Assam after the Independence.

Assam had been ruled by various dynasties at various times of the history. The Varmanas ruled from c. 350 to 650 AD), the Salstambhas (Xalostombho) from c.655 to 900 AD and the Kamarupa-Palasfrom c.900 to 1100 AD. Later, in the medieval period two dynasties, the Ahoms and the Koch emerged as powerful empires. The Ahoms, a Tai group, ruled Assam for nearly 600 years (1228–1826 AD). The nerve centre of Ahom polity was upper Assam; the kingdom was gradually extended till KaratoyaRiver in the c.17th–18th AD. The Koch kingdom, a Tibeto-Burmese, established sovereignty in c.1510 AD in western Assam and present North Bengal. Among the other dynasties, the Chutiyas ruled north-eastern Assam and parts of present Arunachal Pradesh and the Kacharis ruled from DikhowRiver to central and southern Assam. With expansion of Ahom kingdom, by c.1520 AD the Chutiya areas were annexed and since c.1536 AD Kacharis remained only in Cachar and North Cachar more as an Ahom ally then a competing force. However, despite numerous invasions, mostly by the Muslim rulers, western powers were unsuccessful in invading Assam until the arrival of the British. Assam therefore has had a distinct political history and dissimilar rule compared to the rest of India (Baruah 1985). Due to its unique geographical location, it was more susceptible to invaders from the (now known) south-east Asian countries. The various reigns left their discrete marks in the socio-cultural matrix of Assam through coercion or integration. This separate history has influenced the socio-cultural imagination about Assam and about its corresponding demographical constituent. The demography of Assam is commonly believed to consist of people from wide ranging ethnic groups. As has been mentioned, every study of Assam, official or non-official, anthropological, sociological or political, inevitably subscribe to the idea that the land is "culturally divergent and ethnically variegated". Assam has inevitably been considered to be a repository of people inflowing from various regions, mostly from south-east Asia. Being a land frontier and because it is connected to the rest of India only by a narrow strip of land, the people and their culture are generally believed to have closer affiliations with the people of adjoining border countries rather than that of rest of India. These sociological writings along with, government records, the prevalent stereotypes, all conform to the view that Assam, so also the entire north-east region, as a geographical and cultural entity is distant from mainland India. India, in this book, is not just an "ideological apparatus of state power;" neither is it a nostalgia for a national culture. It is more Bhabha's sense of a nation that is narrated and Assam is at least one of its ambivalent margins[5]

The present official demographic constitution of contemporary Assam includes: the "ethnic" Assamese, 14 Scheduled Hill Tribes, 9 Scheduled Plain Tribes, the Tea Garden Tribal community, the immigrants (consisting of the people mainly from Bangladesh and Nepal) besides a section of people who have moved into Assam from other parts of India. The *People of India* project conducted by the Anthropological Survey of India (ASI), a government of India initiative that began in 1985, has identified 115 ethnic groups in Assam. The Austroasiatic are considered to be the earliest settlers, followed by Tibeto-Burman, Indo-Aryan and the Kradai speakers. Forty-five languages are identified to be spoken by different communities, including three major language families: Austroasiatic (5), Sino-Tibetan (24) and Indo-European (12). Three of the spoken languages do not fall in these families. Hinduism, Islam, Christianity, Sikhism, Animism and Buddhism are recognized as the major religions here. Discussing the origin and cultural affinity of the people of Assam, *People of India* says:

> The people of Assam are chiefly of Austro-Asiatic and Tibeto-Burman origin whether they are Hinduised or not, and have contributed to the various aspects of composite Assamese culture. The foundation of the social system marriage laws etc, of the speakers of Aryan languages and Aryanised Hindus of the valleys is based on the cultures of earlier people, including their laws of exogamy, totemism and so on. In the field of economy and cottage industries, there is

evidence of the contribution made particularly by the speakers of Bodo language. In the evolution of the various religious cults, fetishism, animism, cult of fertility and phallus etc, the non-Aryan tribes laid, the foundation of Saktaism and Tantricism in Assam. The harvesting ceremonies of the Assamese people which have Aryan or Hindu affinities also have been greatly influenced by the tribes. The same influence can be detected in some measure in art and architecture. Though Assam is fundamentally allied to the rest of India, it has retained its separate entity with local variation.

The racial composition of Assam has produced its distinct influence on the linguistic map of the state in general; different people and tribes from across the state frontiers, met here and they have, in the course of time, contributed to the growth and development of a common speech called Assamese. The word 'Assamese' is an Anglicised formation. The people call this land Asom, and the word Asomiya derived from it means the language and the people who speak it. Assamese is a composite language into which words of both Indo-Aryan and Indo-Chincse origin have found their way. Besides, other pre-Aryan and non-Aryan influences are discernible, not only in loanwords but also in grammar, syntax and pronunciation. Of all the language groups in the state, the Tibeto-Burman is by far the largest. The largest component of this is the Bodo language group consisting of the Kacharis, the Koches, the Rabhas, the Hojais, the Lalungs and the Morans and the Chutiyas. Most of them speak different dialects, but all of them have together contributed to the growth and formation of the Bodo and thc Assamese languages. The home of the Bodo language group is mainly in the Brahmaputra valley. The Bodos have a wider range of influence on the Assamese language; the survivals of the Bodo place names and name of rivers till today bears testimony to this fact. The prefix *di* or *ti* are used before different river names, *di* means "water" in the Bodo language. The Assamese language, on the other hand, influenced the different Bodo dialects, particularly in points of loan words. In course of time, the non-Aryan speakers were compelled by historical forces to become bilingual. Most of them ultimately became Assamese speakers. The reason why the Mongoloid tribes like the Ahoms, the Rabhas and the rest have, to a considerable extent, forsaken their tribal dialects in favour of Assamese language are not far to seek: Assamese is the language of the Hindu priest; and in the process of conversion of these people from tribal beliefs to Hinduism, the priest

> introduced their own language. The Tibeto-Burmans and the Mongoloids invaded Assam from the north-east; the Aryans came from the north-west. The references to the kingdom of Kamrupa and its people in the epics and the Puranas testify that the Aryan priest and warriors came to Assam at a very early date; they also brought with them their religion and Sanskrit language. These diverse influences from different sources have combined to make the Assamese language an important member of the Indo-Aryan family of languages. (*People of India*: 2003 13, 14)

Similarly, the gazetteers of India had identified the diversity within the population of Assam. This diversity is acknowledged on the basis of their physical traits:

> Out of Assam's population of nearly 9 million (1951), 4.69% are Scheduled Castes and 19.48% are Scheduled Tribes. Classified data are available for 12 tribes like the Arleng, Bodo, Khasi, Garo and others. They are medium in stature in over 50% cases and short in about 30%. The head is mesocephalic in 50% cases, but there are some interesting deviations. The Koc (88), Hill Garo (100) and Plain Garo (100) have dolichocephals in the following proportion 60%, 53% and 47%. This is followed by high figures for mesocephaly, namely, 31%, 44% and 46%. Brachycephalic and hyperbrachycephalic heads are few, though among the Ahoms (19) this rises to very high figure (31%+26%. The Khasi (237) and the Mi-Shing (Miri) (25) have more than 16% brachycephals each, the latter have also hyperbrachycephaly in 8% cases. The nose is mesorrhine in over 60%. The percentage of Chamarrhine and hyperchamarrhine is also fairly high among the Khasi (25%, 2.5%), Koc (24%, 7%), Hill Garo (46%, 4%), Mi-Shing (Miri) (*Gazetteers of India*: 1965)

This description is not much different from the historians' accounts. History of Assam has been made parallel with the history of the people migrating and habituating the region. Historians, within and outside Assam, hold the same view that the inflow and the confluence of varied races is the bedrock on which the history of this region is based. Dr. Balaram Chakravorti, who has contributed a huge numbers of writings on historical, cultural and ancestral matter of India and other countries, writes about the people of Assam while accentuating their difference:

> From the very ancient times different groups of people of different ethnicity, culture, religion and following various customs and traditions began to live in the valley of the Brahmaputra. Some of them were

> autochthonous while others came across the Northern or the Eastern hills or from the plains on the west as, traders or pilgrims. Assam is originally a land of tribal people. We know from the anthropologists that the Khasis and the Jaintias were the most ancient inhabitants of Assam, who were of the Austric race. They were followed by the great Nagas and Danavas who were the descendents of Abotani spreading across to Polynesia and Transpacific countries. Then the Kiratas of Mongolian stock followed them. There after came the Asuras from Mithila headed by Naraksura who brought in the Sanskrit speaking Brahmanas (Devas) from the interior states of India. The land grants of Asura testify to this.
>
> The larger modern Assam is occupied by various tribes like the Bodo, the Kachari, the Garo, the Chutia, the Morans while the Adis, the Apatanis, the Mithings, Meiteis etc. belong to the Danava race. They are off-shoots of the great stock of the Kirata race with different titles.
>
> In the 13th century A.D., at the time of the Ahoms the two powerful branches of Bodos named the Kacharis and the Chutias were ruling over a large part of eastern Assam. At last the group of Sanskrit-speaking people entered Assam with their own distinct culture and heritage through the North-Eastern and the Northern passes from Pamir region, called the Alpines. Some of the Deva groups, who were also Sanskrit speaking came directly from the North from the mountain passes and began to reside in the eastern regions of Assam including Kamrupa. The culture and civilization of Assam is a composite mixture of Sanskrit-speaking Devas and non-Sanskrit speaking elements. (Chakravorti 2000: 10-11)

This view of Dr.Chakravorti, expressing the fragmentary nature of the population of Assam has been the standard way of describing the region. There are innumerable examples which subscribes to the same idea. Historian N.N. Acharyya (Acharyya 1992:272-73) referring to the diversity of Assam concludes that the Karbis, the descendents of Austric race, were the first inhabitants of this region. The Kirats belonging to Mongoloid race migrated from the Western parts of China and speak Sino-Tibetan language. The tribes like Bodo, Garo, Rabha, Deuries, Misings, Morans, Chutias, Dimasas and Koches (Rajbongshi), Lalung, and Hajong also belong to the Mongoloid race. The Kaibartas and Banias from Drabirian race came to Assam from the Mediterranean coast. The Aryans from Caucasian race have migrated from the Gangetic plains to

Assam, as early as the 1st century AD, when the region was under the rule of the Mongoloid kings:

> The majority of the people of Assam are of Mongoloian stock. A range of sub-Himalayan Hills from the north-east to the north-west is inhabited by the people of Tibeto-Burman origin, the Mishmis, the Abhors, the Miris, the Daflas and the Akas. The extreme north-eastern hills are inhabited by the Khamtis and the Singphos while the Patkai Range on the south-east has been permanently the abode of the aboriginal Nagas. Beginning from the extreme south-west the whole area covered by the Garo, the Khasi, the Jayantia, and the various branches of the Naga Hills are inhabited by the peoples of the same names. Further south from the Nagaland dwell the Manipuris.
>
> The most important and numerous of the various Tibeto-Burman races of Assam are the Bodos. These include the Koches, the Meches, the Lalungs, the Dimasa, the Garos, the Rabhas, the Tripuras, the Chutias, the Morans and the Borahis. This stock claims to be the original inhabitants of Assam. Before the rise of the Ahoms, the Bodos controlled the political destiny of Ancient Assam and constituted a synthetic culture over the region bordering the banks of the life-giving Brahmaputra.
>
> In the beginning of the thirteenth century, the Tais or Shans entered Assam through its north-eastern frontier. Among them the Ahoms were the most numerous and powerful and became the ruling clan of Assam for the next six centuries. The other Shan tribes which accompanied them were the Phakials, the Naras, and the Aitonias, most of whom now inhabits the eastern extremit y of Assam. (Acharyya 1992: 10-11)

Delineating the culture and civilization of India, Marxist historian D.D. Kosambi writes:

> In Assam, where every valley has several tribes and different speech, the number of languages or major dialects rises to over 175, mostly tribal idioms, which cannot be related to Mundari or indeed even to any one linguistic group. (Kosambi 1970:41).

This perception and description of Assam as a land inhabited by numerous and wide ranging communities has been the essence of its socio-political matrix. Official, unofficial, historic, anthropological, folk, literary, no context refrains from the narrative that Assam's demography is a variegated composition. While the heterogeneous composition of the population might be considered an irrefutable fact, the depiction of this reality is overloaded with detrimental connotation. The imagination of Assam as a region subsisting with numerous identities is at odds with and definitely inferior to the single Brahmanical/Aryan racial composition seen in major parts of mainland India. This notion, I purport has not changed even after post modernist celebration of plurality. The unitary racial composition was seen as superior and as a strong backbone to building a community. In contrast, Assam is still viewed as a challenge to this national unity.

Assam, located in geographical margin of India, has been ostensibly marginalised from the central idea of the nation. To understand this marginalisation we need to understand the location of Assam.

Recounting Assam's "Ethnic" Problem

The unique feature that differentiates Assam from other Indian states is the embedded narrative that endorses Assam as the homeland of a wide ranging cultures and races. This narrative finds place in every political, social and cultural jargon and imagination. The descriptions not only subscribe to variation in language, religion and traditions but also indicate racial differences. Assam has witnessed scores of conflicts after Independence. These conflicts have demonstrated themselves in various forms. They were sometimes demands for recognition of a particular language as the official language, at times upsurges for separate state, sometimes stir for greater share in development and in the most extreme cases, secessionist demands. At Independence, the Assam plains, the hill districts, the North East Frontier Tracts (NEFT) and the princely states of Manipur and Tripura comprised of the region that we today know as the north-east India[6].

The tensions started immediately after Independence with Naga insurgency demanding secession from India. Naga National Council (NNC) first presented the demand for autonomous status of the Naga in a memorandum to the British colonial rulers in 1945. After Independence this demand took a new turn. The Naga leaders claimed home rule for the Naga tribe on the basis of distinct ethnic identity, customary law, original social system, religion etc. After Phizo took over the reigns of NNC the demand for independence from India started gaining grounds. In 1950 NNC declared that they would hold a referendum to decide whether the Nagas should attain independence from India or remain in India. The referendum conducted in 1951was said to indicate that ninty- nine percent of Nagas wanted independence. Goverment of India rejected this result.

Public disobedience and gradual aggravation to intense violence followed thereafter. In 1957 Naga hill district was separated from Assam and in 1963 Nagaland was given full statehood. Following this, the many assertions were intensified as demand for secession or separate homeland spread to various groups in the region. In 1960 representatives of hill areas formed All Party Hill Leaders Conference and demanded separation of hill areas from Assam. The movement for statehood continued and in 1970 Meghalaya Autonomous State was established and in 1972 Meghalaya became a full-fledged stated. The formation of Meghalaya was more or less peaceful as the hill area was distinctive insofar its population which largely consisted on Khasi and Garo tribes who inhabitated specific areas in the region and demands were made fairly under the constitutional framework. The Lushai hill district that was part of the excluded area during the British rule was renamed as Mizo hill district of Assam in 1954. A separatist movement was already active during the colonial period. However, against the backdrop of Assam government's failure to provide adequate relief during the famine of 1959-61, the Mizo National Front led by Laldenga intensified its demand to separate from Assam. After a prolonged period of violence, Mizoram was given the status of Union Territory of India in 1972 and in 1987 was accorded full statehood. The North East Frontier Agency NEFA) was rechristend as Arunachal Pradesh and was given full statehood through initiative of the Central government. Realizing the distinct ethnic composition and Arunachal Pradesh's strategic importance being adjacent to China, it was accorded full statehood in 1982.

As a result colonial Assam was divided into five states; a phenomenon unique among all the states of the country. The Karbis of the KarbiAnglong district launched a movement for autonomous state (they already had an autonomous district council). After this, the demand for "ethnic" homeland was adopted by various other groups of the state such as the Mising, the Tiwas, the Rabhas etc. Each of these groups today has its own autonomous district council with varying powers, with or without well-defined territorial boundaries. The process has not attained a closure yet. Since many years the Koch-Rajbonshis have been agitating for a separate Kamatapur state, incorporating eleven districts in the Brahmaputra valley and six districts in North Bengal region. The Nationalist Socialist Council of Nagaland (IM) contention for 'Nagalim' (Naga homeland) incorporates a large tract of land which is habitat of several tribes of Assam like the Karbis, Dimasa-Kacharis etc.The ULFA, the Bodoland movement continues to demand for separation. Together with these, there is the looming immigrant's issue that has been propelling immense tension in the social and political context of Assam. In all these assertions, post Independence, two features have been common, first is the shared belief in unique and distinct cultural identity and second is the idea of definite homeland.

There have been various opinions and explanations on this plethora of assertions. All these explanations, however, subscribe to the ideas that Assam is fundamentally a site that houses multiple contesting groups which are essentially "ethnic" in character and that these assertions are inevitably "ethnic assertions".

For Sanjib Baruah, "To be sure, there are no easy solutions to Assam's immigration crisis. But what is striking is the disjuncture between the way the immigration crisis has destabilized Assam — including today's two insurgencies and political and ethnic violence, some of which look suspiciously like ethnic cleansing campaigns —and the low priority given to the issue by India's policymakers". (Baruah 1999: 204). UdayonMisra proposes that, "The reiteration of the polyethnic nature of the Assamese society on the one hand and the rather obsessive quest for a unilingual identity on the other, has been one of the major contradictions which the Assamese middle class has not been able to resolve till date. The struggle for the restoration of the status of the Assamese language is known history. But, the fallout of the struggle spilled over well into the seventies and the eighties". (Misra 1999: 1265). For Paul Brass, after the Independence, violent agitations for linguistic states, and autonomy for cultural regions as Dravidastan, Punjabi Suba, Jharkhand, Telangana, and the North-east Frontier regions induced the Congress leadership and the government to pursue a set of rules and strategy supposed to be more pluralist. Brass earmarks four such informal rules adopted by the central government, which would: (i) suppress any group making secessionist demands, (ii) never accommodate regional demands based on religious differences, (iii) concede to separate linguistic states only when backed by popular support and mobilization, and (iv) not reorganize the states if the demand was made by one language group only. Brass articulates that the regional demands and regionalism, in the later years got expressed in other form of mobilization based on ethnicity. (Brass 1990). Sajal Nag (1990) ascribes the ethnic assertions to economic disparity while Amalendu Guha (1977) to the chauvinism of Assamese middle class[7].

However, the existing explanations fail to bring forth why, none but, ethnic sentiments have been evoked to attain the desired goals, whereas the dissonances pointed out by them have ranged from political exclusion to economic inequity to social discrimination etc. No coherent understanding is available among the present studies pertaining to unbridled ethnic dissidence. The various assertions and conflicts are regarded as subsequent expressions of the different ethnicities living alongside. In contrast to these explanations, the book proposes that the various tensions that have occurred in Assam after the Independence have their own specific epistemic trajectory and particular ostensible goals. The tensions have raised pertinent issues like the question of land rights, unemployment, financial inequity, underdevelopment, education and industrial backwardness, social discrimination etc. However, all the issues have been interpreted as ethnic dissidence. A judicious understanding of the crisis that has plagued Assam's socio-political situation has been circumvented by promulgating them as ethnic tensions. The book emphasizes that there is a dominant ethnic discourse of Assam in place and the asserting group, irrespective of the content of their goals and demands, cannot but appropriate the identities conforming to this discourse during the process of their assertion. The ethnic discourse of Assam contrives in two folds: expropriates the varied assertions within its fold and at the same time dispenses an archetype which the asserting groups replicate in the process of their assertion. This discourse therefore impedes critical understanding of the crux of each assertion. The ethnic discourse of Assam has rarely been examined. The emergence, operative modalities and the reason for assuming such influential pinnacle is yet to be unravelled. The book proposes to analyse this ethnic discourse of Assam through the study of three contemporary assertions which have been termed as ethnic assertions—the Assam movement, ULFA and the Bodoland movement.

The ethnic discourse of Assam has been the prerogative of sociologist, historians and administrative documents. However a new dimension to these studies has been added recently.Political scientist Sanjib Baruah, whose eminent work *India Against Itself Assam and the Politics of Nationality* (1999) engages with the multiple assertions in Post Independent Assam, forefronts the difficulties in unfurling the ethnic discourse of Assam. He, by choice, refers to the assertions as "subnationalist" predicaments and locates these conflicts in the contradictions inherent in the "modern" institution, the nation state. According to him the communities in Assam "coexist and are occasionally in tension with the pan-Indian national community, are best located in the intellectual universe of the nation and nationalism" (Baruah 1999: 5). He treats these sub-national challenges as apparent consequences of India's nation-building process; India grew out of anti-colonial movements and its nationalism was inspired by the nationalism of the West, but in practice, unlike the West, Indian nation building process was to constituent a nation that was by and large opposite to "ethnically and linguistically homogeneous entities" which is standard form of Western nationalism. Baruah considers sub-nationalism as a modern phenomenon which emerged simultaneously with nationalism. The agency that he assigns to sub-nationalism is that, sub-nationalism is a poetics that transforms the geography of an area to a primal, homelike or sacred space and transforms a people into a collectivity with imagined ties of shared origin and kinship.

Well-known Marxist scholar of Assam Hiren Gohain emphasizes on economic reasons for the unprecedented upsurges after Independence (Gohain 1997). In his view the decades following Independence, the democratic constitution and the welfare state whetted the appetite of the masses for a better life, while the actual functioning of the Constitution which was in the grip of the ruling classes in India did not provide sufficient means for fulfilling economical aspirations of the discrete groups. Awakening to a new level of consciousness, these various groups began to organize and clamour for better opportunities for development. Remaining outside the pale of the laboriously constructed nation or nationalities during the colonial phase, they now started demanding an active political role for themselves. In this new environment, he explains, the ethnic movements found a tremendous fillip.

Monirul Hussain (Hussain 2000) who has done extensive studies on post colonial politics in Assam, asserts that the post colonial Indian state has failed in dealing with the in-built pluralism of Assam. He considers Assam to be historically multi-racial, multi-religious, multi-ethnic, multi-caste, multi-class and multi-lingual in composition wherein the *Asamiyas*[8] have constituted the majority national group. Sociologically, Assam's society, according to his view, has been extraordinarily plural in its composition and highly uneven in structure. Ideologues and the leadership of all the ethnic movements have failed to comprehend the hard historical reality that Assam, particularly the Brahmaputra valley has been a shared homeland of innumerable racial, religious, linguistic, ethnic and cultural groups migrated from all the directions at different points of time. It has made not only society in Assam, but also the *Asamiya* nationality highly plural in its composition. Hence, there is no alternative to human and democratic living in a shared homeland. It is obviously possible to maintain one's identity and autonomy in a shared space. He states that privileging the political and social rights of one group over another, both by the asserting group and the state would be drastically ahistorical.

Three of the "insiders" view expressed from different stand points to the same belief that the diversity of Assam is self-evident. These assertions and conflicts are explained by considering that in Assam the cultural and ethnic factors belong to a wide range. The sub-nationalism aspirations explained by Baruah, economic imbalance instated by Gohain or the historical unity emphasized by Hussain, all of these explanation fall short of providing a comprehensive understanding of why and how the ethnic factor in Assam has obtained the level of sole definitive factor of identity formation. The politics and mass mobilization weaved entirely around ethnicity has not been delved satisfactorily, the underpinnings that constitute and inspire politicization of the ethnic factors are left unanswered.

In such an academic and social context where categorization and their consequent politicization are regarded as self explanatory, it is pertinent to ask what constitutes these categories. And why have these categories rendered so influential in the making of the society and state in the region in specific and in the nation in general. Thus we will derive at an understanding of yet another instance of relentless ethnic upsurge in the contemporary world.

The composite state of Assam, when the British left, consisted of: the territory of the last ruling dynasty the Ahoms, Goalpara district ruled in the past by a number of princely families related to the ruling house of Cooch Bihar, certain areas ceded by Bhutan, hill districts inhabited by the Nagas, Khasis and Garos, the Cachar district which used to be ruled by a Bodo dynasty and fragments of Sylhet left inside Assam after Partition. The Assam Land and Revenue Regulation Act (1886) was amended by the Assam Government and a new chapter (Chapter X) called "Protection of Backward Classes" was added. According to this new legislation, the State Government had to specify the backward classes who needed protection, form tribal belts and blocks in compact areas inhabited by these backward classes, and control the settlement of wasteland and transfer of already settled lands in these belts and blocks. Under the authority given by this new law, the State Government classified the following as "backward classes" in Chapter X: the Plain Tribals, Hill Tribals and Scheduled Castes. According to this, 38 tribal belts and blocks were created to safeguard the interest of the inhabitants.

States Reorganization Commission 1955 recommended that besides maintaining the old boundaries of Assam, the states Manipur and Tripura (the two north-eastern states that had not been part of Assam) be merged with Assam. This did not become possible, instead four new states were eventually carved out: Nagaland in 1963, Meghalaya in 1970 and Mizoram and Arunachal Pradesh in 1972. Sanjib Baruah calls these divisions "a lack of fit between the linguistically based nation-province and the ethnopolitical reality of Assam" (Baruah 1999:97). Nevertheless, these separations were the pioneers among the host of autonomy/secessionist movements that ensued in Assam[9]. The problem of "excluded area" in Assam was reviewed by a committee set up by the Constituent Assembly under the chairmanship of Gopinath Bardaloi, the first Chief Minister of Assam. The recommendation of the Bardaloi Committee was incorporated in the Sixth Schedule of the Constitution of India. Among these, the most important one relates to the provision for the establishment of autonomous District councils in some of the hill areas. This initiated a new era of autonomy in the region. Most of the group assertions that followed in Assam were centred around the provisions of the Sixth Schedule.

Amalendu Guha in his eminent work *Planter Raj to Swaraj* (1977) argues that unlike in several other parts of India, the north-eastern region of India was not in the process of forming distinct nationalities even at its initial stage in pre-British days. It consisted of a large number of territories each inhabited by a distinct groups and ruled by its king. Even the most developed group among them—Ahoms had not developed the characteristics of an emerging nation capable of bringing the other groups into its overlordship.

It is my contention that Assam has been a region marked by the presence of discrete cultural groups since the ancient times. These historic communities living in a common space shared interpersonal relationships and cultural dialogues that constituted the composite culture of Assam. The various communities have shared significant similarities in language, social customs, festivals, cultural symbols etc. The cultural interaction and sharing had enabled an inclusivist co-existence. The folklore and other evidence like the Ahom *Buranjis* substantiate that the society in Assam had survived through mutual interchange among the various communities. However, the recent upsurge over territory and autonomy implicates that the identities have adorned an exclusivist tendency that colour their political imagination. This rush for cultural and social distinctiveness is fashioned by aspirations to acquire political mileage through the projection of unique identities. Though the various identities came together at few instances but they scattered very soon. The book proposes that the macro discourse of colonial knowledge had successfully established a micro discourse of ethnicity of the people of Assam. The pervading discourse not only obstructs any other mode of identity formation to emerge but also colours every imagination of the region.

Michel Foucault's proposition of discourse analysis is to unravel the repressive knowledge-power combine and establish newer genealogies:

> By comparison, then, and in contrast to the various projects which aim to inscribe knowledges in the hierarchical order of power associated with science, a genealogy should be seen as a kind of attempt to emancipate historical knowledges from that subjection, to render them, that is, capable of opposition and of struggle against the coercion of a theoretical, unitary, formal and scientific discourse. It is based on a reactivation of local knowledges—of minor knowledges, as Deleuze might call them—in opposition to the scientific hierarchisation of knowledges and the effects intrinsic to their power: this, then, is the project of these disordered and fragmentary genealogies. (Foucault 1980:85)

The present work attempts to unravel the underpinnings that constitute the ethnic discourse of Assam through examining the framing of the ethnic question in the assertions. Thereby, the book foregrounds that the representation of diversity in the discourse constitutes a canon which colours the imagination of the region.

Colonial Categorization and Construction of Identities

All asserting groups of Assam, either while demanding greater share in development, recognition of a particular language, regional autonomy or secession, recounts, a consolidated narrative about their culture and ancestral dynasty. This narrative provides a sense of territorial origin and locates them to a region that they rightfully claim to be their "homeland". Scholars have pointed out that this sense of "homeland" has been the crux of the autonomy and secessionist demands that lurks at the face of contemporary Assam. Many observers have pointed out that this sense of rooting an identity to a specific territorial zone is actually the repercussion of the colonial cartography and their general tendency of adhering communities to a particular geographical location. Sanjib Baruah (1999) points out two colonial policies that made significant impact on the political and cultural destiny of Assam. These were: a) Considering

Assam to be an extension of Bengal, b) Segregation of the hill through the inner line system. These two factors, according to him, remain the most important determinants of Assam's troubled postcolonial political history.

> More than any other factor, colonial geography shaped the projects of peoplehood in Assam: the Assamese subnational narratives and the counter-narratives as well as political agendas that followed from these narratives. Starting from the formation of Nagaland in 1963, the hill ares were gradually separated from Assam... The separation of the once excluded areas from Assam in some ways was the culmination of colonial policy of segregation. Ironically, one factor pushing the alienation of hill people from the plains people was the Assamese desire to have cultural policies that defined the state as Assamese— a desire that was historically fueled by politics of resistance to the other idiosyncrasy of colonial geography: the notion of Assam as an extension of Bengal. The cultural politics of Assamese Assam and the resistance to being treated as a land frontier of Bengal became two central themes in the conflictual subnational politics of Assam in postcolonial times. (Baruah 1999: 43).

While the translation of the colonial cartography to identity formation still is a domain that demands underpinning in Baruah's work, nevertheless his perspective brings to the fore two important patterns in which identities are formulated in Assam. The first is through categories and the second through a continuous validation and negation of the colonial categories.

The British government, as Baruah notes, had not invested in historical or cultural continuity in drawing the borders of the administrative unit of Assam after its annexation in 1826. Instead, the goal was to attain an inexpensive and effective way of administration. Assam was considered to be a land frontier of Bengal and was placed under Bengal Presidency till 1874. In 1874 it was made into a Chief Commissioner's province; yet the idea that Assam was but an appendage to Bengal remained and the Bengali dominated district of Sylhet was added to this new province from East Bengal. Baruah writes:

> But the Lieutenant General of Bengal was obsessed with the idea of Bengal, Sir George Campbell, was obsessed with the idea of the political boundaries of the new unit of Assam coinciding with the natural boundary line drawn up (by) the Meghna and the Surma; following the boundaries of the district of Sylhet and Mymensingh, thence round the Garo hills to the Brahmaputra and then across the

> Duars of the Himalayas. But the resultant decision to bring Sylhet into Assam separated the Bengali speaking people on either side of the Meghna, but endangered rivalry and antagonism between the two valleys of the Brahmaputra and Surma which continued with occasional break ups till our times. (Baruah 1999: 24)

The continuous treatment of Assam as a land frontier of Bengal and colonial policy makers encouraging immigration from densely populated Bengal to scarcely populated Assam[10], set in motion a tussle among the people of Assam and the Bengali speakers. The economic transformation that took place due to introduction of "modern" industrial agencies- tea plantation, petroleum drilling, setting up of the railways etc initiated an economic force that gave further impetus to immigration. The migration that took place during the British period, created competition for new political and economic opportunities, thrown open for the public. The people of Assam became highly apprehensive about the "educated Hindu Bengalis", the "hardworking Bengali Muslims" and "the enterprising Marwaris" (Srikant 2000:4-5). Also, under the British rule, during 1826-1874, Assam was made a new division of Bengal Presidency. The lower rung of this order of administration almost wholly comprised of Bengali Hindus imported mainly from Sylhet. It was then that the colonial rulers established Bengali as the official language of Assam[11]. The Assamese intellectuals vociferously demanded that Assamese should be reinstalled as the official language in the administration and education of Assam. This was finally conceded in 1873. The boundary altercation between the states of Bengal and Assam continued till the Independence. But the most significant corollary of this experiment with the boundary has been, it created the binary category of indigenous and immigrants that till the contemporary times has vexed the socio-political health of Assam.

Another category divide that equally overwhelm Assam is the tribal/ non-tribal binary. This divide further leads to the sprint to establish autochthony and thus the rightful claim over the land. As Baruah had alluded, institution of the line system and segregation of the hills detached the historic interaction and assimilation among the hill dwellers and the plain dwellers. Baruah refers to colonial author Leo Rose and says that the British policy was generally based upon the general principle that all independent hill principalities should be deprived of whatever plain areas they controlled at the foot of the hills. This further accentuates the British idea of overlapping natural boundary with the administrative boundary. The British considered the foothills the natural boundary between "India" and the hill principalities and that all plains areas belonged by right to whoever ruled northern India. This was also to impede the plain dwellers from providing revenue to the hill rulers, thus making these rulers weak and dependent on the British. Baruah analyses this in his writing:

> The logic of British attitudes towards the hills of Assam was the same; however, they considered most of the peoples living in these hills as "primitive tribes". Even in the narrow confines of the hills, there was therefore no pretension of recognizing their independence. They were kept in reservation-like territories called "backward" or "excluded" tracts. The experience of colonial rule in these areas, to say the least, was profoundly different from that of the regular administered parts of British India. (Baruah 1999:28)
>
> A number of discrete laws governed the administration of these marked areas: the Scheduled Districts Act of 1874 and the Frontier Tract Regulation Act of 1880 enabled the government to exclude these areas from regulations like the operation of the codes of civil and criminal procedures, the rules on property registration and transfer etc. The chieftains and customary authorities were restored with the power to try petty civil and criminal cases without the intervention of the modern legal system. The law that concretized the colonial idea of administration was the Bengal Eastern Frontier Regulation of 1873 which empowered the colonial government to prescribe an "Inner Line". The line was drawn along the foothills. The peoples living beyond the line were supposedly "left to manage their own affairs with only such interference from the part of the frontier officers in their political capacity as may be considered advisable with the view to establishing a personal influence for good among the chiefs and the tribes". (Baruah 1999: 28-29)

Before the British had annexed Assam, upper Assam was ruled by the Ahom dynasty and the Koch kingdom ruled the western Assam and parts of present North Bengal. Among other dynasties, the Chutiyas ruled north-eastern Assam and parts of present Arunachal Pradesh and the Kacharis ruled from DikhowRiver to central and southern Assam. With expansion of Ahom kingdom, by 1520 the Chutiya areas were annexed and since 1536 Kacharis remained only in Cachar and North Cachar more as an Ahom ally then a competing force. Despite numerous invasions, mostly by the Muslim rulers, no western power could successfully conquer Assam. When Assam became part of British India, only the area that was ruled by the Ahom was called Assam. But as the British expanded their domain the entire area that was under the Chief Commissionership including the Surma valley, hill districts and Manipur came to be known as Assam. (Baruah 1999: 28).

The colonial state in the late nineteenth century began to introduce some of the major instruments of control of populations and resources tried out in Europe, with suitable modification for colonial adaptation. Simultaneously the colonial administrations inducted cognitive and statistical projects of modern rule, like census and cartography.

The data gathering and enumeration of land and population was processed through questioning and inferring about Indian life; family, religion, language, caste, occupation, marriage, literacy etc. This was a moment when practically all the major aspects of the social and cultural life was questioned and explained. This process, introduced as a part of administrative machinery, lead to objectification and crystallization of many facets of life. The information was ordered in tables and was made referential. These data were utilized in policy formulation and administrative procedures[12].

The first universal census questionnaire adopted for the census of the 1870s included separate items on 'religion' and 'caste or class', besides 'race or nationality or country of birth'. In 1881, a separate item on 'mother tongue' was added and the question on caste was modified to read 'caste, if Hindu; sect, if of other religion'. The schedule adopted for 1901 Census, in addition to items like 'religion and language ordinarily used', provided for the first time recordings of 'tribe'[13] and the relevant question was amplified to read 'caste of Hindus and Jains and tribe or race for others'. Thus the Indian Census during the colonial period can be grouped into three broad categories, namely

1. Population statistics
2. Occupational classification of caste and caste rankings
3. Ethnology including racial classification of the Indian people.

The 1881 census identified the population of Assam mainly into three categories which was based on religion[14]. They are the Hindus, Musalmans and the "tribes". The Hindus were further classified according to caste and the tribes were divided based on the racial affinity. The tribes were included under three generic names: Bodo, Shan Tribes and the Tribes of the mountains east of Bhutan. These were mainly the groups that were racially non-Aryan. 12 tribes were identified as belonging to the Bodo race: Kachari, Mech, Lalung, Hajong, Garo (plain), Rabha, Madhahi, Mahalia, Sarania, Totila, Chutiya and Koch Rajbansi. The Shan race included 3 tribes: the Shan, Ahom and Khamti. The tribes of the mountains east of Bhutan also included 3 tribes: the Daphlas, Miris and Abors. Within the Hindus distinctive castes like the Matak, Kalita, Kewat or Kaibarttha, Dom, Brahmin or Ganak and Katani or Jugi were included. Some castes within the Hindus also were non-Aryan racially but they had been included within the Hindus as they have adopted Hinduism by common consent.

Since its commencement in 1870s the census reports gave short ethnographic account of castes and tribes. But the census of 1901 for the first time provided elaborate anthropological and ethnological data on castes and tribes. At this time the census operations were in the hands of scholar and anthropologist Herbert Risley. The reports of the identification and classification of the castes and tribes in Assam relied upon the ethnographer's accounts working on the particular area. Thereport begins with a note of acknowledgment to these writers[15]. The tribes have been classified in accordance with the phenotypic characters, religion, the language they speak, the social rituals observed by them that are inscribed in the writings about them. The caste Hindus, except the ones who are descendent of the Aryan race, are categorized in accordance to the level that they have been successful at adopting the paraphernalia of Hinduism, the gods and goddesses, rituals and customs, festivals and dressing and eating habits. The report emphasizes that being Hindu is a "mark of superiority" over the tribes. The Hindus of Assam were compared and evaluated with that of rest of India (especially the north and Bengal), their customs and rituals were believed to have been shared with and borrowed from the tribal ways.

This data gathering and enumeration in the process built up a host of elements in the social and political context of Assam. The most important of them were, it initiated: (a) the category "tribal" (b) division between the tribal and non-tribal (c) Hill tribes and Plain tribes and most crucially (d) a ladder of hierarchy amongst the different groups of people.

The colonial administrative machinery in Assam thus put in place a definite idea of peoplehood. Drawing from the phenotypic features and based on the cultural practices the ancestry and racial affinity was traced. The idea of homeland was made prominent in this accordance.

Nicolas Dirks (1992) points out that any study of colonial discourse that fails to examine the historical character and contradictory nature of colonial intervention and the institutional bases of colonial impact must be rejected even if we accept Foucault's emphasis on the fields of power created by discursive practices. The power of colonial discourse was not that it created whole new fields of meaning instantaneously but that it shifted old meanings slowly, sometimes imperceptibly, through the colonial control of a range of new institutions. Although an emphasis on ideas and discourses reveals that institutional hegemony is not based solely, or even principally, on brute force, discourse does not do it alone. Institutions activate ideological changes most often, masking seduction as mutuality, resistance as complicity, and change as continuity. Transformations occurred because of the ways colonial discourse inscribed its peculiar, often masterful, combination of old and new meanings in institutional theatres with major consequences for the colonial subjects. This process, according to Dirks, often involved the paradoxical preservation of old regime forms, creating a shadow theatre in which continuities and changes seemed always to mimic each other. In the same streak Sumit Guha (2003) states that:

> The political norm in pre-British times was that of vertical ties of subordination that converged on the absolute monarch. The aristocratic, the chosen, the best, were necessarily few in number. So fewness, exclusivity, was point of honor. Aristocracy then translated into leadership and honor (and fat dowries). The mature colonial regime inevitably undermined these structures. Vis-a-vis the colonial masters, distinctions among black people were not hugely significant to the average British official or officer. But at the same time, new public forums, including a more active press, were leading to a more vigorous assertion of identity in the public sphere. When limited Provincial Councils were being established in the 1880s, the object was to create representation for specific interests such as British businessmen, the trading, professional and agricultural classes, and the landed aristocracy. Furthermore the colonial fear of loss of control led to the allocation of seats in such a way that the government always had an "official majority". Nonetheless, weighting was achieved via the election/nomination process, and majority voting decided matters inside the assemblies and councils. The early nationalists internalized the norm that majority decisions prevailed, and fought vigorously for elected majorities in decision-making bodies. This political culture was crystallizing in the epoch of the great Imperial Censuses (1881-) and logically extended the idea of majority predominance in adversarial situations to the larger political arena. (Guha 2003: 160).

The old lines of division among the people, in the case of Assam, in the course of colonial regime were made stringent through anthropological categorization and corresponding administrative policies, thereby instituting a new narrative of the region steeped in strict ethnic differentiation. Though one cannot claim that ethnic groups were created by colonial machinery, but the deployment of colonial apparatus and documentation of the population installed the essence of people as naturally variegated—ethnically. To delve why and how ethnic difference became the sole defining character in Assam, it is important to re-visit the colonial sites of history to study the operations of categories of knowledge which had a lot to do with measurement and mapping, classification and quantification. Ethnicity was not exempt from this outreach of knowledge. As Gyan Prakash has pointed out,

> To return to the colonial scene, therefore, is to release histories and knowledges from their disciplining as area studies; as imperial and overseas history; as the study of the exotic other that seals metropolitan structures from the contagion of the record of their own formation elsewhere—in fantasy and fear, in cultural difference and uneven and entangled histories, in contingency and contention. (Prakash 1994: 11-12)

For Assam to be able to insert itself into the narrative of progress, it is important to re-write the narrative of origins and perceive identity as a product of historical relations. My work appears at certain junctures of fissure in post colonial history where various ethnic assertions in Assam have overpowered the state machinery but ultimately failed. I have tried to show that it is important to re-read the movements in Assam in their historic specificity and interpret the plural trends that are emerging. The historian Gyan Prakash has written:

> Thus, as scholars, activists, and intellectuals have fastened on the tensions, anxicties, and intermixtures in colonial discourses to split apart the categories of identity and history associated with racism and western domination, the new sources of knowledge that they have offered remain contextual and contingent. (Prakash 1994:12)

Many recent works delve into colonialism and its role in restructuring of the society which gives rise to identity formation. The political and economic compulsion of the colonial state induces stimuli that lead to the construction and heightening of identities. Gyanendra Pandey in his work on colonial construction, *The Construction of Communalism in Colonial North India* (1990) delineates how colonial configuration constituted the interpersonal meaning among the Hindus and the Muslims in India:

> The all-India 'Hindu community' (and, to a large extent, the all-India 'Muslim community' too) was a colonial creation for, as I have argued, the social and economic changes brought by colonialism,

> Indian efforts to defend the indigenous religions and culture against western missionary attacks, the 'unifying' drive of the colonial state-which was marked at the level of administrative structure and attempted political control ('Muslims' must not be antagonised, 'Hindu' sensibilities must not be touched), and the very history of movements like that of Cow-Protection, widely publicised as they were by the end of the 19th century, tended to promote the idea of an all-India 'Hindu community' and an all-India 'Muslim community' which were supposedly ranged against one another for much of the time. In spite of a widely felt sense of 'Hinduness' and 'Muslimness', I would suggest that until the 19th century at any rate, people always had to work through caste, sect and so on to arrive at the unities implied in the conception of the 'Hindu community' and the 'Muslim community'. (Kumar 1994: 1807)

Pandey refers to writings of the last two decades about the "communal" interpretation of Indian history. According to him, administrators and historians of India from colonial times assumed the existence of readymade, unified religious communities in the past (Hindu, Muslim, Sikh, etc) and exaggerated the existence of conflict between these communities, thus reinforced a communal outlook. He writes that to the colonial writers, communalism was to the East what nationalism was to the west. He cites Theodore Morison [16] and says that the following depicts a wide range of colonialist opinion:

> It is useless to enumerate the grounds of difference between Hindu and Muslim; the only thing that matters is that they do in fact feel and think of themselves as separate people. In all disquisitions on nationality this is the only test which is found to cover all cases... Judged by this standard the Muslims of India are a nation. Communal differences, as they are called, are really national jealousies. (Pandey 2008: 2)

Pandey recounts that, on the other hand, for the Indian nationalists, communalism is equally important, precisely, because it was not nationalism. For them communalism, in fact, was in common with colonialism; the other of nationalism, its opposite, its chief adversary, and hence a necessary part of the story of nation-building in India.

Pandey also holds that the state in the recent times in India has arrogated to itself all the rights of a nation. Thus the relation between the state, as a nation, and ascertained identities has a close connection. In colonial India, he maintains, there was a search for a 'pure' nationalism, among the nationalists. The search for the 'purely' 'political' sealed off, in its ideal state, from all social meaning, from social bases and social consequences. Even though it was a futile search, but has, unfortunately, continued in some quarters down to the present day. Regarding the historiography of communalism, the nationalist historians wrote of the 'tolerance' of Indian rulers from Ashoka to Akbar and the colonialists of their 'intolerance', most marked, it was said, in Aurangzeb's time. The fundamental point is that the history of India (the nation) and the history of the Indian state were treated as being almost identical. In nationalist hands, the unity of India was presented, alternatively, as a metaphysical truth and—since the metaphysical could not stand on its own for long, even in thought—as a historical reality brought about by the state. Pandey also questions other facets of the historiography of Indian nationalism. He refutes, what he calls, 'monist' vision of Indian history—a vision that believed in eternal unities, in natural boundaries and inevitable end, in the history of 'India' as almost a metaphysical entity—affected the colonialist, communalist and nationalist construction of the past in several other significant respects. It led to a quite remarkable collapsing of time, into clear-cut and manageable, if large compartments, and to the reduction of all Indian history to a history of the state. Many other authors also comply with the idea that in the medieval period, society was by and large peaceful and communalism is essential a colonial creation also cites that adult suffrage, mass politics and majority voting that came after 1947 also contributed to the modern day communalism. Dharma Kumar provides a critique of the understanding that communalism took its modern turn during the colonial period. She refers to this understanding as "Left secularist" model and accentuates the fact that there is no proper evidence of harmony among the various religious communities even in the medieval times. The existence of pre-British "composite culture" is another aspect of Golden age myth. Likewise, religious syncretism which is also considered a pre-British norm also has its counters, for example the radical partiality for Din Ilahi is ironic in view of Aziz Ahmad's opposition of Akbar's "imperial and aristocratic" Din Ilahi to the "popular and demotic" Kabirpanthis. According to her, Pandey's grossly overrates the power of colonialism.

> Pandey may rightly object to "the reduction of Indian history to the history of the state", but omitting the need for the state is no better. Even if India had not been a colony, it would have undergone contending nationalisms, more or less successful attempts to construct modern government and states, and mass movements,

> and these would have contributed to the growth of communalism. Moreover, many things that did occur in the colonial period in India were not directly attributable to the policy of the Raj-one obvious example is the rise of Islamic 'reform movements' which homogenised Muslim beliefs and practices all over Asia. (Kumar 1994:1808).

However, it is my contention that, Kumar's work though provides ample evidences that communalism is not a colonial attribute, the alteration in nature of the interpersonal relationships that colonialism brought about with its many facets of urbanisation, industrialization and capitalism, together with the administrative policies of governance cannot be negated. While the British administration did maintain a neutral position between the Hindus and the Muslims, the impulses that were brought about during the colonial period still exist to colour the imagination of the religious communities. Even if disputes and conflicts existed in medieval times among the religious groups, the causes and aims of the present day conflicts assumes a large tone from the developments of the colonial times. For instance, affirmative action policies of the government, appeal for competitive vote bank politics etc.Similarly, an analysis of the contemporary ethnic assertionsprovides anunderstanding of the modern political language that asserting groups utilize to claim their demands. The immediate establishment of a potent discordant ethnic discourse with the coming of the British impeded the consolidation of an overarching identity. This discourse gave the various groups segregated identities which spells out in the contemporary assertions.

Works that documents the emergence of ethnic identities because of colonialism includes Jay O'Brien (1986) work on how ethnic identities were produced in Sudan as a result of capitalist developments that took place during colonialism, Colson (1968) and Asad (1970) who describes that many African tribes were actually colonial construct deliberately created by colonialism to meet the needs of administration through indirect rule, Richards' (1969) work presents that the East African ethnic groups were formalised under colonialism. PremaKurien's work *Kaleidoscopic Ethnicity: International Migration and the Reconstruction of Community Identities in India* (2002) on colonialism and societal change in Kerala puts forward that colonialism imposed a new economic system on the society and introduced unprecedented massive commercialization. The consequent disruption of the economic structure eventually translated into a change in the social structure. Her argument is that over the period of colonialism, the global and systemic character of the social structure and most of the earlier ties of dependency that bound the groups together were dissolved and each of the units of the system began to develop autonomous ethnic identities.

> Colonialism imposes a new economic system on the society and usually introduces large-scale commercialization for the first time. The consequent disruption of the economic structure eventually translates into a change in the social structure. (Kurien 2002: 397)

The classic cases of colonialism[17] have most often been situations where colonial rule was imposed on a pre-capitalist society containing some systems of hierarchically arranged, hereditary, occupational groups. According to Kurien the period of colonialism can, in most cases can be divided into two phases; in the first phase existing social arrangements were harnessed to the exigencies of revenue generation and political control. In this process there was an increase in exploitation of the lower strata and an increase in power of the elite. A combination of factors initiated the process of ethnicization among the labouring groups and among the displaced elites. In the second, capitalist phase, the compulsion of market economy and a modern state necessitated the overthrow of the traditional stratification system. The displacement of groups from their socio-economic niches together with the introduction of new resources into the society carried forward the process of ethnic formation and mobilization. She uses the term "ethnogenesis" [originally coined by ethno-historians Sturtevant (1971) and Newcomer (1972)] for the ethnic formation and transformation that took place under the colonial state. She analyses the changes in three communities the *Mappila* (Keralite Muslim), *Ezhava* (lower-caste Keralite Hindus) and *SyrianChristians* (Upper-caste Keralite Christians) and concludes that the advent of British colonialism led to dismantling of earlier stratification system. Religious and caste identities that had been defined in terms of the position of each group within the larger social order had been reified and made immutable under colonialism and the sub-groups and sub-cultures developed into autonomous and distinct units.

Objective of the Book

The objective of the book is to unravel and understand the underpinnings that lead contemporary dissidences to acquire ethnic trajectory. The book proposes that labelling the various assertions as "ethnic" disables effective understanding of the crux of the problem. The issues raised by the varied asserting groups have been wide-ranging, yet a complex problem has been simplistically explained by attributing it to ethnic dissidence. The book proposes that "ethnic" labelling needs to be probed and arrive at an understanding why the question of ethnic identity has become rampant. In the instance of Assam, this work proposes, colonial intervention has played colossal part in essentializing the region as "ethnically varied". The identity of the people has been determined by the deluging colonial ethnic discourse which still reckons in the imagination of the region. Colonialism here, like elsewhere, was more than simple economic exploitation. Colonialism produced new forms of society that has been "naturalized" as traditional. The salient feature of colonial interpretation of diversity, in the case of Assam, has been that it has rendered the identity of the people fundamentally and essentially as "ethnic". This portrayal of exclusive diversity hindered the integration of the people in the national fold even after Independence. The exclusion, by far, has been facilitated by the unreflective perpetuation of the discourse even in the present times, simultaneously, has provided a trope for the asserting groups to adorn the obtainable identity—the ethnic. The book looks at three recent assertions in the Brahmaputra valley of Assam to probe into the discordant ethnic discourse.

Re-locating the Ethnic Question in Assam

The quickly put together Indian nationalism is largely constituted of dominant discourses. These dominant discourses are mainly concentrated on interests of the mainland. The margins—geographical margins, of which Assam is a part—are included in token ways only. As a result, discontentment is widespread and secessionist demands rampant. These demands have many understandable reasons; to dump them all in the category of ethnicity is to try and suppress the problems of the north-east. "To ethnicise is to treat problems as produced by other cultures" writes Dipesh Chakraborty. It is my contention that the category of "ethnic" is all too willingly accepted by the various players in the Assam scenario (the Central government, the state government and the political parties) because ethnicising the problem is distancing the problem from some other more immediate issues. The state government wants to obfuscate the economic issues, the central government wants to cover over the issues of incomplete nationhood and the political parties want to take advantage of the people's discontent as a result of both.

While there are indications that the prevalent categories in Assam resemble much of colonial administrative practices[18], there exist no systemic or analytical study that provides a lucid understanding of the actual underpinnings that form the ethnic essence. There is a serious ambiguity in the existing literature on the framing and effectuation of the idea of ethnicity. What the existing literature presents is an all accommodating concept of ethnicity that does not go beyond affirming that the present conflicts are rampant of ethnic problem (irrespective of whether they borrow from colonial categorization or not). The impetus and trajectory by which the contemporary identities assume ethnic dimension and how the ethnic identities are framed in the conflicts calls for a deeper understanding of the bedrock, imagination and the subsequent method of deployment of the ethnic idea.

The book will explore the ethnic question in Assam through the study of three contemporary assertions that have been generally termed as "ethnic": the Assam movement, the Bodoland movement and the ULFA stir. Analyzing the discourse within and around these assertions, the book will unravel the crux that forms the ethnic character in Assam. The intellectual belief that the colonial contribution plays a major role in formulating the conflicts will be examined. Drawing from this, the relation of the ethnic group vis-à-vis the state and the latter's importance in creating, maintaining and controlling the former will be examined. The first three chapters will be case studies—the Assam movement, the Bodoland movement and the ULFA stir.

The first chapter will analyze the Assam movement, the United Liberation Front of Assam and the Bodoland movement. It will delve into the inception of the three movements and trace their trajectories. The Assam movement started as an indigenous communities' assertion against the immigrants, but it transformed into ethnic turmoil by the time it ended with the signing of the Assam Accord. The Assam movement started as a collective assertion of the indigenous population against the economic and demographic threat posed by illegal immigrants. But the consolidated movement gradually fragmented into ethnic divisions. It will look into the framing of identity of the people of Assam by the ULFA. The chapter will establish that studying ULFA's idea of identity is important because it thrives upon the broad sense of discontent prevalent in the region regarding its membership in India. ULFA's idea of identity of the people of Assam is different from the Indian identity. The formulation of this identity was possible through underscoring the already existing sense of discontent among the masses in regard to economic deprivation, social marginalization and military cavalier of the centre. Finally the chapter will examine the framing of self identity by the Bodos during the Bodoland movement. The Bodos relied on the already existing discourse to establish their claim as the authentic "sons of the soil". The Bodos raised their claim on the land by evoking an idea of ancestral kingdom in doing so they formulated their identity by challenging the "sons of the soil" of the Assamese.

The second chapter will unflur how the three movements that had arisen with distinctive goals took an ethnic turn. The chapter will argue that in the Assam movement, the difficulty in identifying the "illegal immigrants" amongst the local population transformed into a process of outlining their own identity by the indigenous population. In this process, the identity categories already available were sharpened and this lead to the ethnicization of the purported collective identity of the Assam movement. The chapter will locate the site where ethnicization of the identities took place. They are delineated as: The Elections, Growth of identity based organizations, The Assam Accord. Following this, the chapter will analyze how the identities got ethnicized—it took place in two folds-sharpening the historical rivalry between the Assamese and the Bengalis and eroding of the idea of "greater Assamese nationality". The chapter will demonstrate that the indigenous communities in Assam are sensitive and responsive to the idea of their ethnic identity. Assam movement was an event in contemporary Assam that unbolted the volatile character of ethnic identity. The chapter will demonstrate that the ULFA's idea of distinct identity has evolved from the long circulated view that the people of Assam are diverse among themselves and from rest of India. The chapter will argue that in defining this identity ULFA places (undivided) Assam, as a region, at par with India. ULFA bases the identity of the people dissociated from India on the idea of difference, as a people and the long nurtured sentiment of deprivation and marginalization. The chapter examines the idea of economic and demographic marginalization of the people of Assam and understands how the sense of separate identity from India has evolved. The chapter will argue that the Bodos formulated their identity based on the existing large body of writing and idea about their origin. The chapter will analyze how the Bodos formulated their identity, through the eroding of greater Assamese nationality and attempting a separate tribal identity. The chapter will conclude by demonstrating that the greater tribal identity though was attempted by the Bodos to consolidate their claim on Assam, fragmented into smaller units, once again bringing to the fore that a discordant ethnic discourse is prevalent.

The third chapter will show that the ethnicization of the three movements have been possible because there is already an all pervading ethnic discourse in place in Assam and the ethnic groups irrespective of their original mode of expression, inadvertently or not fall in the ambit of ethnicity. The chapter will weave the three case studies together and infer the indices that determine the deployment of ethnicity in the process of their assertions. The chapter will argue that while the content of "ethnicity" keeps shifting (the Assamese is a citizen in Assam movement, a non-Indian in the ULFA and a non-indigenous in Bodoland movement), the identities are framed on a perception of a dominant "other". Though the assertions emerged on the sense of deprivation and generic identitities were attempted to be formulated in the three assertions, the groups eventually projected the interest of a specific ethnic unit.

The fourth chapter will present that a fragmentary ethnic discourse exists in Assam. The chapter will trace the episteme of this discourse and lay out that it emerged during the colonial period. The emergence of ethnic categories can be traced back to the history, to the time when the people were identified and categorized based on the perceived idea of their origin. It was this practice, started by the British administrators that translated into concretization of the ethnic identities. The identification and categorization of people was put in practice in three interrelated ways—Census and Cartography, Anthropological Studies and Administrative Policies and Acts.

The fifth concluding chapter will present an alternative understanding of the ethnic tensions in Assam, as not "ethnic" problem but as a discursive field that has to be understood epistemologically and in relation to the process of knowledge production.

The objective of this work is to unfurl the idea of "ethnic identity", specifically of the people of Assam and that of the entire north-eastern India, in general. The book foregrounds that the question of ethnicity that has been unquestionably accepted is not a natural and pre-given concept. But, this perspective has been put in place at a definite time in the history, namely in the colonial period; when the identities of the people was concretized. The present ethnic discourse on Assam and on the other north-eastern states has its sources in this idea of ethnicity installed by the Britishers- mainly for administrative purposes. The book looks at the archival documents as well as the contemporary writings on Assam and forefronts that there exists a ubiquitous ethnic discourse of the north-eastern states. The asserting groups, irrespective of their initial objectives and goals, cannot but assume the ethnic mode of expression during their demands.

This work questions and unravels the "naturalized" ethnic identity of the people of Assam. This book emphasizes that existence of diverse ethnic identities does not ensue competition/problem but their narration and contextualization do. This work grapples with the ongoing strife and secessionist movements in the north-eastern states and understands whythey are not"ethnic" problems *per se*.

Reference

1. Connor (1973: 1-21).
2. West Bengal: Gorkhaland, Kamtapur
   - Assam: Karbi Anglong, Bodolandland
   - Gujarat: Kutch, Saurashtra, Bhilistan
   - Uttar Pradesh: Braj/Harit Pradesh/Paschimanchal, Awadh/Central Uttar Pradesh, Purvanchal, Bundelkhand
   - Bihar: Mithila or Mithila Rastra, Bhojpur
   - Karnataka: Kalyana Karnataka, Tulu Nadu
   - Jammu and Kashmir: Kashmir , Jammu/ Dogradesh, Ladakh
   - Madhya Pradesh: Vindhya Pradesh, Baghelkhand, Bundelkhand, Mahakoshal, Gondwana, Malwa
   - Odisha: Kosal
   - Maharashtra: Vidarbha, Khandesh, Marathwada, Konkan
   - Tamil Nadu: Kongu Nadu
3. Foucault, M. *The Archaeology of Knowledge* (A.M. Sheridan Smith, Trans.). New York. 1972.pp. 4-19. See also M Foucault, 'Politics and The Study of Discourse' in Foucault *et.al.. The Foucault Effect: Studies in Governmentality* ed. Graham Burchell, Colin Gordon and Peter Miller. Chicago. University of Chicago Press, 1991. Page 53-72. The meaning of discourse, objectification, subjectification and so on is best epitomized by Foucault himself in his after-word, 'The Subject and Power', in Dreyfuss, H & Rabinow, P (1983).*Michel Foucault. Beyond structuralism and hermeneutics* (2nd edition). Chicago. University of Chicago Press. pp.208-19.
4. Recent work on ethnicity from a variety of perspective include Archdeacon 1983; Banton 1983; Cohen 1978; Dinnerstein, Nichols and Reimers 1979, Francis 1976; Glazer 1983; Hall 1979; Heisler 1977; Keyes 1981; Lieberson 1980; Mason 1982; Pettigrew 1978; Rex 1981; Simpson and Yinger 1985; A. Smith 1981; Thernstrom 1980; Williams 1978; Wilson 1980; Wolf 1982; Young 1976.
5. The marginal or 'minority' is not the space of a celebratory, or Utopian, self marginalization. It is a much more substantial intervention into those justifications of modernity — progress, homogeneity, cultural organicism,the deep nation, the long past — that rationalize the authoritarian, 'normalizing' tendencies within cultures in the name of the national interest or the ethnic prerogative. In this sense, then, the ambivalent, antagonistic perspective of nation as narration will establish the cultural boundaries of the nation so that they may be acknowledged as 'containing' thresholds of meaning that must be crossed, erased, and translated in the process of cultural production. (Bhabha 1990:4).

6. In the wake of transfer of power on 15thAugust 1947 the administrative jurisdiction of the excluded and the partially excluded areas in the hills of Assam was transferred to the Government of Assam which acted on behalf of the Government of India. The constitution promulgated in 1950 contained a special provision in the form of Sixth Schedule for the administration of "tribal" areas that was meant to protect the tribal people who were living scattered throughout the country. The provision was applied to the ethnic groups living in the hill regions of the North East. Under it, the "tribal" areas of the North East were divided into two parts, Part A and Part B. The United Khasi and Jaintia Hill districts, the Garo Hill district, the Lushai Hill District, the Naga Hill District, the North Cachar Hill District and the Mikir Hill District were placed in Part A as autonomous districts administered by the Government of Assam, with a limited representative in the Assam State Legislative Assembly and the National Parliament. The North East Frontier Tract, the Balipara Frontier Tracts, the Tirap Frontier Tracts, the Abor and Mishmi Hill Districts and the Naga Tribal area came under Part B, which was administered by the Governor of Assam acting as agent of the President of India. Tripura and Manipur were not promoted to states but they were made special administrative regions under the control of central government. Sikkim was ruled by monarch at the time of arrival of the British. In 1891 British India signed a treaty known as the Titalia with Sikkim through which the British was able to exercise influence on Sikkim. In 1947 when India became Independent, a treaty was signed between India and Sikkim under which Sikkim was able to retain a special status of a protectorate of India. Sikkim became a full fledged state of India on 16th May 1975, the institution of king was abolished and Sikkim was merged with India. (Singh 1984: 14-51).
7. The various existing perspectives on the tensions of Assam will be discussed in details in the subsequent chapters.
8. He uses this term to distinguish other linguistic groups that have embraced Assamese nationality from the Assamese speaking "Assamese" people. I will elaborately delve on this characterization in my following chapters.
9. "The strategies adopted by these movements have also differed at different stages of confrontation with the Indian state. The Hill-State movement and the Karbi-Dimasa movement have been exemplary in the use of peaceful and democratic methods of agitation. The Assam Movement, though initially largely non-violent, went through an unprecedented violent phase of group and communal clashes during the boycott of the February 1983 election to the State Legislative Assembly. The Nagas and the Mizos organized armed resistance against the might of the Indian army, whilst the Bodoland agitation has been marked by large-scale violence, arson, and killings of civilians". (Misra 1998: 107).
10. Sanjib Baruah (1999)
11. This was done, as the Assamese saw it, under the influence of the Bengali petty officials of the East India Company who argued that Assamese was not an independent language but only a dialect of Bengali.
12. Cohn (1996).

13. The notion of "tribe" was not only associates with nature and the primitive, but it also infantilizes tribals and considered their culture to be the raw primeval base from which arose certain strains of Hinduism and Jainism. (Wolf 2001).
14. Report on the census of Assam. Chapter VI (1881).
15. "The chapter on Caste in the Brahmaputra valley has been drawn up by Mr. E. Stack Director of Agriculture, the note on the Kacharis (para 118) has been contributed by the kindness of the Rev. Mr. Endle of Tezpur, and that on the Miris (para 132) is from the pen of Mr. C.J. Lyall, Secretary of the Chief Commissioner to all of whom the thanks of the Chief Commissioner are due. No data however has been furnished on which to write an account of the castes of the Surma valley"(Report on the census of Assam 1901).
16. Morison, Theodore. "Mohammedan Movements", in J. Cumming (ed.). *Political India.* London 1932.
17. This mainly explains British colonialism more than the colonist strategy of other countries.
18. Sanjib Baruah (1999), Sajal Nag (1990), Sudhir Bhaumik (2009) etc.

Chapter - 1

Recounting the Assam Movement, the United Liberation Front of Assam and the Bodoland Movement

Assam in the recent past has witnessed three major turmoils that had threatened to destabilize its socio-politico fabric: the Assam movement, the United Liberation Front of Assam and the Bodoland movement. The three movements were of different constituent and nature; the Assam movement was an indigenous people's revolt against unchecked immigrants, Bodoland movement was a "tribal" uprising demanding autonomy and the ULFA upsurge, an extremist stir with the aim to secure secession. The three movements had emerged along the common sentiment of neglect and deprivation, had large mass support and were associated with varied levels of violence. It is interesting to note that while trying to annul the perceived/real exclusionary attitude, they grounded their demands by formulating a specific notion of identity that is based on belief in discrete cultural identity and a corresponding homeland. These three movements, that have been called "ethnic" assertions, provide an ample arena to decipher the underpinnings of ethnicity of Assam. This chapter will recount the socio-political situation of the cause and emergence of the three movements and understand how the idea of peoplehood was framed by each of them.

The Assam Movement and the Contest of Citizenship

The Assam movement had an impact on othernortheastern states as well, where similar, but much less sustained, protest took place. One of the legacies of the Assam movement is a sustained crisis of governmental legitimacy that continues to this day. The perceived failure of the Assam movement to resolve Assam's immigration crisis led to a radicalization of Assamese subnationalism, giving it a

> separatist turn. Another effect of the sustained campaign was the rupturing of the ties between a number of ethnic groups. There are episodes of violence between "indigenous" and "immigrant" communities. The campaign also led to friction between the ethnic Assamese and some of Assam's "plain tribal" groups—the Bodoland movement of today is in some ways an outgrowth of the Assam movement. (Baruah 1999: 117).

The Assam movement is marked as the most stringent mass movement in contemporary Assam. This was the culmination of dissidence by the civil society against the enfranchisement of, who they believe were, illegal immigrants. The anti-government campaign that continued from 1979 to 1985 is termed as "Assam movement", Assam Agitation or *AsomAndolon*.

The movement was ostensibly an upsurge of the "people of Assam" against the foreigner, citizens against the non-citizens; indigenous against the foreigners. The native Assamese speakers, who started the movement, were supported throughout the Brahmaputra valley by tribes like the Bodo, Tiwa, Mising, Rabha etc. The various section of the population irrespective of their affiliations responded to the call and actively participated in the movement to drive out the illegal immigrants.

However, what started as a consolidated struggle, fragmented into various ethnic strands by the time the movement ended with the signing of the Assam Accord in 1985. Further, the developments that took place after the movement deepened the chasm among the various communities, ushering in a plethora of similar upsurges demanding cultural and political exclusivity. The "ethnic" disorder that the movement opened up raises the questions regarding the ethnic factor as the most immediate character of expression in Assam. Why did every demand and claim percolate to ethnic interest? And why no other manner of identity assertion, other than ethnic, becomes possible in the region.

Assam movement was, at the foremost, a protest movement against what was alleged to be a *de facto* policy of the Indian government of admitting and enfranchising "foreigners". The agitators called it as "Assam's last struggle for survival" against the "cultural, political and demographic transformation" of Assam by the onslaught of unchecked immigrants which threatened to "reduce the indigenous to minorities in their own land"[1]. In the words of Prafulla Mahanta, one of the leaders of the movement who eventually became the Chief Minister of Assam after the Assam movement ended, the "tussle" between the indigenous people of Assam and the immigrants has existed since a long time. He describes the "malady" of unchecked immigrants as follows:

> The tussle has been in existence since a long time and has gathered cancerous roots. But the position has materially changed since 1979. The usurpation has been duly noticed and the dimensions or erosion and corrosion have been fully appreciated. The avowed objectives to cure the malady have been defined and the battle lines are already drawn. The battle is going to be fought on all sectors—constitutional, legal, social, administrative and even military, if need arises. Actually, this tussle should have never occurred. But as the battle has been imposed, it shall have to be repelled with all the might that we can muster. Once it is won, it is all the better for the nation and for the people of Assam. (Mahanta 1986: 117).

The leaders of the campaign argued that immigrants from foreign countries—mostly from what was East Pakistan and then became the sovereign state of Bangladesh, and some from Nepal— unless were explicitly given citizenship status in India, were "foreigners" or illegal aliens. It was alleged that these "non-citizens" were inappropriately enfranchised and were included in the electoral rolls. Along with the cultural and political threats posed by the immigrants, the movement also was instigated by economic reasons, as the immigrant communities were believed to have attained a strong hold on the jobs and businesses of Assam. This movement is also important not only in the milieu of Assam but in the entire north-eastern India as it catapulted a host of anti-immigrant strikes all over the zone[2].

Though it started as an endeavour of "the people of Assam" to safeguard their interest, the proceedings and trajectories that the movement covered, eventually got the movement represented as an attempt of the "ethnic Assamese" to perpetuate their hegemony in the region. The tension among the various communities, especially after the signing of the *Assam Accord*, surfaced and got pronounced, which still looms at the face of contemporary Assam. In this chapter we engage with the "ethnic" question that emerged during the Assam movement and analyse three key concerns: A) Why has the conflict been termed as "ethnic" conflicts, B) How was "ethnicity" articulated in the movement? C) What was the content of the term "ethnic" in the movement? The chapter will delve into the chronicles of the Assam movement, revisit it and through them will analyze the location and ways by which ethnicization of various sections of identities of Assam took place. Following this, the chapter will examine how contestation of citizenship led to fragmentation of ethnic units. The chapter argues that the difficulty that arose from the inability to distinguish between citizens and non-citizens actuated a process of employing the already existing categories as a mode of distinction.

Chronicle of the Assam movement

Assam movement, even though, started off as a reactionary movement against the government's inability to check infiltration, its effect was manifold. Political, economic and cultural issues were enmeshed to produce disastrous consequences. Antecedent to this anti-foreigner movement can be found traced back to the colonial times; however, the immediate event that propelled the Assam movement can be recounted as follows: the sudden demise of Lok Sabha member Hiralal Patwari necessitated by-elections in the Mangaldai constituency. During the preparation of the electoral rolls it was noticed that there was sudden massive increase of electorate. Subsequently, articles in newspapers like the *Dainik Asom*published news and statistical data over the massive influx of illegal settlers.

> According to government estimates the population of Assam increased from 14.6 million in 1971 to 19.9 million in 1981, or 5.3 million (36.3 percent). The all India growth was 24.7 percent, in accordance to this Assam's population should have been 3.6 million. Also, according to the "Sample Registration of the Government of India", the natural population increase of Assam was .5 percent less than the all-India figures in 1970-72 and 1.2 percent less in 1976-78. On the basis of these figures, the immigration into Assam from 1971 to 1981 was on the order of 1.8 million, though these figures do not say whether the immigration had been from elsewhere within India or from Bangladesh. Also, Emigration of Assamese from Assam is virtually nil. According to the 1971 census only 0.6 percent of all Assamese-speaking people in India lived outside of Assam. The Election Commissioner in 1979 reported the unexpected large increase in the electoral rolls. According to the 1951 census, 56.7 percent of the population was Assamese speaking, in 1961 62.4 percent, and in 1971 61 percent. The Bengalis were 16.5 percent, 18 percent, and 19.7 percent, and the Hindi-speaking population was 3.8 percent, 4.8 percent, and 5.4 percent. Between 1951 and 1961 the population of Assam increased from 8 million to 10.6 million (a 35 percent increase), but the number of Assamese speakers rose from 4.6

million to 6.7 million, a 48.5 percent increase, suggesting the magnitude of language "switching". In the 1931 census only 1.7 million people reported Assamese as their mother tongue. Between 1961 and 1971 the proportion of Assamese declined for the first time, as the proportion of Bengali speakers increased.This shift, though small, was in a direction that aroused the anxieties of many Assamese. If a large proportion of the Muslim population (24.6 percent of the population in 1971), most of whom are of Bengali origin, declared themselves Bengali, the position of the Assamese and Bengalis could be reversed. In 1961, of the 913,000 living in the urban areas of the Brahmaputra valley, 38 percent were recorded as speaking Bengali, 33 percent Assamese, and another 13 percent Hindi. In their own urban centers the Assamese were outnumbered by the Bengalis. (Visaria and Visaria 1981: 10-13).

However what affirmed the notion of unaccounted immigration, was the statement by India's Chief Election Officer S. L. Shakdher on 24th October 1978. His views accentuated and reinforced the idea in the psyche of the people of Assam that the inexplicable rise in the electorate was purely due to the inflow of the "foreign nationals". The statement was as follows:

> I would like to refer to the alarming situation in some states, especially in the North eastern region, wherefrom reports are coming regarding large-scale inclusions of foreign nationals in the electoral rolls. In one case, the population in 1971 census recorded an increase as high as 34.98 percent over 1961 census figures and this figure was attributed to the influx of large number of persons from foreign nationals. The influx has become a regular. I think it may not be a wrong assessment to make that on the basis of the increase of 34.98 percent between two census, the increase would likely to be recorded in the 1971 census would be more than 100 percent over 1961 census. In other words, a stage would be reached when that state may have to reckon with the foreign nationals who may be in all probability constitute a sizeable percentage if not the majority of population in the state. (Quoted in Hussain 1993:102).

Following this, a number of complaints were filed from members of civil society demanding a revision the electoral rolls. There were discussions and debate within the academia about the graveness of the problem. The student community took active part in generating consciousness among the masses and developing public opinion. The first organized opposition was in the form of twelve-hour general strike (Assam *bandh*) called All Assam Students Union (AASU)[3] on 8thJune 1979. AASU demanded "detection, disenfranchisement and deportation" of the foreign nationals; those who had entered the state after 1961 should be expelled from the state and their names were to be expunged from the electoral rolls. On 26th August 1979 a number of political and cultural organization came together to form AllAsomGana Sangram Parishad (AAGSP) or Committee for the Assam People's Struggle, which included AASU and Assam's premier literary body the Asom Sahitya Sabha[4]. The objective of AAGSP was to particularly focus on the unchecked immigration issue and demand Assam's economic development, in general. This was the formal call for the Assam movement or Assam Agitation to begin.

The initial phase of the movement was marked by wall writings against government's exclusionary attitude and call for protest. This instantly saw assembling of lakhs of people. Mass sit-ins, picketing, *satyagraha*, strikes and mass signature campaigns, black-outs at night followed soon after. The "National Register of Citizens", 1951 was considered to be the index to locate and identify the illegal immigrants from East Pakistan (and what became the sovereign state of Bangladesh in 1971) and Nepal. AASU called days long Assam *bandhs* which were observed by the masses. As many as 18 lakhs people took oath to carry out the struggle until the foreigners are ousted.

The unprecedented massive civil non-cooperation, strikes and total unlawfulness resulted in the collapse of the Janata Party state government in September 1979. Leaders of the movement called for boycott of the parliamentary elections of December 1979 until the electoral rolls were revised. "No deletion, no election" was the demand. School and colleges were closed. Hundred and thousands of people came together to rally against the central government. The gazetted officers on election duty refused to co-operate with the government. Printing press refused to print the electoral rolls. Even the police were reportedly taking orders from the leaders of the movement[5]. Assam became the first state in Independent India to not have taken part in the parliamentary elections. As a result 12 of the 14 constituencies' seats remained vacant in the elections of 1979, which brought Mrs. Indira Gandhi to power in centre.

Crude oil from the oil fields of upper Assam was refused to the rest of the country through formation of human chain. *Tez dim telnidu* (will give blood but not oil) was the slogan written in their own blood by many youth. Other natural resources such as plywood and teak were also stopped to other parts of the country. The rigid attitude of the agitators to end the movement till their demands were met and the impairing economic blockade made the centre establish President's rule in December 1979, which continued for a year. Towards the end of 1980, the centre became more stringent in dealing with the agitation. Indian army was called to break the oil blockade; the press which was believed to be sympathetic to the cause of the movement came under censorship.

As constitutionally President's rule cannot be extended for more than a year, it became imperative for the centre to hold elections by December 1980. Sanjib Baruah (1999) states that "the decision to end central rule and form a state government in December 1980 indicated the centre's decision to challenge the power capability of the movement and to back electoral institutions that reflected the demographic realties of the state". The Congress (I)[6] ministry headed by AnwaraTaimur[7] was formed. The supporters of the movement refused to accept the new government as a legitimate, elected ministry. The general hostile atmosphere and deflection of the Congress (I) by other parties led to downfall of this government within six months. President's rule was once again imposed in June 1981. In January 1982 another Congress (I) ministry, this time headed by Keshab Gogoi, was formed. This ministry lasted even for lesser time and fell in two months and was replaced by President's rule yet again.

"Fraud in Assam" (1983), the editorial article in *Economic and Political Weekly* at the helm of the Assam movement noted the general hostile atmosphere of Assam as such:

> The situation in Assam even considering that abnormal conditions have prevailed in the state since the end of 1979 when the agitation against the 'foreign nationals' can be said to have formally begun, is truly extraordinary. Paramilitary forces of the Centre as well as well as armed constabularies from other states have now been drafted to maintain law and order in view of the presumed unreliability of the police forces of Assam itself in performing this routine task. The cities and towns of Assam, especially those in the Brahmaputra valley, have become virtual armed camps. Gauhati streets are constantly and relentlessly patrolled by these armed personnel; there is a premium on not being an Assamese during the evening in the streets in Gauhati. The Republic Day parade was held in Gauhati in the midst of 'Janata Curfew' called by the leadership of the agitation, with only the officials attending and being made to sign the attendance registers. The parade marked by a show of tanks, 76 mm

mountain guns, 105 mm field guns and other armaments was itself turned into a blatant display of military muscle against the citizen. (EPW 1983: 125).

The situation in Assam visibly turned into a state crisis. It developed into a terrain where various quarters contested with the elements of nationhood; state, citizenship, governmentality and identity. The tussle that started as a drive by the indigenous people against the foreigners soon became a greater matter of political crisis and cultural contest. State machinery failed on all accounts; Transportation, Law and Order, Health, Emergency. Holding the elections became necessary for the state to sustain its domain on the region, whereas for the agitators averting the elections till the revision of electoral rolls, determined the success of the movement. Though the centre invited the leaders of the movement for several round of talks, yet no decision was reached regarding the impasse. In such a situation the centre announced holding of the elections in January 1983. This saw a rampant violence among the various communities. 1983 witnessed xenophobic bloodshed phase of the Assam movement which until then was by and large peaceful. In the same *EPW* article the editor noted that, "Under the guise of 'constitutional and democratic rectitude' an enormous fraud is being perpetrated in Assam where in conditions in which the election commissioner himself conceded are far from normal, elections are sought to be held for the 126 seats and the12 still unfulfilled Lok Sabha seats" (EPW 1983: 125).

Around this time, the following the trail of the AASU, students belonging to the immigrant communities also organized themselves with political agenda and called themselves the All Assam Minority Students Union (AAMSU). AAMSU which attempted to include both Bengali Hindus and Bengali Muslim descent had come into existence in May 1980. By September 1980 it had become the third front to reckon with in the negotiations between the centre and the agitators. The leaders of AAMSU were also formally invited by the centre along with the leaders of the Assam movement for talks. AAMSU demanded that all the immigrants who came before 1971 were to be given full citizenship and that the state protects the interest of the immigrants and safeguard them from unnecessary harassment. The cut off date of 1971 was not acceptable for the agitators and they continued to demand that the "National Register of Citizenship", 1951 be the index to determine citizenship, the immigrants who have entered after 1961 are deported back. This caused immense tensions between the agitator and the AAMSU. In many places, which were supposedly stronghold of the immigrants, violent incidence started erupting since the beginning of the 1980s between the AASU and the AAMSU. However, most gruesome were the 1983 riots that took place just after the announcement of the elections.

On 18th February 1983, an indigenous tribal group Lalung (also called Tiwa), along with some Assamese, attacked the village of Nellie[8] and several nearby villages with spears, swords, sticks and guns. The tribal group had long resented occupation of the tribal land by the immigrants. The victims were mainly Bengali-Muslim women and children who had mostly migrated from the Mymensingh district of Bangladesh. The official record stated the death toll as 1,200 but according to journalist reports it was as high as 3,000 (Hussain 2000: 4520)[9]. The pogrom is regarded as one of the worst and severest that the post second world war history has witnessed. This unleashed a chain of similar mob attacks. In ChaoulkhowaChapori of Darrang district there was similar attacks on the Bengali-Muslim immigrant population, in Silapathar of Lakhimpur district there was attacks on the Bengali-Hindus, who were ex-refugees/displaced people from East Pakistan (Hussain 2000: 4521). During the same time, members of Bodo tribal group, supporter of pro-poll Plain Tribal Council of Assam (PTCA) attacked Assamese at Gohpur in Darrang district. This violent outburst demonstrated the rift between the Assamese leadership and the Bodo support to the movement, the latter had by now grown sufficiently suspicious of the Assamese hegemonic tendency within the movement (Weiner 1983: 279-281). This was followed by Assamese attack against the Bodos in the same area.

The central government decided to take stern action against the law and order disorder. Several state government employees who had boycottedthe elections and refused to obey government orders were arrested. Polling agents were brought in from other states. In this situation of emergency, leaders of the AASU and the AAGSP who had taken part innegotiations with the central government were also arrested.

The year saw a sanguinary phase of the movement which until now, the violence had been restricted to attacks against bridges, government offices and policestations. Though there had been individual killing; the bomb attack on E.S. Parthasarathy, a high ranking civil servant is one of the most crucial murders. But the year saw organized mob violence, communities pitting against each other, building and breaking of community allegiance. All these were easily identified as "ethnic conflicts".

The electoral turn out and voting pattern in the various locations within the state depicted the tale of demographic polarisation with respect to pro-election or anti-election population. The state elections could not be completed in 16 out of the 126 constituencies, and in one constituency the election had to be countermanded because a candidate was murdered. Elections could not be completed for 7 of the 12 already unfulfilled parliamentary seats. The voter turnout in the various constituencies was marked in accordance with the population settlement and their allegiance. The turnout was above 50 percent in predominantly Bengali-speaking constituencies and as high as 70 percent in several Bodo-populated constituencies. But in the Assamese-populated constituencies the turnout was low; in 25 constituencies less than 5 percent of the electorate voted and in another 20 constituencies the turnout was between 5 and 20 percent (Weiner 1983:281). Mrs. Gandhi's led Congress (I) Party was declared victorious which won 90 out of 108 declared seats, in 4 constituencies the Congress(I) candidates were elected unopposed as no other party contested their candidates.

The election led Congress (I) form the state government headed by HiteshwarSaikia. After the assumption of the ministry, the immediate task of the Saikia government was to confront the agitation. It is alleged that the government played significant role in targeting the weak links and breaking the support base of the Assam movement. For instance HiteshwarSaikia, himself belonging to Ahom community[10], was seen to represent and reinforce a distinct identity, separate from the "upper caste" Assamese. This was to consolidate the idea which had been around that the Assam movement was indeed an assertion of the upper caste Assamese Hindus to perpetuate their hegemony by whipping up traditional fears about a huge influx of Bangladeshis and their assorted crimes, particulary through manipulation of the press and news reports.The fear was instilled by citing instances of theindigenous people of Tripura and Sikkim who had been overwhelmed by a flood of outsiders. The real interest, as many claim,was actually to retain the Assamese Hindu majority in the legislatory Assembly, so that the Muslims and other community did not team up and reduce the Assamese Hindu to minority in the Assembly. The Saikia government offered patronage to the Bodo Sahitya Sabha which emerged as a rival to the Asom Sahitya Sabha, in an effort to weaken the support of the Bodo community to the movement. It also assured general masses about its seriousness to curb infiltration and remove the names of the people who had entered Assam after 1971; this cut off date was by now agreed upon between the leaders of the movement and the centre after several rounds of negotiations. This was asssociated with coercive measures, especially the press was once again brought under censorship and many journalists were arrested.

The cohesion within the movement had been dwindlingafter the ministry was formed, headed by AnwaraTaimur, The Muslim support to the movement had reduced remarkably during Taimur's alleged dual agenda of coaxing and corecion. The Assamese Muslims had started giving second thoughts about participation in the movement after the large victimization of the Muslims in the riots. Several Muslim members within the AASU issued an ultimatum to the AASU leadership demanding a correction of a "pro-Hindu communal tilt". Their memorandum demanded a "firm definition" of a foreigner. The movement also was gradually reducing its popularity among the general masses who had grown dispassionate after the 1983 violence. (Baruah 1999: 134-138). However, the power of the movement refused to wane with the state ministry facing constant protest. Strikes and *satyagraha* continued to be observed until the central government eventually called the leaders for final negotiation in mid 1984. A total of 855 students lost their life in the struggle duing hunger stike, police lathi-charge and other such measures. This was also a time when the central leadership had changed with the assassination of the Mrs. Indira Gandhi. Rajiv Gandhi's leadership began a new phase in the process of the Assam movement.

The eighteen month negotiation between the leaders of the Assam movement and the central government led to the signing of the Assam Accord on 15th August 1985. As a concession to the movement's influential capability, the state government was kept outside the negotiation table and was dissolved with the signing of the accord. The accord came about with many clauses and agreements to assure the leaders of the movement and the general masses. However, the same clauses and agreements are regarded as the root of the rift among the various communities residing in Assam just after the movement ended. AsomGana Parishad (AGP) came into existence from the yoke of AASU. "Upper caste", Assamese speaking Prafulla Mahanta became the youngest and the first student Chief Minister of the country.

Re-viewing the Assam Movement

The Assam agitation has been the most popular post Independence-studentscampaign. It originated within the academic ambit through ample exchange of thoughts. The movement, therefore, that had generated large amount of debate and discussion within the intelligentsia today forms a vital archival source to comprehend the movement.

Marxist scholar, Amalendu Guha in his much discussed article "Little Nationalism Turned Chauvinist: Assam's Anti-Foreigner Upsurge, 1979-80" (Guha 1980), and also in his prior work *Planter-Raj to Swaraj: Freedom Struggle and Electoral Politics in Assam, 1826-1947*, (1977) clearly demonstrated that the Assam agitation was factually an attempt of the Assamese bourgeoisie to secure their political and cultural edge in Assam. He defined "Little Nationalism" as "a spiritual sentiment that holds together a group of people claiming a common cultural-regional identity (to distinguish themselves from others)". Emphasizing on the "class" aspect of movement, he asserts that the prime motives of the agitation was to serve the Assamese middle class in threefold:

(i) Elimination of Bengali and other competitors
(ii) Opportunities of intensification of labour exploitation, unhindered by trade union
(iii) Unhindered control over the state administration for the creation of bureaucratic capital of which the Assamese upper classes could be made beneficiaries.

He argued that Asam Sahitya Sabha and All Assam Students Union did not represent the toiling peasants and workers but the bourgeois-landlords and petty bourgeois elements. They, through careful mediation with the communication media were able to secure a "mass" character to the agitation with the inclusion of peasants and other working sections. He insists that the ethnic outlook or the "little nationalism" that the movement assumed was indeed a manipulative political stance applied by the Assamese middle class.

This write-up published during the helm of the agitation, instigated tremendous intellectual debate. Scholars responded with immense passion; many critiqued Guha's position, others provided rejoinders. This string of exchanges today presents an important tool in deciphering theoretical answers to the baffling multi-layered nature of the movement. Well-known political observant of Assam UdayonMisra (Misra 1981) provided a sharp eight point critique to Guha. Providing statistical and analytical counter arguments, he raises the issues of assimilation and affirms the political and cultural threat posed by the immigrants. According to him, Guha's assumption that like in the eighteenth century, assimilation of the current immigrants into the broader Assamese identity is the possible antidote to the present cauldron is impractical; as the conditions are very different under feudalism (Ahom rule of eighteenth century), imperialism (British rule) and post colonial situation. He also disapproves Guha's reading of a speech by Tarunram Phukan, popular pre-Independence congressman of Assam, in 1927 as sowing the seeds of chauvinism in the Assamese psychic. The lines "*Uthi aha jatirjibonorcinhaisepuraruparatprabhava bistar kora*" (*Asom Sahitya SabharBhasanawali*, Vol I, Jorhat, 1955), Misra recounts have been misconstrued by Guha and what Tarunram Phukan actually meant was, "The sign of life of a rising nationality is the influence it extends over others" and not, "A rising nationality shows signs of life by extending domination over others" as interpreted by Guha. The debate within the intelligentsia, at this point of time presents a figurative aspect of how the question of Assamese nationality was getting framed at that point of time. Gail Omvedt counters Guha on the chauvinistic dimension of the Assamese and affirms that the Assam movement indeed involves a question of nationality. Omvedt repeals Guha's position that the Assam movement is not a nationalist movement as it does not involve the demand for secession. She recounts that from a Marxist-Leninist position the right to self-determination is fundamental and the movements of oppressed nationalities to exercise this right against an exploitative State are a crucial part of any general revolutionary movement. In the case of Assam movement, she affirms, the Indian State and the stronger Bengali nationality cannot be negated to have played an oppressive role. Finally she argues that given all the objective indicators of Assam's continuing backwardness, impoverishment and dominance of semi-feudal relations in comparison to other Indian states, the Assamese middle class,possibly, could not have suddenly become strong. Also, the immense mass support that the movement is able to generated implied that there are genuine material base (of losing land and political power) unlike other divisive bourgeoisie stirs (like the Shiv Sena that do not enjoy popularity in the Maharashtrian countryside). One more vital rejoinder came from Hiren Gohain (Gohain1981), another Marxist scholar of Assam. He agrees with Guha that the main thrust and character of such movements depend on its more stable features, on its actual programme and its class-leadership. From this point of view, he affirms the current movement in Assam definitely serves the interest of the Assamese small bourgeoisie and landlords, and is most likely to profit the big bourgeoisie but he defies Guha on the point that the latter has failed to capture the class character of the national Congress leadership because of which the national question has not been amply dealt with and the conflicts between "great" nationalism and "little" nationalism is a failure of the bourgeoisie-democratic revolution of India.

> Thus his treatment necessarily fails to throw any light on the exact relationship between the regional bourgeoisie and the "national" big bourgeoisie. Guha also fails to be sufficiently critical of the class character of the Congress leadership on the national scale. Hence, while he makes much of the chauvinist tendencies in the Assamese middleclass, he is unable to see that this can be connected with the failure of the all-India leadership to solve the national question with wisdom and foresight. The tendency to dominate and browbeat the aspirations of small national groups was there among a considerable section of the national leadership from the very beginning. Guha does not draw relevant conclusions from the data supplied by himself... For instance, on many occasions the Assam leadership failed to agree with the views of the national leadership... This may be of course considered in terms of the vested interests of the provincial leaders. But a more pertinent point is the inability of the national leadership to appreciate the difficulties of a neglected, backward and weak national group... Against such a backdrop, the fears and worries of the Assamese are understandable. Seen in this light the conflict between "little nationalism" and great nationalism… appears as a portentous failure of the bourgeois- democratic revolution in India. (Gohain 1981).

Finally contribution came from the political scientist Sanjib Kumar Baruah (Baruah 1981). He disputes Guha's statement that the Assam movement was "national in form, chauvinist and undemocratic in content and proto-fascist in its methods". Through his contradiction of Guha's three major assumptions,he establishes that the Assam movement was indeed a sub-national movement (these he further details out in his later work *India against Itself: Assam and the Politics of Nationality*, 1999). The three points are: first, that Assam movement is not a struggle for self-determination in Lenin's sense of the term. Second, the notion of a threat to the cultural identity of the Assamese is a myth. Third, and this follows from his first two points - the primary explanation for the Assam movement lies elsewhere; it is a conjuncture of crisis of the dominant economic classes in Assam, which explains the "undemocratic content" of the movement. Baruah argues that the Assamese constitutes one of the smaller nationalities in contemporary India. Though the Bengali culture and the Bengali people do not currently enjoy the privileged position in the higher echelons of bureaucracy and official parameters as in the colonial Assam, the historical elements and sense of domination-subordination still persists and is not snapped by a cut-off date. Moreover, the recent fate that similar "frontier" people met in Tripura; of losing their rights as "basic population" to the immigrants from Bangladesh, further aggravates the danger. He quotes Lenin (whom Guha repeatedly invokes) who calls great nations chauvinistic for "treating the national movements of small nations with disdain". Hence he negates Guha's first assumption and affirms that the current movement is indeed a movement of self-determination and not a "picnic style movement" as some had scornfully opinionated about it. Regarding the question of identity threat which Guha had relegated as a myth, he quotes Susanta Krishna Dass, (who has done extensive statistical study on the demographical changes and population growth in Assam and whose statistical findings even Guha had cited), "If the proportion of immigrants to indigenous people is taken as the criterion of assessing the weightage ofimmigration it will be found that nextonly to Brazil, Assam as a geographical region bears the heaviest impact of outsiders. Also among Indian States, it has accommodated the largest proportionate number of people from elsewhere". (Baruah 1981: 677). According to Baruah, Guha's opinion is heavily borrowed from the Census reports, which, he says has its own pitfalls. Baruah compares the immigration situation in West Bengal and in Assam and refutes Guha's claim that though influx is similar in West Bengal too, the Left politics has kept the immigration issue under control. Baruah, on the other hand, states that unlike Assam, Bengalis in West Bengal are not culturally threatened by the immigrants from Bangladesh and the Bengali "bhadralok" have kept the immigrants away from positions of power. Baruah repeats that contrary to what Guha believes that Assamese little nationalism has "acquired an aggressive tone" way back in the 1920s, Assamese nationalism was in fact helpless at the onslaught of cultural threat posed by uncontrolled influx in their own land. He quotes from the same lecture by Tarunram Phukan delivered in 1927, "Alas!", continued Phukan, "it is otherwise; we are incapable of self-defence today. The latter sentence, Baruah repeats is a pointer to enquire into the context in which Assamese subnationalism was growing. The question according to Baruah is whether or not, the Assamese had to defend themselves as early as in 1927, Guha entirely misses the significance of the fact that Phukan's speech was made at a time when migration from East Bengal was reaching record levels and Assamese political protest against it had started. In regards to the class axis, Guha's assumption that it is held by "Indian industrialist, traders, petty landlords, and various sections of petty bourgeoisie urban and rural" and that it was because of this middle class' quest for hegemony that the "Indian nationalism as well as regional nationalism originated". In this assumption, Baruah notes, Guha slips into the sociological theories of social stratification rather than Marxist class analysis, as he had set out to do. In order to define the middle class in Assam, Guha uses the pyramid of social stratification and strikes out the big bourgeoisie at the top, for in Assam it is held by North Indians and is in collaboration with the foreign capital. Even the next stratum is eliminated because a negligible number of the middle bourgeoisie in Assam speaks Assamese. Therefore the middle class according to Guha "virtually consists of small capitalists and other sections of petty bourgeoisie including professionals and service-holders many of whom are also simultaneously small landlords". Guha, according to Baruah, did not pause to think if the relative backwardness of Assam, which shows up in the weakness of some of the classes, could have produced a situation different from that in other states. The Assam movement, according to Guha, was a programme lead by the Assamese middle class at a conjunctural crisis. According to him, hardpressed by big capital from above and the rising labour and peasant movement from below, the Assamese upper classes are terribly agitated about the economic stagnation. Incapable of competing with big capital, they aspired to monopolise the small industries, petty trade and the profession and services.

Baruah cites that Guha considerably expands on his notion of the middle class when it comes to explaining the Assam movement. At places he uses terms such as "upper classes" or "bourgeois-landlord chauvinists" - terms which include, apart from the middle classes, some gate-crashers from the top stratum. Therefore, the "undemocratic content" of the movement, propelled by class bases, as established by Guha is misleading, rather, he emphasizes that this mass movement is in fact a sub-national movement.

Sanjib Baruah in his much acclaimed work on Assam*India against Itself: Assam and the Politics of Nationality* (1999) has delved into the question of Assam's identity in details. He calls the Assam movement a subnationalist upsurge[11]. He locates the crux in the very idea of "nation" which subscribes that political entity should neatly coincide with that of a cultural formation. According to him the subnational conflicts of today are part of that bloody history of nation-building–of trying to create a global order of nation states. According to him "the fit between the formally federal structure of the Indian polity and the emotive power of these subnational narratives is hardly perfect".

> Yet these movements have led to serious and sustained albeit localized, political crisis. This has happened largely because, even though separatists may be a small or a fringe group, they have large constituencies in their region. These movements are located in historically constituted subnational ideological fields and have a dialogical relationship with pan-Indian political institution, processes and values. Regional militants often raise issues that are intertextual in the sense that they allude to are continuous with the mainstream social discourse of a region. As a result there is often a pattern of complicity between insurgent groups and may supposedly mainstream political actors.
>
> ... If nations and nationalities are "imagined communities", subnational narratives, like national ones, are often premised on a poetics about a homeland and its people. It is a poetics that transforms the geography of an area into a primal, homelike, or sacred place and transforms a people into a collectivity with imagines ties of shared origins and kinship. Historically in India, subnational narratives arose simultaneously with—even sometimes predated—pan-Indian national narratives. Like nationalism, the cultural foundation of India's regional based subnationalisms was the language of the region—to be precise the language that were emerging as, or were aspiring to become, regional standards. (Baruah 1999: Xii-8).

Baruah's idea of two tiered nationalism; one pan-Indian and the other regional, is not different from Amalendu Guha (1977) and Sudhir Chandra's (1982) formulation that Assamese identity consciousness based on regional cultural homogeneity developed along with the all India cultural homogeneity and anti imperialism in the beginning of 19th century. Baruah however succeeds in drawing attention to the fact that the conflicts in Assam are symptomatic of failed subnational aspirations in Indian nation building process. He refers to instances in which movements of self-determination have proved to be difficult[12] and asserts that concept of nation is inherently unstable. Baruah work is significant as it details an account of the colonial policies of geographical demarcation which has today become the bone of contention among the various communities of Assam[13]. However, Baruah though points out that the identities in contemporary Assam are "ethnicized", by means of the various movements, he does not go further to give details of why and how this phenomenon has succeeded in dominating the socio-political domain of Assam.

Myron Weiner has raised pertinent questions on the Assam movement in his work *Sons of the Soil* (1978) and later in "The Political Demography of Assam's Anti-Immigrant Movement" (1983). At what point does immigration— legal or illegal— trigger a community response? Is there some numerical threshold of "over foreignization" that prompts a nativist reaction? Is there some point when a native population fears that it is being culturally overwhelmed by outsiders? Or is the triggering mechanism competition for employment and land in a society where population is expanding more rapidly than can be absorbed either in industry or agriculture? According to him, all of the factors suggested by these questions seem to have been at work in Assam, But he points out that a review of the history of ethnic conflict in the region suggests that the issue of who has control over the state apparatus, and whether that control is threatened is often the decisive factor in the forms and intensity of ethnic conflict. Weiner traces the eruption of the Assam movement from the colonial times. He marks the beginning of significant wave of immigration to Assam shortly before the middle of 19th century when the British created tea plantation in hill areas. Unable to persuade the locals to work in the plantation as menial labourers, most of whom owned their own lands, the British brought in a labour force from the tribal region of south Bihar. Together with this, there was an influx of educated Bengali Hindus into positions in the government administrative services and in the professional services. The 1891 census estimated that one fourth of the population of the Brahmaputra valley was of migrant origin. However, Weiner recounts that the largest influx took place after 1900 when Bengali Muslims moved into the Brahmaputra valley from East Bengal. Assam was sparsely populated than east Bengal. Bengali Muslims reclaimed thousands of acres of land, cleared vat tracts of dense jungle along the south bank of Brahmaputra and occupied flooded lowlands along the river. The largest influx came from Mymensingh district, one of the mostly populated districts in East Bengal (presently in Bangladesh).

These waves of immigrants however did not create political uproar until the 1930s and the 1940s when electoral politics was introduced. Weiner describes that at this junction the numerically strong Bengali Muslims had won substantial control over the state government and attempted to use their position to facilitate further migration of Bengali Muslims from East Bengal to strengthen their political position and then finally to press for the incorporation of Assam into the proposed Muslim majority state of Pakistan. The British rejected this demand of the Muslim League, but agreed to partition Assam by transferring Sylhet district to Pakistan. Once Sylhet was removed from Assam, the Bengali Muslims lost their political grip on the state mechanism. After Independence, the Assamese, particularly the Assamese Hindu middle class won control over the government of the newly formed state of independent India. For the first time in hundred and fifty years the Assamese were back in power. They used that control to assert the paramount of Assamese cultural identity and to seek economic and social equality in relation to the Bengali Hindu middle classes-their rivals for jobs in the administrative services, in the professions, and in the private sector.The Assamese-dominated government of Assam made Assamese the official language of the state and established a policy of giving preference to "sons of the soil" (i.e., Assamese) in employment in the state administrative services; appointed Assamese teachers in the schools; and pressed for the use of Assamese as the medium of instruction in schools, colleges, and universities. In this campaign to assert their culture and improve the employment opportunities of the Assamese middle classes, the Assamese won the support of two migrant communities, the tea plantation labourers from Bihar, and the Bengali Muslims. Both declared to census enumerators that Assamese was their native tongue, and both voted for the Assamese-dominated Congress party. As a result Congress easily won every one of the state assembly and parliamentary elections from 1952 through 1977. Even in the 1977 parliamentary elections, when Congress was defeated nationally with only 34.5 percent of the vote, in Assam Congress won 50.6 percent of the vote.After partition, Bengali Muslims turned to the state government for protection as Muslims did elsewhere in India. Many feared expulsion to East Pakistan, especially after the passage of the Immigrant Expulsion (from Assam)Act by India's parliament in 1950. This act, combined with an act passed by the Assam legislature declaring squatter settlements illegal, led many Bengali Muslims to fear that they could be removed from lands illegally held or expelled from the country. In an effort to dissuade the Assamese from taking these steps, Bengali Muslims sided with the Assamese on issues that mattered to them, by declaring their mother tongue as Assamese, accepting the establishment of primary and secondary schools in Assamese, supporting the government against Bengali Hindus on the controversial issue of an official language for the state and for the university, and casting their votes for Congress. This coalition of the Assamese and the Bengali Muslims remained till 1977. Though there had been major language riots between the Assamese and the Bengali Hindus in the early 1970s, the Bengali Muslims evidently sided with the Assamese. It was in 1978 that the sudden death of Hiralal Patwari necessitated by-election in the Mangaldai constituency. The process of the election drew public attention to a rapid expansion of the number of voters since the previous elections two years earlier[14]. As stated earlier, the influx became politically alarming when the Election Commissioner reported the unexpected large increase in the electoral rolls.

> To many Assamese it appeared as if the Bengali Hindus and Bengali Muslims together were now in a position to undermine Assamese rule. Many feared that the census would show a sharp decline in the number of Assamese speakers as Bengalis who had previously declared their language Assamese would now officially revert to Bengali. (Weiner 1983:286).

Weiner considers realization of this demographic transformation at this junction as the impetus that launched the Assam movement. However, he marks another political transition that was enfolding in the national level which had equal impact on the interpersonal relationship among the communities of Assam. This was the break-up within the Congress party after the 1977 elections[15]. This split within Congress ended the post independence coalition of Assamese Hindus and Bengali Muslims.Because what had attracted Bengali Muslims to Congress was the certainty that Congress would govern the state. Some Bengali Muslims subsequently shifted their support to other parties, as did some of the Bengali Hindus who had earlier supported the Congress.

The Assam movement was in many ways significant in the political and cultural milieu of Assam. However, the significant effect that it ushered in was the fissure among the various communities which until now had existed in political and social conciliation. The land which had been historically described as a composite land, housing numerous "ethnic" groups now witnessed tension among them. The agitation studied as demonstration of Assamese chauvinism by Guha, subnationalist upsurge by Baruah and a reaction to the political and demographic transformation by Weiner has still not been analysed for its role in heightening the "ethnic" factor of the identities. It was during and after the movement that the identities organized, consolidated and formulated their ethnic expression to reckon with the components of belonging to the nation: citizenship, identity and rights. The cultural identities pronounced themselves in the political arena contesting head on with national life. The Assam movement brought in a fresh wave of identity consciousness among the people of Assam. This idea of identity, however, was not new but already existent in the socio-cultural milieu of Assam.

Tracing the Genesis

The Assam movement, like all other movements, did not erupt suddenly. Glimpses of dissidence on similar issue could be seen during the language riot in 1960-61. These riots occurred between the patriots of Assamese and Bengali, before and after passing the Official Language Bill (which sought to establish Assamese as the only state language in Assam) by the state Assembly, resulting in large scale violence with deaths of youth, both Assamese and Bengali[16]. The riots broke again in 1972 when the Gauhati University decided to switch the language of instruction to Assamese as language of undergraduate education[17]. However, the language question had much deep rooted concern that had been vexing the people of Assam since the colonial times.

In 1826, The East India Company annexed lower Assam and tried to establish its hegemony in upperAssam through a puppet king, Purander Singh. This setup however, did not prove to be beneficial and the Company annexed the entire territory and placed it underthe Bengal Presidency. Assam was administered as part of Bengal from 1826 to1873. In 1874, Assam was made a Chief Commissioner's province and three districts of Bengal: Cachar and Sylhet and Goalpara came under the provincial administrationof Assam.

Later, the boundary re-organization done at the behest of Lord Curzon in 1905 proved crucial in opening up new vistas in the socio-political facet of Assam, which in many ways can also be marked as the beginning of the immigration issue in Assam. In accordance to this re-organisation, the British partitioned the densely populated province of Bengal into a predominantly Bengali Muslim province in the East which incorporated Assam and named the unit 'East Bengal and Assam' with Dacca as the capital, and a predominantly Bengali Hindu province in the West: the 'West Bengal'. Bengali Hindus reacted stringently at the partitionof their province. The Assamese also strongly resented its incorporation as a portion of Bengal. This anti-partition movement of Bengal soon came to be known as Swadeshi movement. As a result of the strong opposition, in 1912 the British annulled the partitionand re-established Assam as a separate Chief Commissioner's province that included the predominantly Bengali Muslim district of Sylhet and the predominantly Bengali Hindu district of Cachar.

These new boundaries remained intact until the partition of India. However, during the partition, Assam was included in Group C by the Cabinet Mission, this inclusion was almost agreed by the Indian National Congress. Assam Congress leaders like Gopinath Bordoloi vehemently opposed this proposal and were successful in securing the support of Gandhi. Finally Assam was excluded from the plan and only Sylhet district was conceded to Pakistan.

The British establishment had started new industrial enterprises in Assam, significant among them were the Assam tea industry and jute trade. These new enterprises required a regular supply of labour. Thousands of labourers were annually recruited from Bihar, Chotanagpur,Uttar Pradesh and Madras, most of them did not return. Another significant stream of migration was that of peasants from East Bengal districts, 85 to 90 percent of whom were Muslims (Barua 1978: 70). Noting the apprehension of the Assamese during these times, Sandhya Barua (1978: 70-71) writes that, "Though the process of assimilation of these migrant groups was extremely slow, they aspired to be on par with the Assamese in the valley. No doubt the immigrants contributed to Assam's economy by bringing large tracts ofwaste land under cultivation, but their rising number made the Assamese anxious about their social and political position".

The clear approach of British administration in settling more immigrants in the land of Assam was evident as labour legislation related to the recruitment of workers brought in to Assam, their journey to the designated districts and their status while working under contracts were passed, as early as 1863.

One of the features of British rule was to discount local languages and arrange provincial boundaries for facilitating cheap and simplified administration. In April 1831, when Assam was part of Bengalad-ministration, the Government of Bengal replaced Bengali in the place of Persian as the Court language of Assam. The services of the Bengalis immediately became indispensable in the anglo-vernacular and vernacular schools. The preference of Bengali caused a social dominance of the language and its speakers over the people of Assam, Orissa, Chotanagpur and parts of Bihar, where it was established as the official language.

However these areas, eventually, began to produce their own youth equipped with modern education. These ambitious youth grew eager for a share in the opportunities in their own land, which they assumed were being snatched away by the Bengalis. They attempted to redress the balance by stressing that their own languages be recognized as the languages of administration and law. Bengali supremacy was challenged by the patriotism forlanguages like the Assamese, Oriya and Bihari.In 1852, Assamese nationalist Anandaram Dhekiyal Phukan petitioned to Moffat Mills against instruction in the vernacular schools being imparted in foreign language, that is, Bengali (Baruah 1999: 71).

Assam lagged behind many parts of India during the medieval times. Low level of economic development, geographical inconvenience and the isolationist policy of the Ahom monarchy were some of the causes for its relative backwardness which could not be recovered even with the downfall of the feudal order. The absence of native capitalist in Assam, was the main reason why Marwari merchants were successful in setting up commercial monopoly who had followed the British into Assam and diligently tapped the few opportunities for money making opened by the British, like money-lending, supplying provisions to the tea-gardens, procuring mustard and jute for the market outside Assam, and meeting the demand for new cheap and mass produced household implements. This was objected to by Maniram Dewan in his memorandum to A J Moffatt Mills, during the latter's visit to the province in 1853, "Under the revenue settlement of military officers, while a number of respectable Assamese are out of employ, the inhabitants of Marwar and Bengalees from Sylhet have been appointed to Mouzadarships; and for us respectable Assamese to become the ryots [tenents] of such foreigners is a source of deep mortification". (Mills 1854: 607).

The socio-political conditions that emerged in the colonial rule planted a latent fear in the minds of the people of Assam of being swamped by the Bengali-speaking people. As a consequence, "Bangali" (Bengali) became synonymous to "foreigners". Infact the Britishers were called "Boga Bangali" (white Bengali) by the common people of Assam (Gupta 1984: 100). In 1937, during the Indian freedom movement, two leading Assamese intellectuals, Ambikagiri Roy Choudhury and Nilmoni Phukan, had submitted a formal representation to Jawaharlal Nehru which stated that the Congress would get the whole-hearted support of the people of Assam only if it backed effective steps to fight the influx from Bengal; otherwise, they maintained, the Assamese intelligentsia might favour secession from India. (Misra 1979:1993).

Assam movement, hence, can be seen as one more expression of the historic Assamese-Bengali rivalry that had been occupying a significant place in the socio-political life of Assam since the colonial period. The encouragement to immigration during the colonial period, re-organization of boundaries, language bills etc contributed in the commemoration of the Assam movement in 1979. Nevertheless, many other features had emerged and were enmeshed in the new political conditions. The Assam movement ramified the identities and positioned them in a new emergent context, the context of citizenship, ethnicization of the identities was the most significant aspect of the movement.

ULFA's XhunorAxom[18] and Negation of the State

> The people of Assam have been the worst sufferers as a result of the ongoing conflicts. Three decades of widespread human rights violation in the form of arrests, detention, killings and at times genocide have made life miserable for the democratic civilian population. As a result, over the years, various political and non-political organization, intellectuals and various cross sections of the civil society have been demanding for a political solution for the long standing arm conflict known as "Indo Assam Conflict". (Borbora 2008:3).

The above paragraph from the *Comprehensive Note on Armed Conflict in Assam (India) and Political Resolution through Peace Process* presented at the 9th Session of Human Rights Council in Geneva by Arup Borbora, Spokesperson, People's Consultative Group (PCG) represents the United Liberation Front of Assam (ULFA) not only as a civilian armed aggression but also as a quandary that has emerged as a challenge to the process of nation building itself. In more than three decade of its existence, the ULFA has thrived on its foundational basis of articulating an idea of discrete peoplehood for and about the people of Assam, accentuating the question of economic deprivation by the Indian State to incur its demand for secession from India. It is ULFA's argument that India's failure to address and redress the deplorable economic condition of the people of Assam negates its sovereign power over Assam. The chapter identifies three interlocutors that exist in the common parlance of Assam, which was used by the ULFA as its medium to frame a separate identity of the self. The chapter argues that ULFA is a rejoinder of the already existing narrative of injustice and exclusion. This narrative was endowed with a violent ethnicized turn by the ULFA.

The United Liberation Front of Assam vehemently invaded the socio-political scene of Assam in the early 1980s with a series of political assassination and bank robberies[19], though it claims to have founded itself in the late 1970s. It is today a banned extremist group. The ULFA, as it is commonly known as, has been successful in acclaiming itself as the most intimidating form of military nationalism which continues to spur terror and violence till present day. The idea it adheres to is that Assam as a territory, people and culture has never been a part of India. Further, the colonial pattern of exploitation of the resources of Assam without paying dues to the development and progress of the region and its people nullifies the Indian State to rule over the region.

ULFA emerged right after and as a contrast to the Assam movement which had placed great optimism on the Indian State and constitutional amendment. ULFA categorically refused the authority of the State. Unlike the Assam movement, which evoked its strong socio-cultural links with the rest of India and which often adopted largely Gandhian strategy, the insurgency led by the ULFA is blatantly secessionist in nature.In its official website ULFA states that, "To liberate Assam, (a land of 78,529 square K.M.), through Armed national liberation struggle from the clutches of the illegal occupation of India and to establish a sovereign Independent Assam"[20] as its objective and goal. In the same website ULFA validates its choice for violence as a measure to counter the "colonial occupation" of the Indian state in Assam.

> Assam was never a part of India at any point of time in history. The fact is independent Assam has been occupied by India, and deploying occupation forces they are oppressing our peoples and persecuting them. ULFA itself and all freedom fighters of Assam are neither planning nor conspiring to break up India! We are not conducting any armed operation inside India. Freedom fighters of Assam are only trying to overthrow Indian colonial occupation from Assam. (http://www.geocities.com/CapitolHill/Congress/7434/ulfa.htm).

The ULFA since its inception has been responsible for innumerable deaths, bomb blasts, kidnapping and extortion. The key issues that it earmarked were control over the natural resources of the region, the rate and pattern of development, demographic changes and the question of preserving the traditional culture from being contaminated.In August 2011, India's Ministry of Home Affairs in New Delhi welcomed seven top leaders of the banned United Liberation Front of Assam (ULFA). In a meeting with the home minister, the ULFA delegation submitted a "framework" for negotiation to resolve "the issue between Assam and India". The document calls for an honourable, meaningful and peaceful resolution of those issues. ULFA's platform of restoring Assam's sovereignty—which it regarded as non-negotiable till recently—was now replaced by a call for a "fresh look at the issues of sovereignty, also as to ensure that the people of Assam can assert their inalienable rights to control their land and their resources therein.[21] In meetings with the press, these leaders have since been speaking of constitutional change, and constitutional safeguards to protect the rights and identity of the people of Assam. Press reports quoted Home Minister P. Chidambaram assuring the leaders that there is no "problem which cannot be solved within the framework of the Constitution".[22]

It is believed that ULFA does not possess the lethality that other insurgent groups in India do. Its armed activities are, in general, more in the nature of selective assassinations and acts of sabotage against State-owned economic assets like the oil pipeline, rather than aimless terror tactics.The Indian intelligence agency reports reveal that it possesses thrice the number of weapons suitable for guerrilla activities. However, the importance of ULFA lies not on its terror activities but in the all pervasive effect on the society of Assam. The support and sympathy it received from the masses during the initial phase of its inception has been phenomenal. In those years, criticizing the ULFA was an assured means of earning unpopularity in Assam. For M.S. Prabhakara (1990), "ULFA is a state of mind in Assam".

The emergence and popularity of ULFA not only provides a rejoinder in understanding the rise of politics in the ethnic lines in lesser developed societies but also raises questions about the relationship between development and mobilization of the people along ethnicity. Jyotindra Das Gupta puts forward that ethnicity is not merely as a non-rational action impinging on the rationality of Indian planned processes of development, on the contrary, the centralized planning for economic development in India has selectively dispensed benefits of development to certain ethnic groups, encouraging ethnic dominion and subsequent ethnic mobilization by the other groups. Democratic rules, as exists in India, provide options to such access through its inclusionary avenues. (Das Gupta 1991:145-47). Partha Chaterjee echoes similar thoughts with regard to the process of planning for economic development in India, is of the opinion that among the other functions that the process was conceived would perform; it was also a modality of the post colonial state to illustrate a critique to the colonial reign. As alien rule instilled exploitation and large-scale poverty, self-rule would do the reverse-development and progress. It was a means of generate national consciousness (Chatterjee 1997:276-77) Failure of which, would then follows, the sense of colonialism still persists. If this is the economic base for assessing the success of post colonial nation, then rise of ULFA and the immense popularity it gained among the masses during its initial period of emergence alludes to the fact that the Indian State has not been able to deliver its goals of post colonial economic prosperity in Assam.

An overview of Assam's economic background presents an apparent picture of disparity. The state lags far behind both industrially and commercially. In contrast to the state's relative poverty, it is rich a rich source of oil, tea, coal, and plywood. Though Assam supplies 60% of India's crude oil, it receives from the central authority only 3% of its value in the form of royalty. Assam is major centre for tea in India, only a small portion of the tea produced is sold in Assam through auction, 85% is sold through West Bengal and London auction. In fact Assam's share of tea royalties is less than half that which west Bengal receives. Assam supplies 60% of India's plywood but only a very small part of the return from the product is retained by the state- an inappropriately large share goes to the centre in the form of taxes (Das Gupta 1991:157, Misra, T 1980: 1354-64). A general feeling of deprivation and neglect among the masses was already in place much before the ULFA raised it scrupulously. The preceding Assam movement was also on the issue of control of the resources within the state and access to national resources by those who considers themselves as "authentic" citizens of India. The Assam movement also, before the ULFA raised the issue of under development but the fundamental divergence was the difference of attitude towards the Indian state. While the Assam movement saw the Indian State as an apostle of justice, the ULFA rejected the authority of the Indian State. By the invocation of the long history of disjuncture, demographically and emotionally, they appropriated their claim for complete secession from India. This feeling in many ways resonated with the deep seated grievance of exclusion which heightened the acceptance and popularity of the ULFA among the masses at the time of its emergence. The Indian State however did little in terms of its responses to the political and ideological challenge posed by ULFA. The reaction to ULFA from the Indian State was mostly military.

ULFA's demand for secession was fostered by its ability to repudiate Assam's political and cultural history with that of India. By articulating a distinctive disjuncture, it elucidated that ULFA was not a mindless terrorist organization but was an outcome of the gross malevolence that was being meted out to the people of Assam since a very long time. Its goal was to achieve the apostle of dignity of a people- "freedom". Three important interlocutors can be marked as the terrain that enabled the ULFA to formulate its idea of separate peoplehood for the people of Assam. These three inter-related interlocutors which buttressed its claim for uprising and vindicated its subsequent goal of secession can be pinpointed as: the idea of colonial pattern of exploitation of the Assam's natural resources, social exclusion by mainstream India and India's illegitimate occupancy over the land and people of Assam.

"Colonial Pattern of Economic Exploitation of Assam": Mapping the Hinterland.

The idea that Assam is a land neglected and exploited throughout the history is not a notion introduced by the ULFA. The social discourse within Assam contains deep seated resentment towards the attitude of the Centre in regards to its interest.

A vast body of post Independence writing on Assam has critiqued the socially exclusionary and economically disparate attitude of the State towards the region[23]. Tilottoma Misra (1980) in the article "Assam: A Colonial Hinterland", resonated the censure of a large section of Assam's intelligentsia in regard to the economic policies of the government towards the state. She termed the economic strategy of the Indian state as "colonial pattern of exploitation of Assam's natural resources". Misra, points out that Assam despite being the country's largest producer of tea, oil, plywood and forest products is one of the poorest and industrially most backward states of India. Her article was published at the peak of the Assam movement detailing out the putative economic exploitation of the resources of Assam, "A positive outcome of the nine-month old agitation on the foreigner's issue in Assam in the growing awareness among the Assamese people of being subjected gross economic exploitation on a scale comparable to, and sometimes even worse than in, the pre-independence days" (Misra 1980: 1357). She describes the economic situation of Assam vis-à-vis the national and points out that:

> Despite being the country's largest producer of tea, oil, plywood and forest products, Assam is one of the poorest and industrially most backward states of India. India annually earns millions of rupees as foreign exchange from Assam's products, but the per capita income (at current prices) of Assam in 1976-77 was only Rs 816 (one of the

lowest in India) as against the per capita National Income of Rs 1,049 for that year. Manufactured goods from the metropolitan centres in other parts of the country are sold in Assam at three to four times their original price. About 23 percent of the per capita income of Assam is spent in buying consumer goods from outside the state. (Misra 1980: 1357).

Misra in her article delves into all the major economic resources of Assam namely tea, petroleum, natural gas, plywood, fertilizer and jute and underscores the "extractive enterprise" of the central government in each of these industries.

To understand the extent of exploitation, the Assam tea industry is an important source. The Assam tea industry was established by the British colonial rulers in 1834. It is the country's highest and one of the world's highest tea producing regions[24]. However, the total annual profit and foreign exchange earned from the tea gardens of Assam is several times more than the total annual revenue received by the state. In 1980, at the helm of the Assam movement and beginning of the ULFA stir, Jyotirmoy Basu (CPI (M)) in Lok Sabha session while speaking on Appropriation Bill of Assam Budget pointed out that Assam gets on 22 crores of the tea produced in the state whereas West Bengal gets 42 crores as sales tax for the tea from the Assam gardens auctioned in Calcutta[25]. Assam is entitled to an agricultural tax imposed on 60 percent of the profit from the tea gardens, while the Central government is entitled to an income-tax on 40 percent of the total profit. But it is widely believed that the Indian and foreign capitalists conceal most of the profits, thus robbing the state from its due share of revenue and taxes (Borgohain 1980: 43-47). It was only in 1970 that Guwahati Tea Auction Centre was inaugurated. Even the main office of the Tea Board, which is the highest authority in relation to the tea industry and which besides implementing the Tea Act of 1958 is also responsible for approving grants, loans, and labour-welfare projects, is situated in Calcutta.

Assam is rich reservoirs of crude oil and natural gas. During the 1980s Assam had an estimated reserve of 70.46 million tonnes of crude oil and 23,000 million cubic meters of natural gas. About 43 lakh tonnes of crude is produced by the oil fields of upper Assam and since the crude has very high percentage of aromatic content, it is rated high in the world market. According to the international price standards, Assam crude should cost at least 1.5 times more than the low grade Organization of the Petroleum Exporting Countries (OPEC) crude. But despite possessing such rich resources, Assam's economy gets little from its oil. The Centre has time and again refused to establish large public sector refineries in Assam in spite of mass movements[26]. Alongside, the by-product kerosene produced in the refineries of Assam is carried by a product pipe-line all the way to Siliguri in West Bengal where the marketing division of the product is situated and from there it is distributed to the north-eastern states for their consumption. As a result of this, not only do many areas in Assam suffer from acute shortage of kerosene but the state is deprived of the sale revenue which goes to West Bengal. Furthermore, the royalty given to Assam for petroleum is meager[27]. Similarly, about 50 million cubic feet of natural gas is being flared off daily in different oil fields of Assam for several decades. Had these been properly used, Assam would have turned into one of the richest states regarding power generation and production of various industrial goods like different types of rubber, plastic, nylon, polyester fibres, paints, dyes, lacquer, pesticides and various other chemicals. Due to almost non-utilization of the natural gas and the by-products of the crude refined in Assam, no ancillary industries have been set up in Assam.

Another economically viable industry of Assam is the plywood industry which like the other resources is severely extractive in nature. Almost 80 percent of the plywood produced in the factories in Assam is transported by road and rail to depots in other parts of the country. Not one sale depot was situated in Assam during the 1980s though the state produced several lakh cubic meters of plywood. Not a single plywood factory was owned either by the local people or by the state government; neither was a single plywood sale agency was given to anyone from Assam. Gross discrimination was meted out against the local in the employment in the plywood factories. More than 76 percent of recruitment in the highly paid managerial category, the recruitment was from outside the state while more than 42 percent of the lower category job-holders are also from other parts of the country. (Misra 1980 1357-1362).

The story is not much different regarding other resources of Assam, namely jute and silk. Nothing substantial has been done regarding these two rich resources which have much economic potential. West Bengal, Assam and Bihar are the only three jute producing states in India which together produce the highest quantity of jute in the world. There were 68 jute mills in operation in India in the 1980s of which only one was in Assam. West Bengal had had 56 and Bihar three, rest of them were in states which did not produce jute at all. Moreover, the Jute Corporation of India and STATFED bought jute at Rs 175 per quintal from Assam while they paid Rs 225 per quintal to West Bengal for the same quality of jute. Assam produces a wide variety of silk. The primary ones being the Assam silk, Endi and the Muga silk. It is among the largest silk producing states of the country. No measure has been taken up to organize the silk industry on a commercial edge.

The economy of Assam represents a unique case of poverty amidst plenty. It is often alleged from various quarters in Assam that economic development after the Independence has done little to alter the colonial pattern of exploitation—exploitation of the natural resources of the state by outside forces for their profit and the use of the state as a captive market for goods from outside sold at inflated prices. Right after the Independence, till the 1950s Assam was considered to be one of the prosperous states of the country. The per capita income of Assam was a higher than the all-India level. It consequently slipped down and has remained substantially lower than the national average in recent decades. Along with it, the gap between the state's average level of living and that of the national average has been increasing in recent years. The average per capita income of Assam stood at Rs 1374 for the triennium 1980-81 to 1982-83 at 1980-81 prices. It was about 18 per cent lower than the corresponding national estimate of Rs 1672 for India as a whole. The difference widened to more than 45 per cent in recent years when average per capita income of Assam and all-India stood at Rs 1702 and Rs 3211 respectively at 1980 -81 prices for the triennium 1999-00 to 2001-02.

ULFA's aggressive intervention beckoning the unscrupulous exploitation of the resources of the state struck a chord with the general masses and the intelligentsia which had been witnessing the pillage and nurturing a sense of resentment since a long time. Nilanjan Phukan has written about the abdication of the government in fulfilling its duties and in the same vein supporting the path of the ULFA writes:

> Instead of controlling the floods and arranging for irrigation for winter crops, which would have helped numerous small peasants living from hand to mouth, the central government can only think of draining off the 'surplus water' to feed the rich farmers' fields in the UP and south India. The income from oil royalty for the state is still a very negligible fraction of the price of the oil and petroleum products. The top posts in the forest services are being shunted off to people from outside the state, and there are plans to shift the oldest forestry institute in the country from the state to a location in

south India. Tea gardens do not pay wages to the hapless labourers on Sunday on the grounds that they do not work on Sundays. All that the tea company has done for the vaunted development of the state serves after all primarily their own interests. Not a *paisa* was given in donation to the college and universities of the state until the ULFA started its campaign of extortion, out of hundreds of crores earned as profits. On the other hand the Saikia government has so far exempted the gardens from taxes to the tune of Rs. 130 crores, and that too at a time when all development work has ground to a halt for lack of funds. The state of underdevelopment, aided and abetted by nationalized banks tha pumped out several times more money than they care to deploy in helping local development, makes self-employment a chimera and the dignity of labour an empty slogan. For thousands of frustrated and unemployed youth the only source of income are crime and shady business of all sorts. The state government seems to be encouraging these trends by promoting daily lotteries which are another name of gambling.

While in the rest of the country extension of railway routes is almost a routine affair, in Assam most big towns are still to be linked to railway lines, or at most are poorly served by the existing connections. Only a small percent of the railway track is broad gauge. Even the national highways are badly maintained. As for power, with a recent 200 percent hike in electric tariff few local industries are left with hope of prosperous growth. The hike was forced apparently by the state government's refusal—under instruction from the centre—to continue and annual subsidy. Now that the World Bank is insisting on a reduction in a share of the states in funds regularly distributed under the Finance Commission's dispensation, the state government is bound to experience unprecedented penury. As it is, last year more than 600 crore out of a total of central grants amounting to 800 and odd crore were kept back as repayment of earlier debts. (Niranjan Phukan 1993:2014).

Agriculture is the mainstay of more than 70 percent of the state's population. According to 2001 census, 2.66 crores of the total population of the state depends upon agriculture fully or partially. Nearly 40 percent of the state's income is contributed by agriculture. However the share of agriculture in state income has undergone sharp fluctuation. In the 1950s the share was approximately 60 percent, in the 1980s it was 50-55 percent and it was only 35 percent after the 1990s. The production of food grains, oilseeds and other important crops in the state has been reported to be far below the targeted level during the 9th plan period. The annual production of rice has maintained an upward growth but the total production has not been adequate to provide food security to all the people of the state. Inadequate irrigation, floods and archaic methods of agriculture are identified as the major causes for the low levels of production and productivity in agriculture in the state[28].

ULFA's mouthpiece, its website, reiterates that, "The British as a colonial power with a history of looting and exploitation of underdeveloped countries all over the world, did the same in Assam. The Indian colonial govt. has been perhaps the most ardent students of the British and continued this exploitation of all of Assam's natural resources, however in a more subtle and secretive manner"[29]. The ULFA resents that the special clauses inserted in Indian constitution such as the Articles 246 to 248 that ensured that Assam did not gain much from the its naturalresources[30]. The ULFA accuses the central government of plundering the wealth of Assam and not giving its due share[31].

The idea of Assam as a colonial hinterland has existed in the psyche of common people of Assam since and long time. ULFA intervention only accentuated the existing sentiment of resentment, which is many ways explain the support base of ULFA among the general masses. ULFA's envision of retrieving *XhunorAxom* (golden Assam)[32] from the clutches of plunderers struck chord among the public during the initial phase of its inception.

During the initial days of the ULFA when it had not yet paved its way in the socio-political realm of Assam, in November 1980, there was an armed bank robbery in Assam involving Manipuri and Assamese youth. When the Manipuri People's Liberation Army (PLA) leader Biseswar was arrested in this context, one of his associates arrested along with him was an Assamese-NarenGohain. On questioning,Gohain told a reporter that he chose the path of insurgency in order to oppose the exploitation and oppression of the region, that is, New Delhi's treatment of the region as a "colony" and because he had lost faith in the constitutional process. This was one of the first instances that the seed of violent resistance evoking the colonial theory was reported[33].

"My heart goes out to the people of Assam" and the Narrative of Exclusion

Assam, so also the entire north-eastern region of India, is located in a geographically isolated zone, connected with rest of the country only by a narrow "chicken's neck corridor" or the "Siliguri corridor", 37 km long and 21 km-40 km in width which connects the landmass of the north-eastern India to rest of the country. This geographical periphery in many ways coincides with the socially exclusionary sentiments, which represents alienation from or by rest of the country towards or with the north-eastern states. Many corners of the region time and again begrudge being "ethnically" and politically sidelined.

The first Prime Minister of independent India, Jawaharlal Nehru's abdication of Assam at the helm of Chinese aggression is an incidence sited with immense antipathy even to present day. The instance is brooded upon to reckon the Centre's seal of exclusionary stance towards the region. On November 20, 1962, Nehru addressed the nation on All India Radio saying, "Huge Chinese armies have been marching in the northern part of NEFA. We have had reverses at Walong, Se La and today Bomdila, a small town in NEFA, has also fallen. We shall not rest till the invader goes out of India or is pushed out. I want to make that clear to all of you, and especially our countrymen in Assam, to whom our heart goes out at this moment"[34]. The words are understood as connoting unconcern and betrayal by the people of Assam. Nehru is believed to have given up on the region, instead of demonstrating a strong challenge against the intruders. He is thought to have turned his back on the region[35]. The words of Nehru, "My heart goes out to the people of Assam" are often iterated in public and social discourse within Assam which has instilled a sense of hurt and has perpetuated feeling of disintegration in the psyche of the people of Assam. Memories of life, social and political, in the nascent nation did not bring about a sense of security and unity to the people residing in this periphery which was already struggling with economic and developmental crisis.

The north-eastern region not only lags far behind from some of other States of India, industrially and commercially, but it also lacks even in the basic infrastructural facilities required for the development of trade and commerce. Most of the north-eastern States do not figure in the railway map of the country. In Assam there has been little development in the sphere of railway transport. The metre-gauge line was laid by the British nearly 100 years ago, with the aim of facilitating the movement of tea and troops. It has only recently been partially upgraded to broad-gauge. The few roads are practically the only means of transport for the common people in both the hills and the plains of the region, these too are in deplorable state due to poor maintenance. The rains, which are quite often, turn vast areas into virtually isolated zones, cut off from the rest of the country.

Udayon Misra in his work *The Periphery Strikes Back: Challenge to the Nation-State in Assam and Nagaland* (2000) engages with the idea of "periphery" and the "mainland". Misra writes that "certain secessionist ethnic movements cannot be explained in terms of simple economic criteria such as uneven or lop-sided development or disjunction between industry and agriculture" (Misra 2000: 157, 183), they need to be understood in a historically imbibed sense of alienation and exclusion. The main promises of India nation building – political participation, equal treatment before the law and protection from the arbitrariness of state power, dignity for the weak and poor, and social justice and security – were apparently not met in the case of Assam.

The north-eastern part of India is also marked by its international boundaries; the region shares more than 4500 km of international border (about 90 per cent of its entire border area) with China (South Tibet) in the North, Mayanmar in the East, Bangladesh in the South-West, and Bhutan to the North-West. Hence it has been historically treated as a "land frontier". The land has been considered to be "distant" and the inhabitants "exotic"[36]. The general imagination about the land in the minds of general "mainlanders" is that the entire north-eastern part of India is a homogeneous entity; the land of savage "head-hunters", dog meat eaters and land of tantra having innate ability to turn human to sheep or goat and enslave in his/her land forever. In every day parlance "racial profiling", stereotyping and prejudices against the people of the north-eastern India raises its ugly face time and again[37]. Yengkhom Jilagamba (2012), himself hailing from Manipur and teaching at the Centre for the Study of Developing Society, Delhi describes the plight of students from the north-eastern states in other parts of the country as:

> The mysterious death of Loitam Richard in Bangalore, the murder of Ramchanphy Hongray in New Delhi, the suicide by Dana Sangma and other such incidents serve as reminders of the insecure conditions under which people, particularly the young, from the north-east of India have to live within the metros of this country. What these deaths have in common is that the three individuals were all from a certain part of the country, had a "particular" physical appearance, and were seen as outsiders in the places they died.

> ...For north-easterners who look in a particular manner, everyday living in Indian cities can be a gruelling experience. Be it the mundane overcharging of fares by autoricksaw-*wallahs*, shopkeepers and landlords, the verbal abuse on the streets and the snide remarks of colleagues, friends, teachers, or the more extreme experiences of physical and sexual assaults. It is often a never-ending nightmare, a chronicle of repetitive experience. (http://www.thehindu.com/opinion/op-ed/lets-stop-pretending-theres-no-racism-in-india/article3466554.ece).

The feeling of discrimination and exclusion is a recurrent premise that the people from the north-east region of India identify with while being and travelling in other parts of the country.

ULFA responded to the larger sentiment of marginalization and exclusion within the nation by delineating an idea of separate peoplehood; exclusive of the nation. The idea of a people within a nation, adorning the triple attributes of—people as a sovereign entity, which exercises power by means of democratic procedure; the people as citizens ofa state, holding equal rights before the law; and the people as an ethniccommunity undifferentiated by distinctions of honour and prestige, butheld together by common political destiny and shared cultural features, was fragmented by ULFA's formulation of identity. For the ULFA, the people of Assam were not sovereign or citizen subjects of India but were complete nationals belonging to a territory unfairly occupied by the Indian forces[38]. SS. Khaplang, self-proclaimed president of the Government of the People's Republic of Nagaland (GPRN) which is a confederation of ultras of north-eastern India, and hassheltered in eastern Nagaland several rebel outfits during Indian and Bhutanese military operations against them, in an interview published in *The Week* restated that the north-eastern India was never a part India. He claims that groups like the ULFA, United National Liberation Front, People's Liberation Army and few other organizations from the region have been working in close collaboration;"If we work together, it would be easier to achieve independence, sovereignty and recognition in international fora. A united front would benefit us, in terms of sharing information and operational coordination"[39].

While on one hand the "mainland" has substantially undermined the social integration of the north-eastern region in the national folds which was already struggling with underdevelopment and economic wretchedness, ULFA overturned the sense of marginalization to articulate an identity of the people of Assam that completely negates correlation with the "mainlanders".

"...why they have chosen the path of the jungle?" Understanding the indices of violence

The South Asia Terrorism Portal (http://www.satp.org/) lists twenty nine inactive, thirteen active and two proscribed terrorist/insurgent groups in Assam[40]. The two proscribed groups are the National Democratic Front of Bodoland (NDFB) and the United Liberation Front of Assam (ULFA). These numbers are illustration of the mushrooming insurgent groups in the north-eastern region of India. The complex grid of terrorism and violence in the region is still critical and has been intractable even after stringent and draconian anti and counter insurgency measures have been executed by the Centre to repeal the violent agitation. Extremism in the region has been only controlled temporarily at times but has never been completely eradicated. In the present day, fear and terror, both from the insurgents and from the anti insurgent activities, looms large in the minds of the common people. Yet, ULFA has never been dismissed as a band of anti-social goons by the local masses.

ULFA remained more or less dormant till the signing of the Assam Accord in 1985, after the Assam movement was over. But soon after, it invaded the socio-political arena of Assam avowing that Assam movement was battling with the symptoms rather than the disease. The main cause of Assam's woes according to the ULFA, was the "infected and decayed system" itself, from which the Assam movement was seeking remedy. In an attempt to rationalize the path of violence and armed agitation, ULFA subscribes the following:

> If Assam would have been an independent country then we could have brought (about) progressive change by means of agitation or elections. But in the present context, if we agitate or participate in parliamentary politics then the government formed by us (will) have to work as per the Constitution of India and guidelines fixed by the Government...This system is prone to exploitation and corruption. This is proved by the gradual change in phase from the (All Assam) Students Union to the (Assam) Gana Parishad...Therefore, to create an exploitation-free society, our next step (must) be a national war of liberation... We have no alternative to arm revolution. (Verghese 1996: 57)

B.G. Verghese in his book India's Northeast Resurgent Ethnicity, Insurgency, Governance, Development (1996) summarizes the issue of insurgency in the north-eastern region as, "The answers lie in more rapid and innovative economic development and not in division of a limited cake into smaller and smaller portions. That would be to share poverty. Development is an essential though not sufficient consideration to break the vicious cycle". He marks the causes of unrest in the region as, rapid social change resulting in a civilization gap, new value systems, land alienation by outsider or foreign immigrants, unemployment and unrequited aspirations. The stress on developmental agenda for ceasing violence has been a common thread in many of the contemporary writings. However, lack of development and poverty cannot be accepted as the only crisis and the only remedy for the region.Verghese in his book gives a detailed account of the network and support base ULFA created in carrying out its activities. He recounts that in 1986 first contacts were established with the Kachin Independent Army and the National Socialist Council of Nagaland in Myanmar for training and arms. This entailed raising money for payments and gradual set in motion a train of extortion, kidnapping and demands for ransom that soon menaced a widening circle of traders, businessmen, tea gardens, both Indian and foreign-owned, and others. Simultaneously, public relations were promoted through a campaign of social welfare and vigilantism, helping villagers to build roads and flood embankments through self-help, and fighting social evils such as liquor, molestation of women, corruption, drug pushing and rhino-poaching. The police and lower administration had been infiltrated and were unable to intervene against as incipient parallel government, while the Robin Hood image attracted a measure of public sympathy. Pressures in Myanmar led ULFA a couple of years later to establish contacts with the ISI and Afghan mujahideen in Pakistan and still later with the Bangladesh Field Intelligence in Dhaka and, less successfully with the LTTE. As ULFA extremist activities rose, the Centre imposed a number of measures to curb the organization. ULFA attempt to blackmail and extort money from industrial houses and tea gardens incited the Centre to impose President's rule in 1990, army was mounted and Operation Bajrang was carried out throughout the state. It was in 1990 that ULFA was declared a terrorist organization and was banned. This period also ensued a time of disturbance in the public life, the general masses of Assam got caught in between insurgency and counter-insurgency imbroglio. Military checks and searches became the order of the day. The normalcy of day to day life was effected as the army observed strict vigil at every nook and corner of the state[41].

The mass grave discovered by the army in the abandoned camps of the ULFA narrated a story of torture and death. Though the top brass fed to safer havens of Bangladesh, many member of the ULFA were nabbed by the army in Operation Bajrang. Meanwhile in the 1991 state assembly elections AGP was defeated and the Congress formed ministry. The defeat in many ways was the outcome of the general masses disenchantment with the student turned politicians of the AGP government who failed to provide a secured life to the public of Assam. No sooner did Congress assumed office than ULFA struck again, this time more blatantly[42]. This led to the Centre to launch Operation Rhino in 1991. This second extensive anti-insurgency operation attained higher success compared to the first[43]. ULFA's chain of command was broken and many youth were caught in the dragnet. The public, press and the intelligentsia however were caught in the cross roads between their ideological responses to the ULFA and their aversion towards mundane violence.

The Congress Government led by Hiteshwar Saikia, by now sensing the nerve of the youth within the organization, lured them to shun the organization through double enticement of coaxing and coercion. The disillusioned and demoralized youth were offered tempting offers of clemency which led to the surrender of many members in the early 1990s[44].

During the stringent army operations in the early 1990s, in an issue devoted to the ULFA stir, the editor of the Assamese magazine Aami (We) put forward his views as, "ULFA did not drop from the sky, nor is ULFA a wild animal. ULFA is our child. [The members of] ULFA are our brothers, they are our kin. [We must understand] why they have chosen the path of the jungle" (Baruah 1999: 149). The sentiment that the ULFA is not an outsider but an integral part of Assam's society has been widely shared[45].

Insurgency and violence in Assam and in the other north-eastern states of the country is not new. Since Independence this region has been marked by violent aggression from separatist insurgencies, fights between different militia factions, group riots, State's high-handed responses through army operations and continuous violation of human rights from both the State and non-State agencies. This sustained violence has caused irreversible loss of life and property of the civilians. Impediments of growth and development, restriction of foreign investment in the region and perpetual threat and fear in the minds of the common masses have been the subsequent ill-effects of the prolonged violence.

ULFA's violence strategy includes selective terror, assassinations and taxation. Its emphasis on "scientific socialism" and "two-phase revolution" advocating "de-nationalization of ethnic communities" and promise to implement "scientific socialism to build Assamese society after the liberation from Indian colonial rule", are substantiated by evoking the UN Charter:

> According to the UN Charter of Human Rights, freedom and independent is basic human right. National self-determination rights are also fundamental and collective human rights. The occupation of Assam by colonial India, is directly the denial of the basic human rights and so is the breech of the UN Charter. India is continuing the rape,arson, torture, and above all the genocide in Assam by deploying occupation forces to continue their occupation ignoring all humanitarian appeal of the world community.(http://www.oocities.org/capitolhill/congress/7434/HRights.htm).

The use of violence then, for the ULFA, is a legitimate means to attain a legitimate goal.

The approach towards the presence and rise of violence in the region within the public discourse of Assam can be found in the words of social scientist Hiren Gohain. According to him violence are a markers of a) alienation and disenchantment from the State and lack of guarantee in the Constitution of providing decent life and b) weakness of the Assamese national base that made it impossible for the ULFA to negotiate within the national paradigm:

> The ULFA phenomenon is the product of the total alienation of Assamese youth from the Indian state. The vast majority of young people find in the Indian Constitution no guarantee of a right to a reasonably decent life. But the support for ULFA does not mean necessarily support for secession from India. The weakness of the Assamese national base has made it impossible for the ULFA to formulate a programme for national reconstruction. And in the past, it was easy for Congress(I) governments at the centre to find support among the conglomeration of ethnic groups and maintain a semi- Fascist regime by suppressing the Assamese with virtual army rule. Given this, a talk initiated by a genuinely democratic government sympathetically aware of the crisis of the Assamese nationality but capable of firmness when it degenerates into chauvinism is the best hope of solution to the problem posed by ULFA. (Hiren Gohain 1996: 2066)..

Violence for the ULFA is a tool to address the national question- to assert and validate its form of national identity and repudiate the supposedly imposed "Indian" nationality.

Conceptualization of the self— Framing of the identity by the ULFA

The term "United" in United Liberation Front of Assam (ULFA) is believed to be a deliberate adoption. ULFA, though emerged at the same point of time as the Assam movement, its appeal was to all *Axombaxi*— people living in Assam, rather than to the indigenous/citizens. In this way the ULFA distanced itself from the core issue of the Assam movement— the problem of illegal immigrants and engaged itself in what it believed to having plaguing Assam—the colonial rule of India. In a document meant for its cadres ULFA says it recognizes as *Axombaxi* anyone who, irrespective of his or her "prior identity, regards Assam as motherland, treats Assam's problems as his or her own, embraces Assam's culture and is prepared to fight for Assam's future". The same document states that ULFA would even consider changing the name *Axom* (Assam) or the term *Axomiya* (Assamese) "should it be necessary to do so in order to build revolutionary unity of the people who live in Assam" (Baruah 1999: 148). Detachment from "India" and unification with the north-eastern states has been ULFA imagination of identity of Assam. It regards the breakup of Assam into several states right after the Independence as a symptom of Assam's powerlessness. In May 1990 ULFA, the Nationalist Socialist Council of Nagaland (NSCN), the United National Liberation Front of Manipur (UNLFM), and few Burmese insurgent organizations signed a memorandum of understanding. According to Indian military intelligence, the objective of these organizations was to establish an independent state comprising the north-eastern states of India and north western Burma. They formed a common organization called the Indo-Burma Revolutionary Front (IBRF). It was noted in their agreement that the people living in north-eastern India and north western Burma are of the same racial stock and that historically and culturally they are set apart from the inhabitants of mainland India and Burma. The governments, they said, have neglected these far-flung regions, "which must unite and fight their war of independence" (Abidi 1990: 15-16). For the ULFA, evidently, the imaginations of the identity pursued what Ernest Gellner conceptualized as Nationalism, that is,"not the awakening and assertion of these mythical, supposedly natural and given units. It is, on the contrary, the crystallization of new units... admittedly using as their raw material the cultural, historical and other inheritances from the pre-nationalist past" (Gellner 1983:48).Self imagination or the framing of identity of Assam by the ULFA was not sectional and corresponding subnationalist but it was in entirety—the National. Unlike its precedent, the Assam movement, ULFA's contest of identity was not within the parameters of citizenship but it was right outside and in actual negation of it.

The ULFA sought to implement its idea of national identity by what Sanjib Baruah would call "A localized regime crisis" (Baruah 1994). Apart from its envision of securing as independent Assam, ULFA intervened in the social and cultural realm of Assam to "cleanse" it from apparent corruption and from the influence of India. It conducted trials of people involved in drugs and prostitution rings. It punished corrupt government officials and those neglecting public responsibilities through extortion and blackmail, including government doctors who were engaged in private medical practice or teachers employed in government schools who were making money through private tuition at the expense of their classroom duties. ULFA raised huge financial base through extortion from the tea companies and other business organizations within Assam. Apart from money, ULFA made other demands to the industries including employment of local youth, establishment of high schools and colleges at tea plantations, commitment to basic needs of neighboring villages, moving corporate headquarters to Assam, support for higher education for deserving children of tea workers, and improvement in the quality of food and housing provided to tea workers. ULFA made these demands on behalf of the "people of Assam". It established itself in rural Assam through the *JatiyaUnnayan Parishad* (National Development Council), an organization that undertook public interest work like flooding and erosion, industrial pollution, illiteracy, land management ensuring its support base within the masses. ULFA cadres have provided relief to flood victims, and in the post-Ayodhya tensions between Hindus and Muslims, they intervened successfully to control violence in certain areas (Prabhakaran 1993: 9). In April 1990, on the eve of the Assamese new year celebration, *Bohag Bihu*, the ULFA issued a writ asking people not to corrupt the spirit of the traditional festival by playing Hindi film songs and disco music. In many colleges and universities it enforced the traditional dress code of *mekhela sador* for the women in place of "Indian" and western *salwar kameez* or *saree* and jeans respectively. Celebration of Independence and Republic Day in Assam had been banned by calling for Assam *bandh* every year without fail.

ULFA thus adorned itself the role of custodian of the interests of what it called "nationality" which bypassed the functions of mainstream organizations such as the All Assam Students Union (AASU) or *Axom Sahitya Sabha* (Assam literary society), which until now had been the harbingers of cultural identity. This nationality which sought to embark upon the grand unification of the various sections of people living in Assam, soon was challenged by groups such as the Bodos, Karbis, and Misings, but who are increasingly seeking autonomous political futures, in many, instances outside the framework of Assam. For them it was the nationality framed by the "artificial" Assamese that had historically impeded their freedom and growth and had pushed them to utter distress.

Disenchantment towards ULFA'S *XhunorAxom*

A folk song that received immense popularity as Assam stepped into the 21st century was by popular Assamese singer Loknath Goswami- *Moghaibuledholarmaatdhimikidhindhau,xhonorAxomnalagemukmaatirxhojau*[46] (the traditional drummer reckons, I refute the dream of golden Assam, would till the soil to build my home[47]). This song which evokes the spirit of various communities living in Assam- Bodo, Rabha, Mising, Adivasi, tea garden communities etc. clearly undermines the enterprise of ULFA of installing "golden" Assam. The essence of the song encapsulates the aversion of the common masses towards violence, bloodshed and conflict in the enchanting dream of securing independence. This, in many ways, was the mood and attitude of the common people towards the persisting violence unleashed by the ULFA (and other organizations) which until now had enjoyed spoken and unspoken support from the locals.

The local press, more often than not, had been sympathetic towards ULFA since its inception. Sanjib Baruah explains the general sympathetic attitude of the press as "the organization's ability to stake out a place for itself in the space that constitutes the mainstream of Assamese public life" (Baruah 1994: 866). The general tendency was of concurrence if not outright support. Though many newspapers were critical of ULFA's avowed aim of independence and its violent methods, they inevitably published statements made by ULFA leaders in their editorials and other articles. ULFA's position on various issues was, many times placed atpar with the mainstream Assamese public life. National reporter, Kalpana Sharma (1990), expressed astonishment at ULFA's remarkably uninhibited style of expression. She found ULFA's presence to be "ubiquitous". She referred to the role of a widely read Assamese newspaper-*Budhbar* (Wednesday), in spreading ULFA's agenda. The newspaper designed a question and answer column to engage its readers with the aims and activities ofULFA. According to the editor, they received 150 to 200 questions each week; from these the editor would select about 15 and the "ULFA boys" would come to his office and drop in their replies, which were duly published the following week. Even less sympathetic newspapers gave ample space and importance to ULFA's positions on issues and engaged it in dialogue in their editorials and articles. The general concord of the masses with the ULFA could be felt by the grieve that spread at the death of its members. One of the deaths of ULFA members by army operations that created much public sympathy was of its commander-in-chief Hirokjyoti Mahanta[48] in the early days of the organization. His death anniversary on 31 December was celebrated collectively[49] and was mourned across the state. However, gradually this fervor was replaced by a feeling of indifference. The general masses grew averse of the violence and bloodshed that had become mundane and the general public were often caught in the cross fire between the ULFA and the State[50].

ULFA, in the backdrop of massive combing operations and enticement of good life after the "golden handshake" of surrender, started losing the initial rigour by the late 1990s. Though the foundational basis of the uprising was to upturn the injustice and exploitation, the established left parties often ridiculed the ULFA for the latter's ideological immaturity. ULFA did try to acquire ideological orientation through the trappings of a Marxist-Leninist system of ideas. They were reported to have received help from Naxalite splinter groups to some extent.However, even though ULFA tried to adapt Marxist ideas to the overriding goal of "liberating Assam from Indian imperialists", its revolutionary activity largely confined to political assassinations, abductions for hefty ransoms, extortions and intimidations.

Around the same time sharp differences started arising among different sections of the organization on the issues of association with Bangladesh. The top leaders sought refuge and assistance in Bangladesh which did not go well with the some of the cadres[51]. The members were also divided regarding their views about talks with the government of India. As the vision of securing independent Assam started to look difficult, more and more ULFA wished to give up arms and come to negotiation table; at one point this had been perceived as a "clever means employed by the capitalist group and the State of disarming ULFA" and of "creating rifts within its ranks". In the middle of 1991 when the second military operation was at its heights, the ULFA was divided on the question of whether to enter into dialogues with the State. The difference of opinion led to identify certain member as "moderates" and some other as "extremists" within the organization (*Budhbar* 30 October1991). As cadres were in deliberating on talks and surrender, on 22 July 1992, a full general body meeting was held in Bhutan. The meeting was attended by Paresh Barua, Arabinda Rajkhowa, Anup Chetiya and other ULFA top notch leaders. The delegates reached a unanimous decision that the members "will not fall into the trap laid by the Indian State through deceit and treachery in the name of discussion". The attendees also decided to prepare a list of the cadres who were seeking to talks describing them as "counter revolutionaries" and resolved that the people would judge and punish them (*Budhbar* 29 April 1992). ULFA struck to its formulation of "Sovereignty and Independence of Assam" as the only matter of discussion and held that any discussion with the Indian State is possible in a third country decided by the United Nations.

Along the same time, ULFA resorted to sporadic bombing and other disruptive act to keep its presence felt. The loss was, many times than not, felt by the local underprivileged section of the people of Assam. The indigenous population now began to apprehend the fact that ULFA's initial goal of securing the interest of the tormented people of Assam has been lost and they are now just a terrorist outfit. The All Assam Students Union (AASU) and the ManabAdhikar Sangram Samity (MASS), two public interest groups which had until now been supportive of the ULFA's activities, started being vocal against the terror activities of ULFA. One of the most horrendous violent activities which substantially eroded the sympathy of the masses towards the outfit was the bombing at a school ground at Dhemaji which killed 17 people that included 10 school children on 15th August, Independence Day celebration in 2004. Though the initial response of ULFA was of denial, the masses were confirmed that it was the works of the outfit. It took ULFA 5 years to accept the responsibility for that act calling it the "biggest mistake of ULFA"[52].

In November 2004 the late Indira Goswami, Professor of the Delhi University and a respected litterateur of Assam in a formal letter to the Prime Minister Manmohan Singh offered to mediate talks between the Centre and the ULFA in order to end the long withstanding conflict in the state. Arabinda Rajkhowa also offered to come to the discussion table on the condition that the Government of India sends an official invitation for the talk. In an email to the local press Rajkhowa offered to constitute a plebiscite on the crucial issue of independence of Assam. Prof. Goswami met many legal advisors to seek the interpretation of "sovereignty" within the Indian Constitution, among them Soli Sorabjee, the Solicitor General of India. The Telegraph (Calcutta) reported that, "Though the Constitution leaves no room for negotiating the country's sovereignty, legal experts here are of the opinion that the term itself has several connotations.There is economic sovereignty, for instance. It can be discussed and even granted. A state with greater economic freedom is possible"[53]. An eleven member People's Consultative Group (PPG) was formed by the ULFA from the members of the civil society to mediate the talks between itself and the government in 2005[54]. The PPG made substantive effort to mediate the talks between the ULFA and the Government of India. After a year and three rounds of talks between the PCG and the Centre, the Government announced a 15-day unilateral truce on 13 August 2006. Hope of long awaited peace was seen to be finally realizing. But as the talks derailed, the Centre revoked its military operations[55]. Assam again was gripped in erratic terror and bloodshed. For the people of Assam, ULFA now is an aging force. The euphoric goal of *XhunorAxom* lost much of its shine after its linkages with the Pakistan came to light during the Kargilwar when the ULFA was reported to side with the infiltrators. Also, the outfit is also suspected of maintaining bases in Bangladesh, illegal immigrants from which has been the bone of contention for the people of Assam.*More* and more, the public has come to look upon the ULFA as interest-driven, wanting to capitalize on its earlier "sanctified" image of fighting for Assam's liberation for its own economic and political ends[56]. It no longer captures the imagination of the masses. The PCG was dissolved in February 2011. The goal of peace and stability in Assam seems to be wanting of direction and intentions.

Challenging the "Sons of the Soil": Bodoland Movement and Regeneration of the Tribal Question

> Wherever and by whatever name the Bodos may be known to others, now, after all, the allied tribes belonging to the great Indo-Mongoloids living in the proposed Bodolandterritory are often the same Bodo ethnic groups. Ethnically speaking, the majority population of the proposed Bodoland territory is composed of the great Bodo race origin. The proposed Bodoland territory has got its own distinct and quite separate ethnic identity and background which is completely different from that of Assamese. (A Memorandum of the Three Member Expert Committee on the Bodoland Issue by ABSU and BPAC 1991:2)

The Bodoland movement has been the most stringent tribal movement in contemporary Assam. This movement seeded during the colonial times and culminated into a radical assertion in the late 1980s had its source in the ostensible feeling of discrimination, deprivation and injustice. In the campaign to recoup the lost political, economic and cultural suzerainty, the leaders of the Bodoland movement emphasized that the Bodo people are ethnically completely different from the rest of the people of present-day state of Assam (Narzary 1976) and hence entitled to political acknowledgment[57].

The Bodoland movement in its present form emerged in the 1960 demanding to secure a homeland for the Bodo tribal population of Assam. It took a severe turn in the 1980s, after the Assam Accord was signed and propelled immense political and social furor throughout the 1990s. The Bodo homeland question still continues to create political upheaval and terror in present day Assam. The demand is to carve out a separate state within Assam for the Bodo community. This movement is yet another dissent of the tribal community within the state after Nagaland, Mizoram, Meghalaya and Arunachal Pradesh have been successful in carving exclusive tribal states for themselves from Assam in the 1960s and 1970s. The Bodos framed their demand on their claim that none but the Bodos are the indigenous people of Assam. In this purview, the "Assamese"- as a people, in relation to Assam, no longer remained a natural pre-given category. Their right over the land and the political power were questioned and challenged. The Bodoland movement in many ways blanched the authority of the Assamese to speak for Assam. The preceding Assam movement and the ULFA though claimed to represent all the various sections of Assam, were initiated and lead by the Assamese speaking people. Both these movements sought to encompass the various tribal communities in its fold to represent a *brihatarAxomiyajati* (greater Assamese nationality). The Bodoland movement undermined this representation to emphasize the distinct identity of the Bodos and thus challenging the identity of the Assamese. "We are Bodos, not Assamese" is the slogan of the Bodoland movement. The existence of dissidence from the Bodo community (which has now spread to other tribal communities of Assam) foregrounds that the unsettled tribal question and the avowed indigenous right of the non-tribal population within the state. The chapter traces the Bodoland movement since its inception and analyzes how the separate Bodo identity was expressed. Following this the chapter argues that the Bodos relied upon the existing belief of their origin and ancestry in establishing their discrete identity.

Who are the Bodos

The Kachari, Boro-Kachari, Mech-Kachari, Dimasa-Kachari, Thengal-Kachari, Sonowal-Kachari, Rabha-Kachari, Deori, Miri, Mikir (now called Karbi), Lalung (now called Tiwa), Garo, Hajong, Motok, Moran, Abors, Mishimis, Duffla, Singpho, Khamti, Aka, Naga or Kuki Tribe, Tea Garden Tribes living "outside garden areas" are constitute the Plain Tribal People of Assam. The term Bodo is used to denote a large number of tribes living in and outside the state of Assam- the Garosof Meghalaya, Tippera of Tripura and Boro-Kacharis, Koch, Rabha, Lalung, Dimasa, Hajong, Chutia, Deuri and Moran of Assam and other parts of North-East India[58]. The Bodos are considered to be the earliest settlers of Assam. They are thought to belong to the Tibeto- Burman speaking Indo-Mongoloid group. The Bodos have been practicing wet cultivation for a long period, and are well known for their traditional skills in cultivating paddy by irrigation and also for sericulture of Endi and Muga silk of Assam. The people who lived during the epic age of the Ramayana and the Mahabharata in the eastern region of India are supposed to be Bodos who were known as "Kirata" at that time. In some ancient Sanskrit books, including the Vedas, they are believed to be referred to as "Mlecha" or "Asura".[59] In regard to the origin of the Bodos it is agreed that they have migrated to India from southwest China via Tibet and Bhutan[60].

At the helm of the Bodoland movement in the early 1990s, Bodo scholar Bijaya Laxmi Brohmo Choudhury published a detailed account of the Bodos in her work *Bodoland (Kachari) At a Glance*(1993). This work, in many ways reflected the self description of the Bodos during the Bodoland movement. Her study advertently borrowed from the description of the colonial writers' works: S. Endle- *The Kacharis* (1911) and Sir Edward Gait- *A History of Assam* (1906). Choudhury traces the origin of the Bodos as follows:

> The Bodos are one of the earliest settlers of Assam. They are the descendants of the ancient Mongoloid family. The people who lived in Siberia and Mongolia around 2000 B.C. were known as Mongoloid. In course of time these Mongoloid people were divided into three groups. One group of them went towards Europe and liked to settle in Turkey and Italy. According to some historians, the people who are still living in Italy and Turkey are the descendants of Mongoloids. The second group migrated towards North America and Mexico and settled there. Again a small section of the second group went towards Japan and lived there. The people who are now living in

> Erich, North Japan and Mexico are the people of Mongoloid group. The people who migrated from Siberia and Mongolia of the third group through South West of China gradually settled in Hoang-ho valley of China and Tibet. Some of them migrated to foothills of Bhutan. At first they were known in Tibet as the "Bod".
>
> During their course of migration from the foothills of Bhutan they changed their direction towards west and gradually settled in Cooch-Behar, Rangpur, Dinajpur districts of present West Bengal. A section of them went towards Garo Hills, Mymonsingh, Sylhet (Bangladesh) and Tripura. The word Mymonsingh is a Bodo word, the meaning of which is to produce more rice (Mai-rice, Monsing- produce more).
>
> Then they moved towards east and began to live in Cachar as Dimasa and Barman. A section of them went far to the east who are known as Moran, Barahi and Chutia. The people who went to Bangladesh (Mymonsingh and Sylhet) were mostly converted to Muslim religion.
>
> From this description it appears that "China and Tibet are the original homes of the Bodos" (S. Endle). Perhaps there were at least two groups of immigrators who entered through north and north-east to settle over the fertile valley of the mighty Brahmaputra, i.e. one entered through north of Bengal and Western Assam by the valley of the river Teesta, Dharla, Sankosh and the other group entered through the river valley of Subansiri, Dibong and Dihong and settled in the eastern Assam where this group of Bodo Kachari race is known as Sonowal, Deori, Moran and Chutia. (Choudhury 1993: 1-2).

According to Choudhury in 1000 B.C. when there was a cultural influence of the Aryans, Dravidians and Austrics in the South-West India, the North- East India was under the influence of the Mongoloid culture. As a result it led to the mixture of the cultures of different communities. This mixture, Choudhury claims, is the basis of present Indian society[61].

Similarly, B.N. Bordoloi in his seminal work *The DimasaKacharis of Assam* (1984) draws from the colonial writers to describe the various sections of the Bodo as such:

> In the Brahmaputra Valley the Kacharis call themselves Bodo or Bodolandfisa and in the North Cachar Hills and also in Hawaipur, Mohangdijua and Dhansiri areas of the Karbi Anglong district they

call themselves Dimasa. It has already been mentioned that in the Cachar district the Dimasa call themselves Braman. According to G.A. Grierson the Europeans called the Dimasas Hill Kacharis to distinguish them from the plains Kacharis speaking Bodoland.

Bodolandfisa literally means children of Bodo or the descendants of Bodo. But the opinions differ in regards to the precise meaning of the term 'Bodo'. It might refer to the first male forefather of the race or to any natural object. According to Mr. Grierson like other tribal names in Assam, the name probably once meant a male member of the tribe. (Bordoloi 1984: 6).

According to the Census of India 2011 there are approximately 3 million people who identify as Bodos in Assam, which makes the Bodos constitute 5.3 percent of the population of the state[62]. Three main religions are followed by the Bodos—the traditional, the Brahma and Christianity. The traditionalist follows the most early belief and customs and worship "Bathou"[63] as the prime deity. The Brahma sect was introduced by Kali Charan Brahma, a disciple of Swami Shiv Narayan Paramhansa in 1906. This sect follows the vedic rituals[64]. A sizeable section of the Bodo population has embraced Christianity after the influence of Christian missionary in the late 19th century and early 20th century.

Inception of the Bodoland Movement

The first demand for a separate state for the "plain tribes" of Assam was proposed in 1967 by the Plain Tribal Council of Assam (PTCA). However, scholars date the history of identity consciousness among the tribals of Assam to the colonial times, when a memorandum to the Indian Statutory Commission was submitted in 1929 by the Bodo community of Goalpara and the "KachariJuvakSanmiloni" (Kachari Youth Meet) demanding political power[65]. Subsequently, the All Assam Plains Tribal League (AAPTL) was formed in 1933 as a political party under the leadership of Rupnath Brahma. The main objective of this party was to protect the identities and interests of "tribal people" of Assam. It was for the first time that the tribal people of Assam had formally demanded political suzerainty.

The AAPTL demanded provision for separate electorate system for the tribals in Assam Assembly. Consequently, an act was passed by the British government which reserved five seats for the Plain Tribals in Assam. The Tribal League became a major political force to reckon with.In a memorandum submitted to the nascent Indian State in 1947 the following points were stated by the All Assam Plains Tribal League on behalf of the Assam Plains Tribes for their safeguards in the future constitution:

(1) That the Fundamental Rights of citizenship shall be equal in the same degree to all the Tribal people, made subject to the limitations prescribed by law in respect of any Fundamental Rights as and when demanded by the Tribal people.

(2) That there shall be reservation of seats for the Tribal people in respect of elections to all legislative bodies- Central, Provincial, urban and Rural- on the ethnological basis, irrespective of religion on the percentage of their population and that weightage of 25 percent of seats thus allotted may also be added to the number of seats thus reserved.

(3) That the following Tribes and Races residing in the Plains of Assam are to be considered as forming the Plains Tribal People of Assam.

Kacharis

Boro- Kacharis

Mech- Kacharis

Dimasa- Kacharis

Thengal- Kacharis

Sonowal- Kacharis

Rabha- Kacharis

Deoris

Miris

Mikirs

Lalung

Garos

Hajongs

Motoks

Morans

Abors

Mishimis

Dufflas

Singphos

Khamtis

Akas

Any Naga or Kuki Tribes

Tea Garden Tribes living "outside garden areas"

(4) That in view of the backwardness of the Tribal people and the fact that majority under all forms of democratic government usually put obstacles to the way of enjoying equal rights and self- determination by minorities and in view of the existing fear, doubts, suspicion, and distrust among the different communities, by the attempts made from time to time by the advanced and influential communities to force their will upon the backward minorities. The Tribal people feel that they should till such time as a healthy atmosphere is not created, be allowed to select and elect their own representatives to the seats reserved for them on a separate electorate system, without the help and interference of any other community or outside political party. The Tribal would however, welcome the day when they would feel secure and there would be no longer be any other personal views.

(5) That there should be a statutory cabinet in the Centre and the Provinces where the number of the Tribal members shall be proportionate to their numbers in the Legislatures.

(6) That the Tribal people should have a sufficient share in the enjoyment and application of any money which may be provided out of public funds by the State, Local, Urban or Rural budget for educational, religious or charitable purposes, so that these backward Tribal people may progress towards equal advancement with other communities, as speedily as possible.

(7) That the Tribal people must be ensured of adequate facilities for instruction in their educational institutions through the medium of their own vernacular, especially in the Primary stages.

(8) That there should be sufficient provisions to ensure that the Tribal people get their due share in all Public Affairs, Trades, Commerce and Industries according to their population.

(9) That there should be sufficient statutory provisions may be made to ensure full protection to the land of the Tribal people, so that, it may not be encroached upon or exploited by Non- Tribal communities and further to ensure that sufficient lands may be provided for them for the future expansion of the Tribal people.

(10) That the Tribal members of the Cabinet in the Centre or Provinces together with the Tribal members of the Legislatures many be entrusted with full powers to see that the provisions of safeguards made in the constitution for the Tribal people are effective.

(11) That as the Tribal people generally carry arms for their protection in the hilly tracts and jungle areas where they mainly reside, there should be such provisions made to allow the Tribal people to keep and bear arms without any restrictions. (Choudhury 1993: 35-37).

The Tribal League formed a coalition government with Muslim League in the new formed Assam state assembly. Later in view of assurance given by the Congress party for protection of the "tribal people and the tribal lands" the Tribal League merged with the Assam Congress.

Following this, another significant step by the Bodos towards asserting its exclusive identity came from its premier literary body the Bodo Sahitya Sabha. In 1952 the Bodo Sahitya Sabha had come to the fore. It raised the issue of language and script in relation to consolidation of the Bodo identity. The Bodo Sahitya Sabha along with the ABSU and PTCA launched a movement in 1968, demanding recognition of Bodo language as a medium of instruction in the Secondary stage of education in the schools of Assam. As a result Bodo language was introduced in the Secondary stage of education. Following this another demand was raised by the Bodo Sahitya Sabha and the ABSU in 1974-75 for Roman script in lieu of Assamese script for Bodo language. There was a clash between the Assam government and the propounders. At this stage the then Prime Minister, Indira Gandhi intervened and according to her suggestion Devanagiri script was adopted by Bodo Sahitya Sabha giving up the demand for Roman script.

However, in the due course of time the "tribal people" of Assam found that all the assurances given by the Congress party though codified were not implemented in true sense. They found it necessary to revive their own political identity. As a result Plain Tribal Council of Assam (PTCA) was formed in27[th] February, 1967. Its aim was to demand a

Union Territory called "Udayachal" in the Bodo dominated areas. They placed their demand several times before the state and central government. But when the demandswere not fulfilled, a movement of dissidence was launched. The PTCA and the All Bodo Students Union (ABSU) boycotted the General Elections of 1968.

The All Bodo Students' Union" (ABSU) was formed on 15th February, 1967 at a time when the Prime Minister of India, Indira Gandhi proposed to reorganize the state of Assam on 13th January, 1967. The ABSU adopted a constitution on 2nd March 1969 with the objectives:

> "We, the All Bodo Students unanimously and with our purest hearts have resolved to organize the students of various Bodo groups into an organization for better and mutual understanding among ourselves, to safeguard and develop the socio-economy, culture, civilization, tradition, language and literature of the great Bodo nationality and this organization is know as the All Bodo Students' Union (ABSU) and on the expediency of having written guiding rules of the organization, do hereby adopt, enact and give to ourselves this constitution on this day of 2nd March, 1969". (Choudhury 1993:59).

Amongst other aims and objectives outlined in section 3 the ABSU gives itself rights to struggle even on political issues:

Section 3 (e) Settle the issues relating to political crisis that may arise among the Plain Tribal Bodo people out of selfish and political diplomacy of the so-called politicians threatening the national existence of their future generation though the ABSU is a non-political socio-economic literary and cultural organization.

(f) Struggle to achieve the just and constitutional rights through democratic process.

(g) Fight for all round security and if the above goals are denied and ignored, the Union further shall not refrain even from struggling for political self-determination within the frame of Indian Constitution. (Choudhury 1993:60).

At the active initiative of the ABSU, the political organization named Plains Tribal Council of Assam (PTCA) came into being on 27th February, 1967. Through PTCA, ABSU raised the voice for a political demand for the UnionTerritory of "Udayachal". But disillusioned by the activities of PTCA, ABSU began to work independently.

Chronicles of the Bodoland Movement

After the exit of the PTCA, the ABSU assumed the centre stage with its radical demand for separate statehood- "Divide Assam Fifty-Fifty". ABSU under the leadership of late Upendra Nath Brahma launched vigorous mass movement on 2nd March, 1987 on three political demands.

1. Creation of a separate State of Bodoland on the northern bank of the river Brahmaputra.
2. Creation of two Autonomous districts, i.e. Nilachal and Lalung on the southern bank of river Brahmaputra.
3. Inclusion of Bodo Kacharis living in KarbiAnglong into the Schedule Tribe (Hills) lists along with the demand for immediate fulfillment of other genuine grievances. (Choudhury 1993: 60).

The Bodos claimed that the attitude of the state government of Assam, dominated by the Assamese has been step-motherly towards them. The constitution provided for the making of laws related to residence, restriction movement etc. in the interest of the tribals, reservation of seats in Central and State Legislatures, recognition of special claims for government jobs and appointment by the President of special officers and commissions to report on the conditions of the tribes from time to time. The state government has been directed to promote education and economic interests of the tribals and protect them from social injustice. The leaders of the Bodoland movement none of the provision and directives had been implemented by the Assam state government.

Several organizations like "Bodo People's Action Committee", "All Bodo Employees Federation", "Assam Tribal Women Welfare Federation" etc actively co-operated with the ABSU in its demand. The ABSU also received strong support from the "Bodo Sahitya Sabha".

During the Assam movement many of the Bodo youth worked along with the AASU. But when the post Assam Accord enthusiasm waned, the tribals began to perceive that the new government's stance towards them is not much different from the previous government (George 1994:880). As disenchantment spread among the Bodo youth, the All Bodo Students Union (ABSU) took over the leadership; it launched the Bodoland movement in the late 1980s, for the creation of separate Bodo state- "Bodoland". Together with it, there has been the rise of a number of Bodo militant outfits like the "National Democratic front of Bodoland" (NDFB), "Bodo Liberation Tiger Force" (BLTF), "Bodo Army" etc.

In February 1993, a Memorandum of Settlement (MoS) was reached constituting a 40–member Bodoland Autonomous Council (BAC). Tripartite talks were arranged at Delhi between the leaders of the movement, Assam government and the Union Government. After eight rounds of talks, Union minister, Ram VilashPaswan, representing the Government of India, put forward a proposal to set up a three member expert committee on the issues. The content of the proposal was:

> "The Government of India is deeply concerned about the problems of Bodos and other Tribals of Assam and is committed to their economic development and other rights. On serious consideration of the Bodo problem, the Government of India proposes that a three member Committee of Experts may be set up to determine the area of Bodos and other Plain Tribals of the north of river Brahmaputra and make recommendations as to the autonomy, legislative, administrative and financial powers that may be given to them. This Committee will consult all groups concerned and submit a report within a period of forty five days to the Government of India". (Choudhury 1993:60).

The Three Member Expert Committee submitted its report to the Union Government in the last part of March, 1992. The ABSU rejected the report on the ground that it was not based on facts and failed to realize the ground realities of the aims and aspirations of the struggling masses. The period between rejection of the report and the Accord is marked by phases of movements and series of discussions with the governments. Demarcation of the boundary for BAC continued to pose serious challenge to its functioning. As boundary issues between the BAC and Government of Assam remained unresolved, election to the BAC was not held. There was large disagreement between the member of the BAC and the Assam government regarding sharing of power, with the members insisting that the autonomy granted to them could not be executed because of the high handedness of the state government. Following this, fresh demand for separate state was raised. This period is marked by the shifting of leadership from the BAC leaders to the hands of the underground terrorist outfits. Terrorist activities heightened as the BAC was thought to have no constitutional validity.In period that followed, the Bodo region became an arena of violence. The government enforced a number of laws to subdue the movement, like the "Disturbed Areas Act, 1955", "Armed Forces Special Power Act, 1958", "The Terrorist and Disruptive Activities (Preventive) Act, 1987" also by promulgating

144 the Cr. P. C. (Criminal Procedure Code). Mass movement gave way to armed struggle. The *modus operandi* of the movement got shifted from *bandhs*, fasts, road blockades etc. to extortion, loot, kidnapping, murder and ambushes.

Expert on the Bodoland movement Chandan Kumar Sharma describes the unrest in Assam at the onslaught of the Bodo militant outfit as such:

> Another important aspect in the present trend of the Bodoland movement is the alleged involvement of the aforementioned underground outfits—both NDFB and BLTF—in the ethnic cleansing operation, the worst demonstrations of which was witnessed in Barpeta in 1994, around Kokrajhar and Gosaigaon in April-May 1996 and near Barama in the Nalbari district in the late 1997 and January 13, 1998. These operations were prompted by the desire to turn these areas to Bodo dominated ones—demographically and influence wise—by compelling the people of other ethnic groups to leave areas which come under the proposed Bodoland state. This is again in response to the often repeated contention that the territory claimed for Bodolandcomprises many such areas where Bodos do not enjoy a majority. The role of the state in the whole affair is one of queer inaction. (Sharma 2000: 138).

Finally, the Union government appealed for talksby July 1999. BLT declared unilateral ceasefire in response to it. On October 2, 2001, BLT gave up its demand for a separate Bodoland state and reconciled itself to politico-administrative arrangements for autonomy under the Sixth Schedule of the Indian constitution. This led to the signing of a Memorandum of Settlement (MoS) for the creation of the Bodoland Territorial Council (BTC) on February 10, 2003 between the representatives of Union Government, Assam Government and a BLT delegation.

Chandan Kumar Sharma in the same piece writes that "the discourse on the Bodoland movement lays in front of us a definite life-cycle of it whose similarity with the preceding Assam Movement can hardly be overlooked" (Sharma 2000: 138). This view resonates with that of Sanjib Baruah on the Bodoland movement:

> Indeed, to some extent the movement for a Bodo homeland was an outgrowth of the Assam movement. It is not surprising that the intensive political mobilization in support of the demand began in 1987 during the first AGP government. The student leaders of the Assam movement, who became the leaders of the AGP, got caught

> in dieir own rhetoric and failed to recognize that Assameseness itself is a contested formation. In failing to select sufficiently inclusionary historical and cultural symbols, and in being insufficiently sensitive to the human impact of their policy demands — as applied to "foreigners" and "indigenous" peoples alike — the leaders of the Assam movement contributed to what I called the process of ethnicization of the Assamese. (Baruah 1999: 175).

The launch of mass movement under the leadership of students' body, signing of accords after period of dissidence and mass struggle, formation of political parties and eventually entry into power politics by the student leaders, emergence of underground terrorist outfits in response to the failure of the leadership of the mass movements are striking features of both the movements. However, the underlying foundation that colours and to a large extent justifies both the assertions is their idea of the "self" identity as distinct from a perceived "other". In the Assam Movement it the other was the outsider Bengali identity whereas in the Bodoland movement it was the Assamese identity. For the ULFA, on the other hand, it was the Indian identity itself.

Situating the Bodoland Movement

The Bodos are the largest group of Plain tribes in Assam. However there is no clear definition of the meaning of "tribe" in India. The Indian Constitution also does not provide any description of "tribe" or "tribal". The Constitution has however empowered the President to appoint a commission after every ten years to review the situation of the scheduled tribes and declare by public notification the scheduled tribes or tribal communities (*The Constitution of India* 1950: Article 342). The underlying idea behind this idea was that the tribal condition would not be perpetual and with the improvement of economic standard and political consciousness, the tribes will gradually be eliminated[66]. In a sharp contrast to this idea was the definition of tribe that members of tribal communities of India gave to themselves in a meeting in Shillong in 1962. They defined tribe as an indigenous, homogeneous unit, speaking a common language, claiming a common ancestry, living in a particular area, backward in the technology, preliterate, loyally observing social and political customs based on kinship (Consultation Findings 1962: 80). The self definition of the tribe is a static body unaffected by the waves of modernity and change.

In Assam the administration of the tribal areas are governed by the Sixth Schedule of the Constitution. This is a provision in the Constitution of India as to the administration of tribal areas in the states of Assam, Meghalaya, Tripura and Mizoram which allows constituting autonomous district and autonomous regions for the tribal groups. The then Chief Minister of Assam Gopinath Bordoloi highly recommended the protective Sixth Schedule when the Constitution was being framed. Scholars believe beyond the apparent appearance of the state Congress to adorning a liberal attitude towards the tribal of the state, Bordoloi and other Assamese leaders were motivated by the hope that in the long run these tribal communities, while maintain their cultural identity would eventually become a part of the *brihatarAxomiyaJati* or the greater Assamese nationality. Being part of one political unit Assam's geographical entity would remain unaltered. In such a situation Assam would have a greater voice in the affairs of Independent India (Misra 2001: 40). This envision of the Assamese leaders did not see light of the day as four tribal states were carved out of Assam after the Independence. Even in the present day Assam many assertions are around the question of the Sixth Schedule[67].

One of the essential factors, which scholars have often pointed out, that contributed in the surfacing of the Bodoland movement is the emergence of the Bodo middle class (Mittal and Sharma 1998; Sharma 2000) in the first quarter of the twentieth century, mainly in western Assam. The emergence and consolidation of the middle class is assigned to the upshot of two basic features: first, the advent of cash economy into the Bodo society and its proliferation under the colonial administration and second is the spread of Brahma movement propounded by Kalicharan Brahma. Cash economy played a significant part in withering the traditional tribalistic social structure among the Bodos and opening them to broader vistas. Brahma movement was a reformist movement that touched not only the religious aspect of the Bodos but its scope was extended to larger realm of their society and brought about a holistic change in the economic and cultural sphere. Besides bringing about social changes in marriage customs, restricting liquor consumption and pig rearing, it made profound impact on the spread of education amongst the Bodo masses. As a result the converted Bodos became more equipped to compete in the modern milieu than the unconverted brethrens and took over the leadership of the socio-political life of the Bodos[68]. This facilitated in the swelling of the ranks of the Bodo middle class. It was also through the consciousness of the college going Brahman Bodos, that the first Bodo students organization was formed in the 1930s—Bodo Chatra Sanmelan. The aim and objective of the organization were to unite the scattered Bodos through conferences and to take up programmes of social service and social reforms.Education enabled the Bodo youth to enter into the colonial job market. Like the Assamese counterpart, the development of the Bodo middle class became job centric.

The Bodoland movement is significant in the socio-political context of contemporary Assam not only because it was successful in mobilizing the masses around the tribal question but also because it provided a diametrical instance to the Assamese narrative of assertion. The Assamese who had framed themselves as the victim in the Assam movement and in the ULFA were constituted as the delinquent in the Bodoland movement. The Bodos in the fad of the Bodoland movement vehemently engrossed themselves to cull out an identity distinct and a plane more organic than the Assamese with respect to Assam. They executed this in two stages:

(a) Reversing assimilation

(b) Eroding of the "greater Assamese nationality"

"We are Bodos, not Assamese" *and the phase of Reverse assimilation*

The Bodoland movement took radical turn after signing of the Assam Accord in 1985 at the end of the Assam movement. The Bodo leadership raised stern objection to the clause in the accord that promised "constitutional, legislative and administrative safeguards…to protect, preserve and promote the cultural, social, linguistic identity and heritage of the Assamese people". (*AssamAccord*:1985). The Bodoleaders accused the "artificial Assamese" leaders of the Assam movement of treachery and vehemently expressed their suspicion that the Bodos and other tribal communities would now be subjected to hegemony by the Assamese—politically and culturally. To secure their position as the autochthons of the land and hence the rightful claimants, the Bodos evoked the myths and legends associated to themselves and consolidate their separate identity, more ancient and greater connected to the land than the Assamese.

The Bodo community, irrespective of the sects, contains in its belief a story of creation of its ancestors. The beliefs entails that they are the first human from whom the entire mankind has been born[69]. The belief about the centrality of their existence is twinned with the idea about their glorious past. The Bodos are believed to have ruled at different point of the history by different names—the Kiratas, Asuras, Mlechas—in the entire eastern and north-eastern sub-continent. "It is evident that Kochari or Bodo sovereignty was exercised in Assam in different ages, in different names in different places" (Narzi 1985: 12). Chandana Bhattacharjee in her work on the Bodo-Kacharis community- *Ethnicity and Autonomy Movement: Case of BodoKacharis of Assam*(1996) gives an account of British administrator Captain Fisher's description of the rule of the Bodo dynasty as follows:

> Captain Fisher observed that "The Kacharis gradually acquired an empire over Assam, Sylhet, Mymensingh and the valleys to the east of the Brahmaputra, their original seat being Kamarupa; and that their rule ultimately embraced everything from Kamarupa down to the sea. They built bricks cities, and it is supposed that the Tippera Raja was the youngest son of the house, the original empire being divided into a northern and southern part". (Bhattacharjee 1996:26).

It has been pointed out by scholars that the powerful Bodo regime got marginalized by the ingress of Ahom and Koch powers in the medieval period. Chandan Kumar Sharma describes the process of assimilation of the Bodo community with the new entrants Ahom and Koch and finally with the Hindus as:

> Although the relatively advanced and dominant Ahom and Koch state systems in medieval Assam permitted several tribal principalities to enjoy limited political autonomy in their respective territories in return for the fulfillment of certain feudal obligation, there were considerable interactions and intermixing among the subjects of these territories and between those of the Ahom and the Koch states in the sphere of polity, economy, language and culture. In fact, this process of interaction can be traced back to much earlier times under different politico-economic and societal arrangements even before the Ahom and the Koch kingdoms came into being. The relatively advanced mode(s) of production and cultural conditions of the semi-feudal states of the central and western Assam created the objective conditions that facilitated the process of sanskritization among different tribes of the region. This process was engineered by the upper caste Hindus, especially Brahmins, who had already settled in the area otherwise dominated by mongoloid people and culture. The Burman kings, who reigned over parts of North Bengal and central and western Assam (known as Kamrupa kingdom) from the 5th to the 8th century A.D. are held as Hinduized Bodos...the neo-vaishnavite movement in Assam propagated by Shankardev and his disciple Madhabdev (other prominent neo-vaishnavite preachers of the era include Haridev and Damodardev) in the 15th and the 16th centuries lubricated and consolidated this process to a considerable

extent. Initially the role played by the Brahmin literati and their brand of Hinduism was commendable in accelerating the pace of social development in Assam. Later on, they lost that progressive character and became proponents and practitioners of an ideology whose sole aim was to perpetuate the social and ritual superiority of the Brahmins and the social order that sustained it.

On the other hand, neo-vaishnavism as espoused by Shankardev was an egalitarian religion. The caste hierarchy and ritual complexities of Brahminic Hinduism enjoyed little significance in neo-vaishnavism. This was indeed in tune with the neo-vaishnavite movement that swayed the most parts of India at that time. The various indigenous communities of Assam were attracted to the egalitarian tenets of neo-vaishnavism. The tribal neophytes were known as *sarania*s (those who take *sarana*, religious shelter, under vaishnavite gurus). A large number of Bodos also became *sarania*s and still they are addressed as such who have over the years been totally assimilated in the *Assamese* society. Neo-vaishnavism then made tremendous inroads in the upper Assam. Many tribals like the Morans, the Sonowal-Kacharis, the Chutias, the Deoris, the Thengal-Kacharis, etc. became devout followers of neo-vaishnavism. All the above mentioned groups, some of which were Bodo origin (e.g. the Sonowals and the Thengal-Kacharis), are now part and parcel of the Assamese society. (Sharma 2007: 4-7).

In the course of time the Bodos and other tribal groups of the region came under the umbrella of the Assamese nationality and began to be regarded as "natural" constituent of *brihattarAxamiyajati*(greater Assamese nationality). The popular metaphor that has been reiterated to build up the position of the tribal groups within the Assamese nationality fold was created by cultural icon of Assam BishnuPrashad Rabha (1909-1968), who was himself a tribal and was rendered the title of *Kalaguru* (exponent of culture) for his matchless contribution to Assamese literature and arts. Rabha envisaged that the Assamese nationality is like the great river Brahmaputra. As innumerable tributaries merge into the Brahmaputra, so will all the ethnic groups, big and small, in the Brahmaputra valley would eventually merge into the greater Assamese nationality. Rabha even added that whoever dared to thwart the above process would be swept away, the way the torrents of the mighty Brahmaputra sweeps away everything that comes its way. Sharma (2007:10-11) is of the view that this metaphor was expressed in a much wider context but was exploited by the Assamese nationalist leadership to justify their assimilationist ideology. It made the cast Hindu Assamese intolerant to any kind of self-assertion on the part of the tribal group.

Tribal leader and scholar, Indibor Deori (2001: 20) has recently interpreted the historic metaphor in a different way. He writes, "The Luit[70] exists as the Luit because of its lively tributaries and the tributaries are flowing because of the Luit. Their existence is mutually dependent... The tributaries may not become the Luit themselves due to certain specific historical conditions and the stages of social development that exists in Assam but they certainly have the rights to attain fullness". This expression resound the popular sentiment of the Bodos after the Bodoland movement was launched. It was a significant departure from the pre-Bodoland movement scholars' views. The Bodos now had begun to shed the aegis of the greater Assamese national and cultural identity and had started to sharpen their unique existence. In this context the view expressed by the President of Bodo Sahitya Sabha Brajendra Kumar Brahma is significant. In an interview based news article published in the popular Assamese daily *Aji* on 15 November 2002, he expressed that it is only because of the chauvinism of the Assamese people that the Bodos are compelled to denounce the process of greater Assamese nationality formation despite their initial willingness to be part of that process. He further states that the Bodo Sahitya Sabha itself is an outcome of the process of alienation.

In the process of constructing a distinct identity, unique from the Assamese, the Bodos relied significantly on the colonial writings about themselves, which has been, until then, the only significant body of work on the "origin" and racial affinity of the Bodos. Writers like Bijaya Laxmi Brohmo Choudhury (1993), Indibar Deori (1995) etc evoked the colonial anthropological description about the Bodo identity to establish a separate identity for themselves. Along with this, the Bodo leadership engaged in a project of "construction" of their own "ethnic" history. Since the Bodos had no written history, the folklore like the myths, legends and folksongs became the sources in the quest for identity markers. The history extracted from these sources assisted the Bodo leaders in their claim that the Bodolands are the earliest inhabitants (*bhumiputra* or sons of the soil) of the region. It also pointed out that the Bodos had their own kingdom and that they had been an influential community in the region in the ancient times. Sanjib Baruah (1999: 183) writes that, "The central theme in Bodo cultural politics today is to repudiate the process of unequal assimilation into the Assamese subnational formation and to seek differentiation from, and equality with, the ethnic Assamese". Baruah attributes ample responsibility to the Assam movement in sparking the Bodoland movement. According to him, the leaders of the Assam movement failing to select sufficiently inclusionary historical and cultural symbols and being insufficiently sensitive to human impact of their policy demand got caught in their own rhetoric which gave fillip to the Bodo to intensify the homeland movement, who were already nurturing the feeling of repression and marginalization since long.

The Bodoland movement ushered in a host of assertions demanding for separate homeland from such groups like the Rabha, Tiwa and Karbi tribal groups.

***Divide Assam Fifty-Fifty** and eroding of the greater Assamese nationality*

LakhiKachari, a Bodo person in response to the ULFA's call for independent Assam, in a letter to the editor of Assam's daily newspaper the *Sentinel* (January 1991) asked what gave ULFA—which represented the upper caste Assamese—the authority to demand an independent Assam? According to him the ULFA has no right to demand anything for Assam. Assam, he claims has been illegally occupied by the "so-called Assamese"[71] who had migrated to Assam from other parts of the country. This expression represented the spirit of the Bodo community at the wake of the Bodoland movement. The Bodoland movement not only sought to establish the Bodos as the aboriginals of Assam but it also questioned the influence of the Assamese over Assam.

The Bodo assertion manifested itself by twofold negation- negation of the Assam state government as representative of their interest and aspiration and refusal to share a particular territory (which they claimed had been their kingdom in the ancient times) with other groups. Though it cannot be denied that not all the Bodos were equally fervent for separate Bodoland, but along with more stringent organizations like the All Bodo Students Union- Upen Brahma group [ABSU (U)] and the Bodoland Peoples' Action Committee (BPAC), the All Bodo Students Union- Ramsiary group [ABSU (R)][72], the Plain Tribal Council of Assam (PTCA) and the United Tribal Nationalist Liberation Front (UTNLF)[73] have also expressed their alienation from the Assamese society and their solidarity for the demand of separate Bodoland.

The Bodoland movement took a radical turn in the late 1980s, however, seeds of resentment and an urge to consolidate their separate identity already existed among the Bodos since a long time. In this context, the contribution of a religious reform movement under the aegis of the Brahma sect propounded by Kalicharan Brahma is significant. Kalicharan Brahma (1860-1938) is rendered the title of *Gurudev* (master) by Bodos and is considered to be the "architect of all round development of the tribal people"[74]. During the first quarter of twentieth century, the Bodos of lower Assam (which include the west and certain parts of central Assam), especially that of the Kokrajhar area, (the nerve centre of the Bodoland movement from the 1980s) were swept by this reform movement. Though this movement was religious in form, the movement in its content was socio-economic. This movement not only was successful in improving the economic conditions of the Bodos but it also was significant in bringing together the isolated Bodo groups under its umbrella and thus infusing in them identity consciousness hitherto unknown. Kalicharan Brahma vociferously opposed the conversion of the Bodos to *Sarania* through the neo-vaishnavism reform movement that was gaining popularity at that time and was contributing in bringing the various tribal communities in the Hindu folds, hereby strengthening the Assamese nationality[75]. Another significant section of the Brahma movement was "Brahma Company" which enabled economic development to the downtrodden tribal people of Assam. Though this company eventually had to face bankruptcy, it facilitated peasants and other underprivileged tribal sections to attain better conditions of living. Also, it was under the patronage of the Brahma movement that the Tribal League of Assam was formed. This organization for the first time gave a platform to the political aspirations of the various tribal groups in Assam. The Bodo, Kachari, Rabha, Lalung, Miri, Deori, Sonowal etc came together under the Tribal League to consolidate the tribal identity. These various tribal groups were appropriated under the umbrella of Bodo stock in the League. These groups were until now considered to be the components of the composite Assamese identity. The greater Assamese nationality began to erode politically and culturally.

In a memorandum submitted to the Simon Commission in 1929 that had come to review the administrative system of Assam, the Tribal League expressed its willingness to participate in political field. In presenting their case for a separate electorate, the Bodos delineated their identity as follows:

> The Bodoshave a distinct civilization of their own. There should be a separate category as "The Bodos" in the census report. History shows very clearly the part this community has been playing in the history since the time of Bhagadatta, who ruled over Assam during

> the time of great epic, the Mahabharata. Many kings who ruled over Assam belonged to this race. Bhismak Raja, Bali Raja, Ban Raja and Viswa Singha all belonged to this race and history will prove now how influential once they were.
>
> ... In our opinion there should not be mixed electorate. Each section of the people should have the liberty of sending their representatives in the local councils. The peculiar position in which we are placed offers us practically no chance of sending our representative in which, in which though there is a large number of voters in our community. Out of the total population of the whole district of Goalpara, which numbers about six lakhs eighty five thousand eight hundred eighty two, three lakhs sixty nine thousand three hundred ninety seven fall under the head of non-Mohammedans. Non-Mohammedans mean Hindus, Christians, Jains, Sikhs, and the like. A liberal view of the things shows that we cannot enjoy the advantages of the reform as the other community does. Inspite of our being in such a large number all advantages of the reforms are being enjoyed either by Brahmins or by the Khatriyas or by the Sudras. So in order to safeguard the interest of our community we should have a separate representative in the council. (Quoted in Choudhury 1993: 26- 27).

Another phase in history that underscored the identity of Bodos against the Assamese identity was from 1952 to 1967. This time it was spearheaded by the Bodo Sahitya Sabha, the premier literary organization of the Bodos. This phase is marked by predominance of the issue of Bodo language and script. The demands of this phase were to introduce the Bodo language in the schools in the Bodo dominated areas and for recognition of Roman script in the place of Assamese. This phase saw a mass movement first time in the history of the Bodoland movement. It was also a phase when the Bodos directly confronted the chauvinism of the Assamese middle class. In 1963 eventually Bodoland language was introduced as medium of instruction in the schools of the Bodo dominated areas. The demand for introducing Roman script met with violent outbreak and as many as sixteen people losing their lives[76]. Finally Devanagiri script was adopted by the Bodo Sahitya Sabha instead of the demand for the Roman script in 1974. In 1977 the Gauhati University recognized the Bodo language as one of the modern Indian languages. The Bodo language was accorded the status of Associate Official Languages of the State of Assam as per the Assam official Language (Amendment) Act, 1985.

An apparent erosion of the greater Assamese nationality came in the third phase, the late 1980s and early 1990s, when the Bodolands reinforced the demand for separate homeland after the signing of the Assam Accord. The Bodos demanded "Divide Assam fifty-fifty" and secure half of Assam's territory for the proposed Bodoland. What followed was an apparent repudiation of the Assamese identity. The Bodos refused day-to-day interaction in Assamese (which had been a *lingua franca*) and insisted on speaking Bodoland language, the Bathou festival began to be celebrated on a large scale, women and men adorned the traditional Bodo attire instead of the Assamese clothes, cuisine, customs and traditions were revived and heightened[77].

According to Chandan Kumar Sharma (2007), the Bodos relied on the folklore as a mode of constructing and glorifying a distinct history and tradition during their self assertion movement. The newly emerging class of litterateurs among the Bodos in the first quarter of twentieth century made attempts to infuse self-confidence among the common Bodo population in order to establish themselves as a homogeneous group deserving sufficient attention. The folk songs, myth, legend, tales etc narrated the glorious past of the Bodos, laments the downfall and evokes the masses to unite to regain the lost opulence. For example the following song describes the ancient kingdom which the Bodos believe they had ruled and now has been taken away from them:

Dimapur was the kingdom of Bodos *Boronijaigayagougou Dimapurimounsou*
O' listeners, was the kingdom of Bodos;*O' aiphorDimapurimounsou*
That Maibang was the capital of that kingdom. *Maibong Kacharao Boronirajadangmounnou*
Bodos had to leave all these. *Boroagoudounougarnaphaidamounnou*
To climb a tree branches are needed, *Dimaphurikhou*
To lead the nation on shiny path *Thangddinnoubungblaboujaigagoumanou*
Education is needed *Binikhainou, bongphuuojaigagoumanou*
To lead a king is needed *Jathikhoudaikhangnoulekhanangou*
So said our forefathers *Harikhoudaikhangnou raja nangou*
O' listeners, arise! *O' aiphorjongthanaijaigayagongarnisounou*
Get united and build the society *Goudoniabouaboianoubungladou*
Aiphoradaphoursirithadou
Khousoijananoiraijoujadou
O' aiphorraijoujadou (Sharma 2007: 17).

Similarly, Mittal and Sharma (1998) collected and analyzed more than a dozen folk songs and poem from different Bodo villages by known and unknown composers. These songs and poems were presented in different meetings and assemblies. This exercise of circulation of folklore, inspiring self pride among the Bodo populace, was to infuse a sense of solidarity amongst them who had been living in different parts of Assam. Mittal and Sharma summarized the central ideas of this folklore as:

In a poem called 'Dimapur' dated 2 June 1973, there is a call to the Bodos to awaken and to remember their glorious past in the social, political and cultural spheres.

In another poem composed before 1970, the poet asks when they will get a separate state. A third one of the same time calls the Bodos to awaken. In June 1971, another big poem was written in which the poet, Kumar Nalin Brahma, praised the PTCA for opening up new horizons.

A famous Bodo artist-singer composed a folk song on 15 March 1973 with the purpose of arousing the community in support of the struggle for Udayachal. Similarly, folk-songs composed for the purpose of inspiring the Bodo people on the issue of their language have played an effective role in organizing them in support of the language movement. Two pamphlet published during 1963 and 1965 contains folk-songs. The later was issued in support of the introduction of Bodo language as a medium in secondary education. (Mittal and Sharma 1998: 324).

The demand for the creation of separate state on the northern bank of the river Brahmaputra and two autonomous council in the southern bank had been placed on the basis that that was the territory where the ancient Bodo kingdom once existed, hence they are the rightful owner of the land. The Bodoland movement however neglected the existence of other groups in the particular area they demarcated. The result has been predictable. Two major hill tribes the Karbis of the KarbiAnglong district and the DimasaKacharis of North Cachar district are demanding autonomous districts for themselves which cover the region the Bodos have demarcated for themselves.

Conclusion

Though the three movements had emerged along the common sentiment of neglect and deprivation, they were of different constituent. Three of them however, grounded their demands by formulating adistinctive cultural identity and a corresponding homeland. These idea about their cultural identity were inclusive; Assam movement demanded on behalf of "people of Assam" or Indian citizens, ULFA assumed itself to be the voice of inhabitants of Assam, including the immigrant communities and Bodoland movement spoke about the rights of indigenous tribals of Assam. But, in the course of time the inclusive claims of the three movements did not sustain and they began to be seen as fringe groups demanding exclusive privileges for themselves.

Reference

1. The anxiety that stimulated the commencement of the Assam movement has been compiled through many personal interviews with participants of the movement, from the casual participants to the most ardent agitators. Some of them are:

   Dhruba Prasad Baishya (25.09. 2008); Presently member of BJP, was Chairman of AGP ministry in 1985.

   Jugal Kishor Mahanta (17.12.2008), participant of the movement and surrendered ULFA member (ULFA).

   Madhab Baishya (17.12.2008), Student participant in the Assam movement who led in the oil blockade in the 1980s.

   Rukmini Choudhury (27.11.2008), student participant.

2. "The antiforeign movement spilled across the borders of Assam into the nearby states of Tripura and Manipur. In Tripura indigenous tribal groups launched violent attacks against Bengali settlers, who, by now, outnumbered the locals and controlled the state government. And in neighbouring Manipur, Manipuri students attacked Bengalis, Biharis, Punjabis, and the numerous and increasingly prosperous Nepali dairy cattle farmers. India's entire northeast has been fragmented by the migrant-ethnic issue". (Weiner 1983: 287).

3. AASU, the umbrella students organization of schools, colleges and universities of Assam, has been an active political body. It commands immense influence on government and the general public. The history of AASU can be traced back to 1916 with the formation of the *Asom Chhatra Sanmilan*, an organisation that was formed to focus on literary, social and economic development of Assam. Since its inception it has been active in the political activities centring around Assam and India, in general. Most important among them has been its active participation in the Non-Cooperation Movement during India's struggle for independence. It had played the leading role in mobilizing the student community in the anti-Simon Commission agitation in 1929 calling for strike and non-cooperation. In 1940, Asom Chattra Sanmilan divided into the All Assam Student' Federation and the All Assam Students' Congress. In 1959 they merged again and formed All Assam Student' Association, which was later renamed to All Assam Students Union in January 1967. In August 1967, it adopted its formal Constitution. (Bora 1992)

   "During 1956 and 1957, students of Assam started formally organizing against the government. This was in relation to the establishment of oil refinery in Assam instead of Calcutta. Guwahati Students' Oil Refinery Action Committee was formed. Massive spate of activities including strikes, non cooperation, and protest march were organized, and ultimately the centre had to change its policy and decided to set up oil refinery in Guwahati. The students started looking into fulfilling the aspirations of the society in a more concerned manner. In 1958, the All Guwahati Students' Union was formed, which paved the way to formally form the All Assam Students' Association in 1959, with the objective of a students body without any political biasness, and to work for the cultural and moral uplift of the students community of Assam."

4. Other organization included Asom Jatiyabadi Dal, Purbanchaliya Loka Parishad, the Sadau Asom Karmachari Parishad, Asom Jatiyabadi Yuva-Chatra Parishad, AsomYuvak Samaj, All Assam Central and semi-Central Employees' Association etc.

   "The Asam Sahitya Sabha was founded in 1917 to promote the culture of Assam and its Literature. Presently it has about one thousand branches all over Assam and its neighbouring state. Its Central office is at Jorhat .

   The primary Objective of the Asam Sahitya Sabha is to make all round development of the Assamese language, literature and the multifarious but indigenous culture of the State.

   With this end in view the Sahitya Sabha is endowed and committed to the following areas:

   - The publications of Dictionary, Grammar, Research works, monographs on languages,
   - literature, culture, tribes and races etc., books on literary criticism, complete works of the
   - great writers of Assam etc.
   - Publication of Assamese Encyclopedia (Bishwakosh).
   - To enquire, collect and research on ancient literature of the State of Assam.
   - To find out and publish the rare books.
   - To recognize and award the outstanding writers, scholars and artists of the state.
   - To provide financial help to the deserving writers who cannot afford to publish their books and literature for financial stringency.
   - To promote music, art and sculpture of the State.
   - To publish a journal of the Sabha on regular basis.
   - To bring out leaflets, pamphlets etc. in order to publicize the Assamese language and literature.
   - To establish Research Centre to develop Assamese Language, Literature and Culture.
   - To promote exchange plans and schemes between Literature and Culture.
   - To do such work which helps in expanding development of Assamese Language, Literature and Culture".

5. Information gathered from personal interview from participants of the movement.
6. The faction of the Congress which was led by Mrs. Indira Gandhi
7. AnwaraTaimur, an Assamese Muslim, who was elected from a constituency populated by Bengali descent was seen as a sympathizer to the immigrants by the supporters of the Assam movement.
8. A small village by the southern bank of Brahmaputra, 45 kms away from the nerve centre of Assam- Guwahati, inhabited mostly by "Plain tribal" group- the Lalung (Tiwa). The Lalung once had their kingdom in this area much of which were encroached by the Bengali immigrants and their descendents. As Sanjib Baruah (1999: 134) notes that the British administration did not view them as

"backward tribe" but as "Hinduised tribe" hence their land rights were not protected by the land system. Subsequently the post colonial government did not secure their traditional land through the policies restricting land transfer in "tribal blocks" which led their easy lose of the land to the immigrants.

9. Monirul Hussain (Hussain 2000: 4520) also notes that, "Notwithstanding the pogrom, severe violence and terror, the inhabitants of Nellie had refused to be displaced come what may. They had no place to go, no alternative to their existing living space. After spending only a few weeks in the state sponsored relief camps the entire people of Nellie who could manage to survive somehow returned to their normal life in an abnormal situation. Ultimately, they succeeded in resisting displacement. Of course, they had to pay a huge price, the lives of their near and dear ones".

10. The Ahom community is one of the dominant "tribal" communities in Assam. The Ahom rulers are believed to have ruled Assam for six hundred years during the medieval times, starting from 1228. They are believed to belong to the Shan race speaking the Tai language, in contrast to the Assamese who are believed to be Indo-Aryan speaking the Assamese language.

11. He uses the term to refer to a pattern of politicization and mobilization that meets some of the criteria of nationalism, but is not firmly to the idea of separate statehood. (Baruah 1999: 5).

12. "It is not surprising that Woodrow Wilson, after proclaiming the right of nation's to self-determination when confronted with numerous petition of sovereignty and statehood admitted that he had no idea that there were so many nations in the world. Granting self-determination to all these nations, he feared might have meant that a vast number of new states would have had to be created which would have threatened the prevailing global political order".

    "Sociologist Amitai Etzioni, in an essay published in 1990 at a time when the cold war was giving fresh impetus to many new nationalisms, argued that it is time to withdraw moral approval from most self-determination movement. While these movements have been a positive historical force for more than two centuries, he wrote, they no longer have the capacity to create more democratic states. Now the thrust of many movements of self determination, he believes, is destructive". (Baruah 1999: 2-3).

13. This will be discussed in the following chapters.

14. According to the 1951 census, 56.7 percent of the population was Assamese speaking, in 1961 62.4 percent, and in 1971 61 percent. The Bengalis were 16.5 percent, 18 percent, and 19.7 percent, and the Hindi-speaking population was 3.8 percent, 4.8 percent, and 5.4 percent. Between 1951 and1961 the population of Assam increased from 8 million to 10.6 million (a 35percent increase), but the number of Assamese speakers rose from 4.6 million to 6.7 million, a 48.5 percent increase, suggesting the magnitude of language"switching." In the 1931 census only 1.7 million people reported Assameseas their mother tongue.Between 1961 and 1971 the proportion of Assamese declined for the first time, as the proportion of Bengali speakers increased. This shift, though small, was in a direction that aroused the anxieties of many Assamese. If a large proportion of the Muslim population (24.6 percent of the population in1971), most of whom are of Bengali

origin, declared themselves Bengali, the position of the Assamese and Bengalis could be reversed. (Weiner 1983 :286).

15. In Assam, as elsewhere in India, the Congress Party split into proand anti-Indira Gandhi factions, with the result that, in March 1978, for thefirst time since independence Congress failed to win a majority of seats in the state assembly elections. In an assembly of 126 seats the pro-Gandhi Congress(1)-I for Indira-won only eight seats and the anti-Gandhi Congress won 26.14 In the 1978 state assembly election, the Communist Party of India (Marxist) won 5.6 percent of the vote (and 11 seats), and the Communist Party of India 4.1 percent of the vote (and five seats), more than twice the combined vote of 4.3 percent won by these two parties in the parliamentary elections only a year earlier.Many Assamese regarded the Communist parties as Bengali because of thedominant pro-Communist vote in both West Bengal and Tripura. (Weiner 1983: 287-288).
16. The tension was controlled by the intervention of Lal Bahadur Shastri who suggested the Assam Official Language Act be amended by giving the local bodies the authority to alter the official language of their area by two-third majority, by allowing communication between the state capital and Cachar and the hill districts to continue to be in English, at the state level to continue the use of English along with Assamese and incorporating stronger provisions for protection of linguistic minorities (Chakrabarty 1981).
17. This immediate crisis was suppressed by D.K. Barooah, member of then Prime Minister Indira Gandhi's cabinet, by suggesting a compromise formula that allowed continuation of English and removed compulsion of Assamese in colleges of Assam. (Chakrabarty 1984).
18. Golden Assam.
19. http://www.rediff.com/news/2001/jan/23inter.htm.
20. http://web.archive.org/web/20091027113256/http://www.geocities.com/CapitolHill/Congress/7434/ulfa.htm.
21. "Peace Talks Last Oppourtunity, Says ULFA Chairman," The Hindu, August 8, 2011. http://www.thehindu.com/news/states/other-states/article2334056.ece (accessed October 14, 2011).
22. "ULFA Presents Charter of Demands, Seek Change in Constitution," The Hindu, August 5, 2011. http://www.thehindu.com/news/states/other-states/article2328147.ece?css=print (accessed October 14, 2011).
23. Misra, Tilottama. "Assam: A Colonial Hinterland". *Economic and Political Weekly*. 9 August 1980. Vol XV, No. 32.

    Das, Amiya Kumar . "Assam's Agony: A Socio-economic and Political Analysis". New Delhi. Lancer's. 1982.

    Bhattacharjee, Mridul and Goswami, Sanjeeb. "Assam: Assam's Agonies and Grievances". New Delhi. National. 1985. Pg. 5-19.
24. Present day Assam has around 850 tea estates and more than 2500 tea gardens. Each year Assam produces around 6,80,400 kgs tea.
25. The Assam Tribune. Gauhati. 15 June 1980.
26. Suggestion put forward by Soviet experts on basis of extensive surveys for the establishment of large scale refinery at Silghat in Assam was rejected outright.

Instead it was established in Barauni in Bihar for refining the crude oil from Assam which has a capacity to refine more than 30 lakh tonnes of crude. Mass movement against the unfair decision of the Centre was staged in Assam in 1956-57 following which a small refinery having capacity of 7 lakhs tonnes was established in Guwahati. Another mass movement shook the state in 1969 following which the Centre set up second public sector refinery in the state. This time too the new refinery-cum-petrochemical plant fell short of the Barauni refinery and had only 10 lakh tonnes capacity.

27. Just before the Assam movement and the ULFA stir commenced, the state government had submitted a memorandum to the Centre demanding the revision of oil royalty from Rs. 42 to Rs. 315 arguing that since crude was a non-replenishable commodity the proprietors of the natural resource should be adequately compensated.

28. Draft Tenth Five Year Plan and Annual Plan. Planning and Development Department. Government of Assam. 2002-2003.

29. http://web.archive.org/web/20091027113301/http://www.geocities.com/CapitolHill/Congress/7434/economy .htm# THE%20 DRAINING %20AWAY %20OF%20ASSAM%27S%20OIL%20RESOURCES

30. Central Government Act

    Article 246 in The Constitution Of India 1949.

    246. Subject matter of laws made by Parliament and by the Legislatures of States

    (1) Notwithstanding anything in clauses (2) and (3), Parliament has exclusive power to make laws with respect to any of the matters enumerated in List I in the Seventh Schedule (in this Constitution referred to as the Union List)

    (2) Notwithstanding anything in clause (3), Parliament, and, subject to clause (1), the Legislature of any State also, have power to make laws with respect to any of the matters enumerated in List III in the Seventh Schedule (in this Constitution referred to as the Concurrent List)

    (4) Parliament has power to make laws with respect to any matter for any part of the territory of India not included (in a State) notwithstanding that such matter is a matter enumerated in the State List (http://www.indiankanoon.org/doc/77052/)

    Central Government Act

    Article 248 in The Constitution Of India 1949

    248. Residuary powers of legislation

    (1) Parliament has exclusive power to make any law with respect to any matter not enumerated in the Concurrent List or State List

    (2) Such power shall include the power of making any law imposing a tax not mentioned in either of those Lists (http://www.indiankanoon.org/doc/1270258/)

31. The people of Assam have never benefited from the oil revenue. On the other hand they have been kept completely in the dark and not informed about the factual reality of the oil reserves, its production, refinement, sales, revenue accrued etc. In 1948 Delhi and its appointed oil companies sold a metric tonnes (MT) of Assam's crude oil at Rs. 1382. Assam received Rs. 61 per MT as

royalty. As taxes the central government received Rs. 532 and gave Assam Rs. 131 out of this. In subsequent years the price of oil increased substantially but the minimal royalty did not, in equal ratio. In 1991-92 the natural gas in Assam was still not utilized fruitfully. 56% was flared off. The official figures in 1992-93 were Rs. 30 lakh per day of natural gas wasted. (http://web.archive.org/web/20091027113301/http://www.geocities.com/CapitolHill/Congress/7434/economy. htm# THE%20 DRAINING %20AWAY% 20OF%20ASSAM %27S%20OIL%20RESOURCES).

32. The romantic idea of Assam being adorned with natural and aesthetic glory has been a strong narrative within Assam which finds its place in numerous poetics. Among them, cultural icon of Assam Bhupen Hazarika, has sung and composed several songs around the idea. "Axomaamarrupohigunorunaixekh…" (Our Assam is laden with priceless qualities…) is one such popular song that has been sung and heard since several generations.

33. M. S. Prabhakara, "Still Largely Symbolic",*Hindu*, February 13, 1985.

34. Naresh Mitra. *Times of India*. Guwahati. 6 October 2012.

35. Though no printed version of the speech is available neither it has been reproduced in the various volumes of Nehru's speeches. The recording of the tape is also unavailable in All India Radio office. Those sympathetic to Nehru argue that the sentiments expressed in the words were Nehru's concern and love for the region but the general understanding among the masses regarding the attitude adopted by the Centre at the time of this emergency was that of insensitivity and uncared for.

36. S.C. Kakati (1954) describes that Mahatma Gandhi too was influenced by such preconception which led him to consider the people of Assam as savage in his *Hind Swaraj* (1909). Later he made amendments "Lovely Assam" published in *Young India* on 1 September 1921 after he visited Assam.

37. http://www.sunday-guardian.com/analysis/delhi-listens-to-northeasts-concerns-for-a-change.

    http://www.thehindu.com/opinion/op-ed/lets-stop-pretending-theres-no-racism-in-india/article3466554.ece.

    http://www.northeastblog.in/north-east-india/does-the-north-east-belong-in-india/.

38. Assam was unfortunately annexed to India because of the trickery and conspiracy of the Congress, the British sponsored association of the "Indian elite".

    The exploitation, oppression and the looting of wealth remain undeterred today as before. The only difference is that, previously the colonial exploitation was manipulated by the British imperialists directly but now Assam comes under direct Indian colonial exploitation and on the other hand under the indirect International Monopolistic entrepreneurs as an alliance of Indian big business.

    The identity of the indigenous peoples of Assam is now threatened because of these double layered exploitations. On the other hand, the Indian government has arranged to form the powerless Assam government with the help of some puppets under the Indian constitution having a governor directly appointed by New Delhi. Elimination of all the basic rights with the help of the direct governing system of Delhi, the Indian government has made their way clear. At the time of power transfer to the loyal Congress leadership by the British, the Congress leadership took the chair of ruler without changing anything of the Indian constitution which was drafted on the model of the British system. The Indian constitution has failed to open any route to the development of other nation-tribes providing self-determination right to them and to eradicate its eccentric character which is amended 85 times up till now. However, it makes a new social base loyal to the colonial India crushing the demographic structure of the nation-tribes. It is the manifestation of the previous social base established by the British. This servant or sycophant class is helping the caretaker government of India stationed at Gauhati making a favorable environment for administration and exploitation by the slogans like "united India" , "India is our mainstream", "we are all Indians" who are totally unsympathetic to the rights, honour and the identity of the indigenous peoples of Assam. This puppet class is creating the environment of hatred, differences and conflicts among the indigenous nation-tribes. This class is more brutal than the British in suppressing the legitimate struggle of the indigenous peoples, the democratic non-violent movement organized with the of hope of emancipation of the peoples of Assam who have been pauperised and deprived of their basic rights in their own Motherland. Therefore, the indigenous peoples of Assam under 51 years of Indian colonial rule have been tasting the bitter experiences of brutal repression upon unarmed movement. Now Assam and the whole of so-called North-Eastern region is subjected to the colonial system of Indian ruling class through their repressive administration behind the veil of fake democracy. They are conducting their cultural, economic and political repression under the cover of Indian constitution. With these rules and systems, the Indian government has closed all the doors to the solution of "Nation Problem of Assam" establishing the right of self - determination of the indigenous peoples of Assam.

That means -

1. the right of national self-determination is not recognized in the Indian constitution.
2. the Indian constitution and the other state systems are founded on the idea of "one nation state" other than the character of "Multi-nation State".
3. It does not empower any nation to adopt any eco-social and cultural planing or program in its own motherland.
4. It does not entrust any power to the national peoples to determine the demarcation of the area where a specific nation lives unaccompanied.
5. The constitution provides for a powerful centralised system (clause 352, 353, 365 ,360) to crush any movement organized by the national peoples to solve their problem by imposing "emergency" without any consent of the people's representatives.
6. In Delhi, the President of India and the Governor in Assam is supreme in power; the people's power is neglected.

39. In Assam, they are enforcing different laws and acts, those are discriminatory comparing with the rest of India. (IMDT Act, AFSPA 1958 Assam, Manipur etc,)

In addition, in 1962 the Government of India almost handed over Assam to China. On 21-11-1962 all the Indian soldiers left Assam. Jawaharlal Nehru said farewell to Assam (by his famous speech "My heart goes out to the people of Assam"). Even, at that time the "conducive pipes" of Burma Oil Company were lifted away to West Bengali, Bihari and Marwari peoples from Assam. Moreover, the indigenous peoples of Assam stayed here contemplating their destiny. After that, is there any legal right of India to rule Assam? However, shamelessly India again established their colonial rule after China declared unilateral ceasefire without encroaching on Assam. India once again re-established its colonial rule in Assam and resumed their colonial economic exploitation of Assam. And till today, the act of looting, and plundering of wealth of Assam is going on. (http://www.oocities.org/capitolhill/congress/7434/history.htm).

40. http://week.manoramaonline.com/Cgi-bin/MMOnline.dll/portal/ep/the Week Content. do? contentId =11534616 & programId =1073755753 & tabId =13& BV_ID =@@@&categoryId=-176321.

41. http://www.satp.org/satporgtp/countries/india/states/assam/terrorist_outfits/index.html.

42. An excerpt from *Asia Watch* report said:

    "The Indian state of Assam, located south of Bhutan and east of Bangladesh, is geographically almost cut off from the rest of India, with its only physical link a narrow land corridor to West Bengal. Home to a number of tribes and ethnic groups, Assam has been the site of separatist movements and violent insurgencies since India's independence in 1947. The most serious has been the campaign waged bythe United Liberation Front of Asom (ULFA) since 1979. In attempting to crush the ULFA organization and several other groups, the Indian government has launched counterinsurgency campaigns that have been faught with widespread human rights violations.

    The Indian army has conducted massive search-and-arrest operations in thousands of villages in Assam. Many victims of abuses committed during these operations are civilians, often relatives or neighbors of young men suspected of militant sympathies. Villagers have been threatened, harassed, raped, assaulted and killed by soldiers attempting to frighten them into identifying suspected militants. Arbitrary arrest and lengthy detention of young men picked up in these periodic sweeps, or at random from their homes and from public places is common, and detainees of the armed forces are regularly subjected to severe beatings and torture. Deaths in custody have occurred as the result of torture, and in alleged encounters and escape attempts". ("No End in Sight: Human Rights Violation in Assam": April 1993:1-2).

43. Fourteen officials and some others were taken hostage. The Government sought to negotiate their release and offered an amnesty to all detents taken during Operation Bajrang. It subsequently freed 400 of them pending reciprocal action by the underground. ULFA played false, liquidating some of the hostages and going on rampage. Within 11 weeks, as many as 166 persons were killed and at least 252 kidnapped. (Verghese 1996: 58).

44. Counter-insurgency grids were laid within 48 hours and a combination of surprise, saturation and pressure resulted in the quick capture of leading ULFA cadres and receipt of specific, actionable intelligence on the basis of which many others

were caught in the net. As many as 431 hard core elements including 46 top leaders were nabbed along with 299 supporters and trainees within the space of some weeks. Sixteen ULFA camps were destroyed. Piles of arms ammunition, communication equipment, documents and photographs were seized. This established KIA, NSCN and LTTE links and the existence of sanctuaries in Bangladesh. Rs. 5 crores in cash and 32 gold bars had been recovered during Operation Bajrang. More was now discovered and there was some indication of money had been used to purchase arms at the rate of Rs. 50,000 for automatic weapons, Rs. 40,000 for pistols and Rs. 45,000 for VHF wireless sets. (Verghese 1996: 58-59).

45. In March 1992, Sunil Nath, publicity chief of the so-called pro-talk ULFA, led 3,500 youth overground. More followed, raising the number of those surrendering to over 4860 by the middle of 1995. These "surrendered ULFA" or SULFA were each offered a cash incentive of Rs. 50,000 and a soft loan of Rs. 2 lakhs for their rehabilitation. Some 40,000 availed the offer or were absorbed in jobs. (Verghese 1996: 59).

46. In 1990 Praful Bidwai writing on ULFA in the *Times of India* states that, "The truth however chilling is that ULFA is not a collection of rejects, lumpens and youth from the fringe of the society. Its presence looms large than life in Assam. Many people attributed almost magical qualities to the group. They really believe that ULFA in some fundamental sense invincible and many Assamese find it hard to think ill of ULFA". (Bidwai 1990).

    The late Chief Minister of Assam who was indeed seen as the arch-enemy of the ULFA, hailing the surrender of members called it "the return of the boys" (Baruah 1999: 149).

    Sanjib Baruah (1999: 149) evokes the popular cultural icon of Assam Bhupen Hazarika's composition to elucidate that the ULFA's position in the mainstream of Assamese public life. Hazarika's lyrics to a song with a marital melody applauds bravery, sacrifice and heroism: I salute mother Assam and I dress up to go to war. I salute the river Luit (Brahmaputra) and offer puja to Goddess Kamakhya; with your blessings and an oath I am off to war". Hazarika's sense, according to Baruah echoes the Assamese sense of how things came to this, persuasion has failed and there are few alternatives but battle to avenge past wrongs.

47. http://www.youtube.com/watch?v=-0e1h63vikE

48. Translation is mine.

49. The local as well as national newspapers reported that he was killed after he was arrested and in army custody, while the army claimed that he was shot as he tried to escape. It is widely believed that Mahanta, against whom there were a number of murder and other charges, was killed because he was a major obstacle to the pursuit of negotiations between the government and the ULFA.

    He was conferred the status of martyr by the ULFA. A general sense of mourning and loss was spread across the state for a long time. Many new born children were named after him. (Personal experience).

50. Though the army and police were able to stop the observations in the capital cities of Guwahati and Dispur, there were several memorial services observed in other part of the states participated by large crowd.

51. "Recently, six Ulfa activists were killed by the security forces in Parulguri village in Netaipukhuri, some 15 kilometres from Sibsagar. Those killed included Pradip Mohan, a front-ranking Ulfa leader and a close confidant of Ulfa commander-in-chief Paresh Baruah. In what was easily one of the more serious encounters involving the ultras and the security forces, two school-boys also lost their lives in the crossfire which took place in the afternoon of June 2. Just a few months ago, the killing of so many Ulfahardcores would have led to a wave of protests in the state, compelling the administration to come out with an explanation, however tenuous. But this incident, apart from being yet another 'success' of the security forces in fighting Ulfa terrorism in the state, brought to light the growing internecine feud between those Ulfa cadres who have surrendered and those who have refused to give up arms. The popular reaction to the killings also seems to have brought to focus the diminishing appeal and the rather shrinking mass base of the United Liberation Front of Assarn. It is significant that the killing of as many as six front-ranking Ulfa cadres did not evoke any major protest in the state". (Misra 1993: 1635).
52. In a personal interview Jugal Kishor Mahanta, one of the key members of the Surrendered ULFA, narrated the unexpected move of the top brass to associate themselves with Bangladesh as a "breach of trust" which "defeated the very purpose of the revolution". (Jugal Kishor Mahanta, Guwahati 27.03.2007).
53. http://articles.timesofindia.indiatimes.com/2011-05-27/guwahati/29590966_1_pranati-deka-ulfa-chairman-arabinda-rajkhowa.
54. www.telegraphindia.com/1050222/asp/frontpage/story_4408414.asp
55. Mamoni Raisom Goswami (Jnanpith Awardee writer), Reboti Phukan (Former footballer and childhood friend of Paresh Baruah), Arup Borborah (Lawyer), Lachit Bordoloi (*Manab Adhikar Sangram Samiti* leader), Mukul Mahanta (Engineer), Ajit Bhuyan (Editor, Aji), Haider Hussain (Editor, *Asomiya Pratidin*), Brajen Gogoi (Doctor), Dilip Patgiri (Adviser to the *Asom Jatiyatabadi Yuba Chatra Parishad*), Diganta Konwar (Journalist) and Hiranya Saikia (Sports organiser).
56. Though no one is sure why such peace talks have inevitably failed, Institute of Peace and Conflict Studies, New Delhi, lists the following reasons for the failure of this particular peace initiative:
    - The Army publicly expressed doubts (through a press statement issued by the Press Information Bureau's Defence Wing) about the ULFA's intentions to launch an offensive even while the so-called truce was on, suggesting that the Union government was talking in different voices.
    - The ULFA sticking to its demand for release of five of its detained leaders saying their presence was needed for any decision on the issue of entering into talks with the Government.
    - The ULFA refusing to name its team of negotiators.
    - The Union government insisting on a written assurance from the ULFA that it was actually interested in talking peace with New Delhi.

    (http://www.ipcs.org/article/india/ulfa-the-deadlocked-talks-and-the-road-ahead-2141.html.

57. The ULFA resorted to sporadic acts of violence: blowing up of oil pipelines, hurling grenades at the Guwahati Refinery, bombing of the high security Republic Day venue at Guwahati Judges Field. These attacks resulted in the deaths and injury of the common masses.On 22 January 2006, the ULFA carried out at least ten attacks on vital installations like oil installations, and gas pipelines. This severely crippled the supply of crude oil and natural gas in the state and the North Eastern Electric Power Corporation (NEEPCO) was forced to temporarily shutdown. ULFA also triggered an explosion in the main gas supplying pipeline of Assam Gas Company Limited (AGCL) during that time.
58. The Bodolands think that they have been robbed of the constitutional protection contained in the provision for tribal belts and blocks (Assam Land Revenue Manual, 1970). The Bordoloi Sub-Committee of the Advisory Committee of the Constituent Assembly recommended that the Plain Tribals of the Northeast India should be treated as a minority and the question of their representation and protection of their land should be considered by the Minority Sub- Committee (Report of the Bordoloi Sub-Committee, 1947). Thus, the Bodolands and other plains tribals of Assam were denied the elaborate constitutional protections contained in the Sixth Schedule of the Constitution. (Mittal and Sharma 1998: 301).
59. Brahma, M.N. "The Bodoland Kacharis of Assam- A Brief Introduction". *Bulletin of the Tribal Research Institute*. Guwahati. 1:1. 1983. pg.52.
60. Choudhury, Bijaya Laxmi Brohmo. *Bodolands (Kacharis) At a Glance*. Bongaingaon. Modern Offset Printers. 1993.
61. Chatterjee, Suniti Kumar. *Kirata Jana Kriti*. Calcutta. Asiatic Society. 1974.

    Choudhury, Bijaya Laxmi Brohmo. *Bodolands (Kacharis) At a Glance*. Bongaingaon. Modern Offset Printers. 1993 Sharma, Chandan Kumar. "Genealogy Contested: Oral Discourse and Identity Construction: The Case of Bodolands in Assam. Muthukumaraswamy, M.D. (ed.) *Folklore As Discourse*. Chennai. National Folklore Support Centre. 2007.
62. Choudhury gives examples of the mixtures as follows:
    1. Duryyadhana, the eldest son of the Aryan Kaurava dynasty married Bhanumati, who was the sister of Kirata king Bhagadatta of Pragjyotishpur or Kamrupa. So in the battle of Kurukshetra Bhagadatta took the side of Kaurava and fought against Pandava with Chinese and Kirata army.
    2. Shri Krishna, the Lord of Hindu married Rukmini Devi, who was the only beautiful daughter of the Kirata king, Bhismaka of Kundil kingdom.
    3. Aniruddha, the grandson of Lord Shri Krishna married Usha Devi who was the only daughter of Ban Raja of Kirata dynasty.
    4. The stone-staircase uptoKamakhya temple over the hill was completed within a night by Narakashura, the Kirata king to win over Kamakhya Devi as his wife. Of course Kamakhya Devi betrayed him.
63. http://planassam.info/Economic_Survey_Assam_2010-11/Economic %20 Survey _Chapter-2_POPULATION.pdf.
64. "Bathou" or "Bathou Barai" or "Khorai Barai Maharaja" is believed to be a form of the Shiva, of the Hindu pantheon. The Bodolands regards the Siju (genus

Euphorbia), Basil and Jatrasi plants as the symbols of Shiva and are placed side by side. This alter is encircled by bamboo fencing. The altar comprising of these is called the "Bathou". During the Bathou festival male and female called the "Uza" and "Doudini" take part in dance and are thought to be influenced by some occult power through which they are able to speak oracle. Sacrifices are performed during the festival.

65. They worship by offering various agricultural products like fruits, vegetables, honey, milk etc to the fire. This mode of offering is called "Jagya-Ahuti".
66. The erstwhile British government appointed the Indian Statutory Commission on constitutional reforms on 8 November 1927. The chairman of the commission was Sir John Simon and all other six members were also British and Member of Parliament. Hence, the commission was also called 'all white commission'. This commission officially called 'Simon Commission' arrived in Shillong on 2 January 1929. Twenty-seven organizations of Assam province submitted memoranda to the commission. (*Fengkha*,Anchalik Committee, All Bodoland Students' Union, Kokrajhar, February 1999). (From http://www.manipurresearchforum.org/tribal_autonomy_assam_arch5.htm).
67. The first commission for the scheduled areas and scheduled tribes (Dhebar Commission) appointed by the President of India in 1961 quoted Arnold Toynbee to define tribal societies as "primitive societies as we know them by direct observation…lying torpid upon a ledge of a mountain-side with a precipice above". But the commission argued that the static condition of the tribal societies was only temporary, for the "tribal people as children of mother nature are subject to the same laws which govern her other children". The commission observed that the static condition of the tribal was caused by centuries of their isolation from the people outside their society. It hope that the tribal would be on move again, because nature did not permit eternal static condition. (Chakraborty 2004: 3).
68. Besides Bodoland land Territorial Council, administration of Karbi Anglong Autonomous Council and Dima Hasao Autonomous District Council are under the jurisdiction of the Sixth Schedule in Assam.
69. For example, the first political elites—such as Rupnath Brahma, who became a minister in the Assam Government — were, educated Brahmas. It was in 1936 that Sitanath Brahmachoudhury became the first Bodoland graduate and later became the first Bodoland M.P. in 1952 on the Congress ticket. His father had as a Hakim (Magistrate) as he could spell his name. The trend of higher education has since grown among the Bodolands, mainly through the converted 'Brahmas'. (Mittal and Sharma 1998: 303).
70. Lord Aham Guru created two birds, one male and one female. The female bird laid three eggs and she heard a divine message from the Guru that from these three eggs different types of creatures would be born after many years. Hearing this she began hatching these eggs. Thousands of years passed in this process, but nothing was born. The she-bird lost her patience broke an egg and to her dismay found no sign of formation of anything in it. Then she again received a message from the Guru not to break the remaining two eggs. The Guru further asked her

to spray around the substance of the broken egg, from which was born the evil spirits, insects, creepers, trees, etc.

After thousands of years four human beings were born from the remaining two eggs. From the first laid egg a pair of old man and woman by the name of *Maunchiching Buda Budi* and similarly from the second egg *Diba Budi* and *Bubi Budi*, another old pair was born. All the people on earth are believed to be their children. (Bhattacharjee 1996: 24).

71. Another name for the river Brahmaputra.
72. Quoted in Baruah (1999: 173).
73. The All Bodoland Students Union divided into two fractions in the early 1990s- The ABSU (U) and the ABSU (R) on the question of tactics and strategies. The ABSU (U) succeeded in catching the imagination of the Bodoland masses and mobilizing thousands for their programmes and action plans.
74. This group is more influential among the Bodoland Christian converts.
75. Choudhury (1993: 29).
76. "He had to face much trouble in preaching this faith. One Mouzadar of Sidli named Jagat Chandra Boro-Kachari brought a Gohain named Ananta Narayan Goswami. Kalicharan Brahma boldly opposed this move and called upon the people not to become Saranias. All the people of that locality except five or six came forward to accept the Brahma faith of Kalicharan Brahma". (Choudhury 1993: 24).
77. http://www.assamtribune.com/scripts/detailsnew.asp?id=sep2812/state05.
78. Personal observation cited in Das, Bitasta. "The Question of Ethnicity in Assam: Ethnic Upheavals and the Ethnic Discourse". *Social Science Probing.* Vol 22, no. 1. Indian Council of Historical Research. June 2010.

Chapter - 2

Ethnicization of the Assam Movement, United Liberation Front of Assam and the Bodoland Movement

The three movements during their assertions culled out a distinct narrative of peoplehoood about them selves. However, these narratives were inclusive; Assam movement demanded on behalf of "people of Assam" or Indian citizens, ULFA assumcd itself to be the voice of inhabitants of Assam, including the immigrant communities and Bodoland movement spoke about the rights of indigenous tribals of Assam. However, the apparent inclusive claims of the three movements did not sustain for long and gradually they began to be seen as groups demanding exclusive priviledges for themselves.The trajectory of dissolution of the putative identities initially framed by the three movements,into specific "ethnic" identities is traced in this chapter.

"Ethnicization" of Identities in the Assam Movement

Joi AaiAsom (Glory to mother Assam) was the call that the leaders of the Assam movement enunciated, imploring all, who identified themselves with the interest of Assam, to "save" it from the clutched of foreign nationals. Every section of the population responded to the call; the Karbis, Dimasas, Rabhas, Bodos, native Bengali speakers, native Muslim communities overwhelmingly participated in the movement[1]. The Assam movement was a success, if success of a movement is measured in terms of incorporation and institutionalization of its ideals into the larger society. The success was embodied in the form of the central government's assurance and promise: the Assam Accord. Yet, till the time the Assam Accord was signed in 1985, the various groups had fallen apart and Assam had become an arena of "ethnic" rifts. Journalist Arun Shourie (Shourie 1983: 56), reporting on the situation of Assam in 1983 wrote that, "each community that was a victim in one place, was the predator in another". Sanjib Baruah (Baruah 1999: 132) writes that, "The ethnic divisions along which the violence took place varied from place to place: Tiwatribals versus Muslims of Bengali decent; Bodotribals versus Bengali Hindus and Muslims; Bodotribals versus the Bengali Hindus; Bodotribals versus Assamese Hindus; Misingtribals versus Bengali Hindus and Muslims; Muslims versus Hindus; ethnic Assamese and Hindus and Muslims versus Muslims of Bengali decent". The categories of the people hence got accentuated. For Weiner, "What thus began as an issue of illegal immigrants soon grew to a broader conflict among Assamese, tribals and Bengalis". What were the denotations within the movement that lead to such ramification? Why did the movement, which founded itself on the cornerstone of "secularism"[2], fracture into an ethnic carnage? Why the consolidated regional identity, "People of Assam", propounded by the idea of "composite" Assam not able to sustain itself?

To understand the trajectory of the fall out among the various communities, we need to enquire the factors that led to such confrontation, what were the situations and conditions that developed the identities, antagonist to each other; how were the identities formulated? If there was any underpinning within the formulations themselves that pitched the identities against one another? What does it mean to be "ethnic" in the context of Assam? The answers to these questions unravel a path that will facilitate an in-depth understanding of the contemporary tensions, marked as "ethnic".

For Fredrik Barth, to comprehensively grasp how ethnic groups generate and maintain themselves, one should shift the focus from emphasizing on internal constitution and history to ethnic boundaries and boundary maintenance, "…the ethnic boundary that defines the group, not the cultural stuff that it encloses. The boundaries to which we must give our attention are of course social boundaries, though they may have territorial counterparts" (Barth 1975: 75). Barth's formulation supposes ethnic groups primarily as organizational bodies. Though Barth has been criticized for discrediting the cultural content of ethnicity, his pattern of analysis has served as a vital tool for understanding societies torn in ethnic strife. The boundaries delineating the communities during the Assam movement were sharpened and heightened. Mahmood Mamdani in *When Victims Become Killers: Colonialism, Nativism, and the Genocide in Rwanda* (2001)applies similar mode to analyse the conflicts in Rwanda in the early 90s. To understand accumulative and institutional form of ethnic expression, we must delve into the synergy between individuals and the structure of their ethnic affiliation. As Barth points out, if the culture-bearing aspect of an ethnic group is considered to be its primary characteristic, one is caught in a presupposed belief both on: i. the nature of continuity in time of such units, and ii. the locus of the factors which determine the forms of the units. The features that are taken into account are not the sum of 'objective' differences, but only those which the actors themselves regard as significant. Ethnic categories provide an organizational vessel that may be given varying amounts and forms of content in different socio-cultural systems. They may pervade all social life, or they may be relevant only in limited sectors of activity. Therefore there is a scope for ethnographic and comparative description of different forms of ethnic organization.

In Assam, during the period of the Assam movement identities were "ethnicized". The ethnic component, as Barth points out, necessarily did not represent the core content of the particular group but were features that got heightened and intensified at the particular junction. The three loci where marked "ethnicization" of identities took place can be recounted as: (i) the election processes, (ii) emergences of identity based organizations and (iii) the proclamation and implementation of the Assam Accord.

(i) The Elections

The two elections, within the span of 1979-1983, had become an arena where "allies" and "antagonist" were decided based upon their participation or boycott of the elections. The population of Assam formed fractions as the Assamese, Bengalis and the tribals pitched themselves against an either at different locations.

The only two constituencies out of the fourteen where polling was successful in the 1979 Lok Sabha elections were the Karimganj and the Silchar constituencies. Both these constituencies were populated by Bengali Muslims immigrants from Bangladesh, underscoring the 'immigrant communities' mandate to defy the poll boycott and harbour the refuge that the central government seemingly provided. In the other places there was clear stir to keep the sympathizers of the immigrants away from power. Abida Ahmed (Congress (I) candidate and wife of former President of India, Fakhruddin Ali Ahmed), had filed nomination for Barpeta constituency. Her nomination paper was cancelled by the returning officer. Immediately after this, other three candidates withdrew from the fray, as their only intention was "not to allow Mrs. Ahmed go uncontested". In the other eleven constituencies, nominees of various political parties could not file nomination papers as they were confined to their residences or party offices for days together by the agitators (Boruah 1980: 44)[3]. In the consecutive 1983 election, turnout was moderate only in the constituencies regarded as "stronghold" of the immigrant population. The stance towards the elections, therefore, became a benchmark of affirming one's affiliation to a particular ethnic group.

Shekhar Gupta (1984) giving an account of the 1983 poll writes that the poll boycott was effective in Assamese and some tribal dominated areas in the Brahmaputra valley. In some strong Assamese majority areas polling were as low as 0.38 percent, 0.40 percent, and 0.68 percent. In some constituencies reserved for "scheduled tribes" and considerable tribal populated areas also, the election boycott was successful. In Mising dominated areas the polling percentages were 0.85 percent (Dhakuakhana constituency), 0.40 percent (Dhemaji constituency) and 9.28 pecent (Jonai constituency). In the Tiwa dominated Jagiroad constituency the turnout was 4.87 percent. However, the hill districts, KarbiAnglong and North Cachar hills, which were mostly unaffected by the Assam movement, the polling was normal, 39.54 percent and 55.91 percent respectively.

In Gohpur, where the Bodos predominated, the Plain Tribal Council of Assam (PTCA) contested the elections, Bodo peasants had a fall out with the local Assamese peasants over longstanding land dispute. The land primary belonged to the state, part of the Gohpur reserve forest. The local Bodos had cut down trees, cleared the forest and had settled in a large area of the reserve forest. The government had evicted them and had allocated some of these lands to the local Assamese peasants for agriculture. This became the bone of contention between the Bodos and the Assamese of the area. The PTCA through contesting the elections and by the anticipated victory planned to re-allocate these areas to the Bodos. Therefore the Bodos welcomed the 1983 elections with the view that they could negotiate their demands with the new government and realized the long held dream of separate homeland- the Udayachal (Baruah 1999: 133).

The choice of Chief Ministers by the Congress (I) in both the term is also seen as a pivotal strategy of political manoeuvre. AnwaraTaimur, Keshab Gogoi and HiteshwarSaikia, three of the nominated candidates belonged to ethnic affiliation other than Assamese Hindu that the leaders of the agitation belonged to, and whose interest was the alleged dominating strand of the movement. By electing the members of the "peripheral" groups as the state's Chief Minister the central government at one hand attempted to weaken the cohesion within the movement while on the other it conveyed its solidarity with the cause of the minority and the immigrant communities. Keshab Gogoi and HiteshwarSaikia both belonged to the Ahom community that ruled Assam in the medieval period. Appointing them to the apex of the state was a definitive step towards incurring the substantial Ahom support to the state mechanism rather than the agitation. Similarly, choosing AnwaraTaimur, an Assamese Muslim, elected from a constituency that was dominated by immigrants of Bengali Muslim and Bengali Hindus decent affirmed the central government's stand that the cause and interest of the movement was not acceptable. Taimur's tenure saw a staunch coercive measure to suppress the movement; removal and arrest of sympathetic officials and bureaucrats and transformation of the Chief Minister's secretariat to individuals belonging to Muslim community. "The process appeared to be one of de-Assamesization of the state bureaucracy, and it reinforced the fear of Assamese minoritization and of immigrant power" (Baruah 1999: 129).

The "pull and push" that emerged in the elections processes thus rendered the identities conspicuous and unfolded a vivid picture of sectarian interest.

(ii) Growth of identity based organizations

Another significant development that took place during and just after the Assam movement was the emergence of numerous political parties, literary bodies, students organization and insurgent groups representing specific identity. Various section of Assam's population, that until then had considered themselves to be part of greater Assamese identity, ramified into discrete identities. Here we can draw parallels with Abner Cohen's (1981) emphasis on group organization leading to pursuance of group interest through social and political processes. The development that started during the Assam movement of grouping under a banner continues till date. Every community in Assam today, has its respective organizations that represent it in various political and cultural premises. This characteristic evinces the specific characteristic of Assam's ethnicity, the significance of structural module to preserve and perpetuate distinct identities. The fact that the various communities of Assam did contain varying level of ethnic consciousness even before the Assam movement had commenced cannot be negated. The Bodos had got themselves organised as early as 1939 under the Tribal League. It sought to overcome the socio-economical deprivations faced by the tribals and demanded direct participation in politics through reserved seats in the legislative assembly. The Naga people under the Naga National Council(NNC) and the subsequent Nationalist Socialist Council of Nagaland (NSCN) had declared themselves as separate national identity and demanded an independent statehood right after the Independence of India. It was through perpetual tension and negotiation with these bodies, that Nagaland was curved out of Assam in the 1960s. Similarly, Mizoram was developed into separate state through the demands of Mizo National Front (MNF) respectively. These organizations through consistent pressure and political pragmatism were able to secure consolidated states which represented their ethnic identity.

However, the form and frequency in which the identities emerged during and after the Assam movement exemplifies how ethnicity in contemporary Assam is formulated, generated and maintained.

The Mising community was among the first groups to consolidate their distinctiveness. The MisingAgomKebang or Mising Sahitya Sabha (Mising literary body) though was formed in 1972, vehemently generated momentum in the early 1980s. Similarly, the All Mising Students' Union or the TakamMisingParinKebang and Bane Kebang or the Mising People's Conference which until now were dormant bodies, formalized themselves. These three organizations came together to place demand for the recognition and progress of the Mising language. They were finally able to secure Mising as a language of study in the primary schools in 1987. They ongoing demand is to establish Mising as the medium of instruction of all the schools in the Mising dominated regions.

The Moran-Matak who is listed as More Other Backward Communities (MOBC) in Assam has been trying to preserve and uplift their Mayamora Vaishnava heritage.The Sadau AsomMatakSanmilan strongly came forward during the 1980s and demanded a separate tribal status for themselves citing historical fact and their present socio-economic condition. In 1979 they placed a demand in the form of memorandum submitted to the Parliamentary select committee and in a separate memorandum to the Prime Minister and Home Minister, Govt. of India, in 1980 stating there is enough historical proof that the Moran-Matak is a tribe who have been living in utter poverty and illiteracy. They asked that they should be scheduled as a tribe and not as a backward community (Pakem 1990:181-185).

One of the most potent identity centric demands that commenced right after the Assam movement was from the Dimasa community. Dimasa Jalairaoni Hosom was formed in 1972 as a non-political cultural organization devoted to protect and promote the cultural identity of the community. The basic demands were to protect Dimasa historical monuments and press for demand towards the adaptation of Dimasa language at the primary school level in North Cachar Hills. However, n 1979, Dimasa Jalairaoni Hosom obtained a political aspect when it passed a resolution to move the appropriate authority to stop settlement of outsiders in Dimasa dominated region. Likewise, Dimasa National Organization born in 1979 passed its first resolution in the general to demand proper preservation of ancient relics and monuments of the Kachari kings lying in various places of Assam and other parts of India especially at Dimapur, Maibang and Khaspur. Another Dimasa organization Nikhil Hirimba BarmanSamity, put forward a political demand in 1980 for the reorganization of the Dimasa speaking areas of the North-east. This organisation believed that the Dimasa nationality is facing a danger of cultural annihilation unless all the Dimasa are brought within a single administrative unit. They claimed that their demands are based on government documents, historical and geographical facts. They proposed that the southern part of Nowgong district including Howraghat, Jamunamukh, Dabaka, Lanka, Hojai, Namti, Jogijan and the area from Dimapur to Dhansiri should be included in the proposed administrative unit. They threatened prolonged agitation in the event of the non-fulfilment of their demand. The Dimasa leaders of North Cachar Hills demand a separate state, to be carved out of Assam. The annual conference of the various Dimasa organizations are organised in various places. Besides having an intellectual objective, they also provide a common platform for the Dimasa youths to voice their hopes and aspirations. Other activities of these organizations are to hold cultural programmes to revive the traditional folk art and culture of the Dimasas. The first Dimasa news journal, *Waimijing*, received active patronage from all these organizations.

The socio-cultural organization of the Oraon community of Assam AssamPradesh Kurunkh (Oraon) Sangha though was formed in 1968[4] added a new division to their organization in 1986 after the student led Assam movement. They established students' home for the Oroan students for supporting them and helping their all round development. Other development and fragmentation around this time was between the Rabha and the Koch communities. The literary organization of the Rabha community All Rabha Sahitya Sabha(ARSS) formed in the early 1970s had remarkable Koch contribution in the composition of members and the acceptance of literature and script. It faced tussle among the various constituent sections in the mid 1980. Rongdani, Maitori, and Pati are regarded as major sections of the Rabha community. Of these three sections the former two have their own dialects. While the last one has already lost their language as well as have adopted Assamese as mother tongue. The tussel between ARSS and Pati who are numerically more than other two sections began in the language issue. The Pati elites vehemently oppose the move of the ARSS in implementing the Rabha medium in the schools. Meanwhile the birth of the Rabha Bhasa Parishad (RBP) led by Pati section is critical to the activities of the ARSS and the process of unity between the Rabha and the Koch. Among the more recent ones, the SonowalKachari community of upper Assam affiliating to Kachari Tribal Sangha are making their entry in Assam's politics. Alongside, various representative bodies have emerged like Sadau Sonowal Kachari Jatiya Parishad, Sadou Asom Sonowal KachariSatra Parishad, Sonowal Kachari Swasyatta ShashanDabi Samity.

These socio-cultural groups most of the times have corresponding political counterparts. In addition to this, each of the communities of Assam today has students organization modelled on the AASU. But what has been most overwhelming within the social life of Assam is the rapid emergence of insurgent organization. The South Asia Terrorism Portal marks as many as thirty five identity specific extremist groups active in Assam[5]. The insolent eruption and existence of identity based groups manifests the socio-political processes that Assam has been undergoing.

(iii) The Assam Accord

The Assam Accord was the memorandum of settlement signed in 1985 between the nascent Rajiv Gandhi led Government of India and the leaders of the Assam movement. This marked the end of six year long Assam agitation.[6]

The main points of the Assam Accord were- all those foreigners who had entered Assam between 1951 and 1961 were to be given full citizenship, including the right to vote; those who had entered after 1971 were to be deported; the entrants between 1961 and 1971 were to be denied voting rights for ten years but they would enjoy all other rights of citizenship. A developmental package for the economic growthforAssam, including a second oil refinery, a paper mill and an institute of technology, wereagreed to be established. The central government promised to provide "legislative and administrative safeguards to protect the cultural, social, and linguistic identity and heritage" of the Assamese people. The existing assembly was dissolved as a concession to the agitators and fresh election was held in December 1985.

A new party, Assam Gana Parishad (AGP) was formed by the leaders of the Assam movement. It was convincingly elected to power, winning 64 of the 126 assembly seats. Prafulla Mahanta, the AASU leader, became, at the age of thirty-two the youngest chief minister of independent India. Extreme and prolonged political turbulence in Assamapparently ended.

After the accord was signed the revision of electoral roll was taken up with new fervour. However, the procedures that were implemented were not devoid of criticism. There was an accusation of a large number of legal citizens being removed from the rolls (Choudhuri 1985). The final roll, on the basis of which the December election was held, had 6,89,715 lesser than the numbers in the updated electoral roll of October 1984.

Along with the AGP another prominent political party emerged after the Assam movement was over and with the signing of the accord: the United Minorities Front(UMF), claiming to represent the religious and linguistic minorities of the state. It sought to bring all the minorities; Muslim of Bengali decent, Hindu Bengalis, Assamese Muslims, Nepalis and the tribals within its sphere. The demand of UMF right after its inception was to scrap the Assam Accord as it was not conducive towards the interest of the minorities in Assam. A clear ethnicization of identities evolved with these political parties; AGP believed to represent the interest of the Assamese people of Assam as opposed to it, UMF emerged as the benefactor of the other groups dwelling in Assam[7].

Sanjib Baruah (1999: 140) noting the positive impact of the accord on the citizenship status of the immigrants writes that, "Apart from disenfranchisement of significant numbers of aliens, the accord also legitimized the citizenship status of a large number of immigrants: those who came before 1966 and those who came between 1966 and 1971, who were legitimized in phases". However, this simplistic optimism has not proved to be beneficial for the interest of Assam and its people. The cycle of policies and acts that were imparted during this phase have been a cause of tussle among the population which have continued even today. The sprint to prove the citizenship status has created irrevocable web of suspicion and rivalry among the Assamese, immigrants and the tribal population of the region that expresses itself in numerous assertions demanding autonomy or secession.

Two counter Acts that the government passed during this vulnerable time have provided an arena where the population of Assam contested their and challenged other's citizenship status. The Illegal Migrants (Determination of Tribunal) or, IM(DT) Act, 1983 passed by Hiteshwar Saikia government at the helm of the Assam Agitation in 1983 was one of them. This was a policy measure extended to safeguard the immigrant community from the onslaught of the anti-foreigner agitation. This Act is unique to Assam as in rest of the country, The Foreigner Act, 1946 prevail in relation to immigration law. The basic difference between the two Acts is that the onus of proving the illegal status of a accused lies on the accuser in case of IM(DT) Act, 1983 whereas in the case of the Foreigner's Act, 1946 the responsibility to prove his citizenship lays on the accused himself. The other directives of the Act were that:the accuser must reside within a 3 km radius of the accused. He should fill out a complaint form (a maximum of ten per accuser is allowed) and pay a fee of Rupees ten. However, even if a suspected illegal migrant is successfully proved, he can secure his legal status by mereproduction of a ration card. If the accuser cannot produce the required document, a system of tribunals made up of retired judges would finally decide on deportation. Moreover, the act also provided the clause that "if the application is found frivolous or vexatious" the Central Government may not accept it.

This Act has been severely criticized by the citizens of Assam and the local media as an obstacle in detecting and deporting illegal immigrants. The IM(DT) Act, 1983 has been held as the prime reason why the illegal immigration influx has not been able to be dealt with[8]. There have been many request made for it repeal. Finally in 12 July 2005, the Supreme Court of India, struck down the Act as unconstitutional. The three member bench verdicted that the rules and regulations of the IM(DT) Act, 1983 "has created the biggest hurdle and is the main impediment or barrier in the identification and deportation of illegal migrants"... (the IMDT Act) is coming to the advantage of such illegal migrants as any proceedings initiated against them almost entirely ends in their favour, enables them to have a document having official sanctity to the effect that they are not illegal migrants". However, the immigration issue of Assam have been so politicised that repeal of the Act poses a counter threat. In the words of Walter Fernandes, "The court judgment has actually polarised Assam as much as the act had done for two decades". (Fernandes 2005: 3237).

The other procedural measure that the government implemented which remarkably highlighted and distinguished the identities of Assam was during the reversal of the electoral rolls in 1985 after the Accord was signed. As a special measure, house to house enumeration was conducted. Then Electoral Registration Officers were asked to prepare two separate lists of the names. List I was to contain "the names of those persons enumerated whose linkage with 1971 electoral rolls could be established directly or through their parentage". List II was to contain the names of persons whose linkage with the1971 rolls was not established. The names of List II were thus all suspect. Patwaris, amins and junior police officials were asked to submit reports as to the whereabouts of these persons prior to March 25, 1971. If the report was favourable the name of the person concerned was to be included in list I, and if not, the name was to be dropped. The government announced that more than two lakh names were dropped out by this procedure. However, minority sections in Assam claimed that the figure was much large.

Together with this, the prescribed form for raising objection removed and a system of plain paper objection was introduced. This decision on AASU's demand, that it was difficult to submit *enmasse* objections in the prescribed form which required a counter signature of a voter of the same locality. The Election Commission also made the significant change that, "Where any objector prefers his objection on the basis of evidence exclusively in possession of government the Electoral Registration Officer then on his own should get and check the record related to such document to satisfy himself". (Choudhury 1985: 2146). Thus, the serious job of submission of objection became a popular pastime for the youth of Assam. However, the claimants were required to submit their claims in the prescribed forms duly countersigned by a voter of the locality and the burden of proving their citizenship also laid on them. Thus, it was criticized that the developments that took place in the fervour after signing the Accord shorn of the Election Commission of its autonomy and independence and transformed into an agency of the Home Ministry (Choudhury 1985:2146).

The tussle during the Assam movement was essentially around the question of Indian citizenship. In this wake to prove and refute citizenship status, the identities got percolated to: Assamese, Bengali and tribal identities. These ethnicized identity were used to preface the idea of citizenship vis-à-vis the issue of immigration. Which category of the population qualified as citizens of India and which were illegal immigrants, formed the crux of the tussle.

Contestation of Citizenship in Composite Assam: Fragmentation to Ethnic Units

The Assam movement was a call of the people of Assam to save it from the domination from the immigrants. The residence of Assam were dispersed into various identity groups like the Assamese, plain tribal, hill tribal, Hindu Bengali, Muslim Bengali etc during the contestation on the question of citizenship.

The immigrant communities came to be associated with two terms *bahiragota* (outsider) and *bidexhi* (foreigner). These two terms were used simultaneously and many times interchangably. The tussle of this period between the people of Assam and the immigrants, keeping the state of India as the interlocutor, can be understood from the speech ofPurbanchalia Lok Parished (PLP) chief,Nibaran Borah, "If the issue of stateless persons could be raised by Sri Lanka as late as 1965, in respect of migrants from India who had moved out a century earlier and if the Government of India could undertake to get these persons repatriated and rehabilitated in India, which the Government of India has done, we do not consider a post-1955 issue as either being belated or closed". (Kamath 1980:9). Here, Assam has been placed on par with the independent nation of Srilanka and immigrants from other places of India have to Assam been compared with the immigrants to Srilanka. The idea of outsider and foreigner conflated in such an understanding.

The difficulty that arose with such a socio-cultural context in which illegal immigrant were impossible to be distinguished from the citizens, the Election Commission declared that entry of name in 1971 or pre-1971 rolls, copies of National Register of Citizens and Citizenship Certificates and Certificates of date of birth of the claimants as the only three documents that can be regarded legal to claim for citizenship status.

Ethnicizing the Narrative of Injustice and Exploitation- ULFA's Violent Rejoinder

> With the state getting tougher and the public turning against them, the militants in Assam are clearly on the defensive today. Militancy in Assam is not a mere law and order problem but a reflection of a deeper malaise affecting the whole society, neither can it be dubbed as radical politics of the marginalized communities against

> hegemonizing forces. Politics of identity in Assam is basically trapped in the world of appearances, fighting imaginary enemies, and drawing strength from prejudices and misconceptions of groups about themselves and others. Without an understanding of the material and ideological roots that gives birth to militancy, restoring peace in Assam would be an uphill task.(Srikanth 2000: 4117).

Present day India is blightedby various forms of armed conflicts; separatist movements, left-wing extremism, religious fundamentalism. Different terms are used to address the various agents of the conflicts. "Terrorist"for (supposedly) foreign miscreants, "Extremists" refers to groups in the Naxal-affected areas and "Militants" refers to groups operating in Jammu and Kashmir and in the north-east India. The ULFA though presently has reduced its terror activities to a large extent, its presence nevertheless, threatens the peace of the region's social landscape and the complacence of its political structure.

ULFA: United Liberation Front of Assam: A Political Analysis (1994) by Samir Kumar Das, is one of the rare academic monographs on the ULFA, where the author covers the political presence of the outfit during the period from 1979 to1991. This work proposes that ULFA has brought to the fore a serious political critique which its adversaries (the Indian State) will find it difficult to ignore or erase it away by force. In his analysis of the ULFA, he locates the problem in the seamless and totalizing nationalism that Indian State subscribes to. According to him this form of nationalism is "inappropriate" in two complementary ways; On the one hand, this is what enables the state to ascend to the much-vaunted hegemonic position. On the other hand and almost in the same vein, the hegemonic state, in the name of ostensibly advancing universality and rationality, actually helps in disorienting the smaller cultural identity- groups and ethnic minorities. Terming the ULFA upsurge as "ethnic problem", he reiterates that ULFA is a response not to the project of nation building, but to the Indian State's failure of building a nation, "To us, ethnic problems are not only a consequence of the state's project of building the nation but also a response to the state's abdication of the very project" (Das 1994: 8):

> If we argue (as does Gramsci) that the nationalist ideology is crucial to a state's exercise of hegemony and that the Indian state is one that abdicates the task of building it then we have to admit that we have a state that can seldom be called hegemonic in character. A non-hegemonic state, in more positive terms, maybe taken to mean, what

> we earlier designated as a *minimal state.* A minimal state, first of all, is one that has already abdicated the task of building the nation. Secondly, it includes an institutionally *loose-ended* state. Its institutions fail to produce the desired harmony. Indeed many of the state's institutions are at loggerheads with each other. Again, the strategies adopted by the state have not only been mutually inconsistent but also at times not properly geared to the objective of nation-building. (Das 1994: 9)

The three interlocutors that we have marked earlier, based on which the ULFA has formulated its demand for secession—exploitation, exclusion and India's illegitimate authority over Assam's territory, sides with Das's view that it is the State's inability or withdrawal to constitute itself into a nation that has insulated various sections of the population, to assert themselves for dismembering from the State.

However, Das's perception that ULFA is an "ethnic" uprising needs further analysis. Does ULFA represent the angst of a group that can be "ethnically" distinguished, if yes then whose cause does it represent? If no then what are the contextual inadequacies that hinders it from being called to represent any other political objective? The inability of the State to find a solution of the critiques posed by the ULFA and the ULFA's vehement rejection to find a solution within the Constitution of India and demand for complete sovereignty to retract its grievances of exploitation, exclusion and territorial subjugation forefronts the need to understand the hindrances within the Constitutional structure in addressing the challenge.

The Indian federal system, which is apparently meant to divide power, has a clear distinction of the roles of the Centre and the states. A "concurrent list" enumerates shared powers such as civil and criminal law and planning; a "state list" enumerates state power such as education, agriculture and welfare; and a "union list" enumerates the centre's lion share of the powers- defense and foreign affairs, income taxation, banking and other residual powers. In addition to the huge powers allotted to the centre through the union list, the vital is the power bestowed upon the Parliament to create new states, to alter boundaries of existing states and even abolish a state by ordinary legislative procedure without recourse to constitutional amendment (Ghai 2000: 57). Also under emergency powers the constitution allows the federal government to convert itself to a "unitary one". Even when the Parliament is not functioning under emergency conditions, it can "make laws with respect to any matter falling in the state list for a temporary period". Partha Chatterjee, in *Nationalist Thought and the Colonial World: A Derivative Discourse* with the use of "thematic" and "problematic" reckons that there are inbuilt ambiguities and contradictions in the doctrines of nationalism in India. He argues that assertion of political possibilities condition the choice of a structure of justifications on one hand and on the other hand the justificatory structure itself conditions the identification of possibilities. In this process, some possibilities are emphasized, other erased, the marks of disjuncture are suppressed and the rational continuity of a progressive historical development is established.

The ULFA emergence and long existence indicates the presence of possibilities that emphasizes it perpetuation. Scholars have often criticized the myopic vision of the State in dealing with the matters related to the insurgency of north-east India, which has been either been "developmental" or "national security" paradigm. As such, the response to the extreme insurgency has led to reorientation of the policies in the recent years. In 2001, a cabinet level Department for Development of the North Eastern Region (DONER) to fast track the economic development of the region. The north-east India has risen to be the only region in the country whose development is a mandate of the national government. Together with this an industrial policy has been put to place that provides tax incentives to invest in this region. The Asian Car Rally in 2004 was to showcase the north-east region as a "gateway to Asia" in the line of "Look East Policy". Yet the existence of insurgency reckons that the malaise is far deep and cannot be redeemed by interim developmental actions.

The emerging difference of opinion between the ULFA on one side, and the All Assam Students Union (AASU) andJatiyatabadi Yuba Chatra Parishad (AJYCP) on the other, regarding the bona fide benefactor of interest opens up another layer of understanding of the complex situation of insurgency in Assam. The two organizations have recently started war of words against the ULFA for its pro-Bangladesh stand. In what looked like a desperate bid to shed out of its pro-Bangladeshi stand, ULFA's commander-in chief Paresh Barua came up with as urprising stance saying that "any person, except those from the north-east, who had entered Assam after 1947 should be regarded as a foreigner". The comment on the foreigner issue did not go well with the AASU and the AJYCP which have since the Assam movement been the custodian of the issue of illegal immigrants in Assam. The AASU has said that the 1971 cut-off year for detection and expulsion of illegal Bangladeshi migrants was reached after consultations with a cross-section of the Assamese society before the Assam Accord was signed in 1985, which ended the anti-foreigner agitation. ULFA's perception of regarding anyone (other than the north-eastern) as foreigners regarded the rest of Indians and Bangladeshis alike whereas AASU's insistence of detection of the Bangladeshi immigrants foregrounds: a) "Foreigners" are impending danger in Assam and b) perception of the "foreigner" is the crucial arbiter in one's imagination of the integration with the nation.

Commenting on the decline of ULFA along the years, in his later writing, Samir Kumar Das states that:

> "If ULFA *appears to have* deserted the critique (or the 'cause') it had produced and so fervently brought to the fore over the years, its adversaries have squarely to be blamed for making it desert what once was so dear to it. As the critique deserts itself, ULFA does not make itself felt any longer through the power of a discourse. It is thus *forced* to clutch on to various non-discursive forms of power. The political critique *per se* has not lost its validity. It has only outlived one of its most powerful agents". (http://www.satp.org/satporgtp/publication/faultlines/volume13/Article5.htm).

ULFA has defined the concept of the "Assamese" (*Axomiya*) as "a people of all communities, the mixture of people who are determined to work for all-round progress of Assam". This definition of the people does remain restricted to those whose mother tongue is Assamese. In this description, the immigrants from Bangladesh are considered as "an indispensable part" of the revised notion of *Axomiya*.ULFA has been accused of having made this turnaround at the instance of its operational requirement of securing a safe haven in Bangladesh, which has been believed to have converted to a space from where the outfit can mastermind and also "hide" from the Indian security forces. Fear is being expressed from various quarters of Assam's public sphere that the dream of a "*XhunorAxom*" (Golden Assam) through independence from India, may soon turn into a nightmare of a "*Brihat Bangla*" (Greater Bengal), if the ULFA continues its undertakings. The present form of ULFA as a mere terror tactic marks the transformation of ULFA's ideology from an end into a mere means.

Bodoland movement- "Sons of the Soil", contesting the premises

The Bodoland movement gave significant shift to the already persisting tussle in Assam. The tension turned from foreigner versus the indigenous to the imperative of establishing the authenticity of the indigenous. In his classic *Sons of the Soil* (1978), Myron Weiner had warned against the "potentially explosive" situation stemming from the idea of the "sons of the soil". According to him, India conceded local autonomy to nativist Assamese. But the victory of the Assamese launched a counter attack by the Bodos, pressing for the creation of a union territory of the Bodo regions outside the ambit of Assam. In the late 1980s, when Upendra Nath Brahma became president of the ABSU (All Bodo Students' Union), he led the entire movement with diatribes against "Assamese Chauvinism". Rajiv Gandhi's government, however, paid little attention to this issue. Next, the aboriginal Koch-Rajbongshi population mostly within the Bodoland staged a protest demanding their right to self-determination. Of the 1.8 million people living in Bodo villages, 1.2 million are Koch-Rajbongshi, and now their fate was, according to one spokesman, "at the mercy of the Bodo leaders in the name of geographical contiguity of the BAC area..." Other Bodo organizations argued about getting as yet excluded villages into the zone of the BAC. State authorities, to the extent that they side with the indigenous, may be in for a never-ending set of autonomy demands. In Assam, it was not only Assamese, Bodos and Koch-Rajbongshis. The Nagas pressed for Nagaland and other tribal groups did similarly, with the result that Assam has been broken up into discrete cultural-political units (Weiner 1978, 120-22).

"Sons of the soil" conflicts in Assam have two core features. First, it involves a competition for political concession against the fear of a dominant other, second, the members of the asserting group think of their group as indigenous, and as rightfully possessing the area as their group's ancestral (or at least very long-standing) home. The question of land alienation has been a defining feature in the Bodoland movement.

The trail of "sons of the soil" tussle continued as Weiner had predicted. One of the most potent identity centric demands that commenced right after the Bodoland movement has been from the Dimasa community. *DimasaJalairaoniHosom* was formed in 1972 as a non-political cultural organization devoted to protect and promote the cultural identity of the community. The basic demands were to protect Dimasa historical monuments and the adaptation of Dimasa language at the primary school level in North Cachar Hills. In 1978 the District council gave some new settlements to a few non-tribals and its annual general meeting on 24.6.79 DimasaJalairaoniHosom passed a resolution to move the appropriate authority to stop undesirable settlement to outsiders. The annual conference of this organization is organised in various places of the district and besides intellectual deliberation it provides a common platform to the Dimasa youths to voice their hopes, aspiration and apprehension. Branches of this organization are found in almost all the Dimasa villages and they arrange traditional cultural programmes to revive the traditional folk art and culture of the Dimasas. The first Dimasa news journal, *Waimijing*, received active patronage from this youth organization.

Dimasa National organization was born in 1979 and the first resolution passed by the general session of the organization on 11 March 1979 demanded “Proper preservation of ancient relics and monuments of the Kachari kings lying in various places of Assam and other parts of India especially at Dimapur, Maibang and Khaspur”. The executive committee of this organization consists of Dimasas belonging to the plains and the hills. Important Dimasa personalities like Nandamohan Barman (President), Sri Phanidhar Gorlosa (Vice-President), Sri BrojendraLangthasa (General Secretary) were connected with this organisation and this was the first attempt to unite all the Dimasa living in different units under a common umbrella. Dimasa lawyers like Sri Anil Kumar Burman of Cachar, and then Assam Minister Sri SonaramThaosen of N.C. Hills and the delegates from Nagaland pledged to work for cultural and social unification of all the Dimasas. The organization, of course, did not pass any political resolution and its activities are even today confined in the social, economic and educational domain.

The Dimasa of Cachar formed DimasaSanskriti Parishad in 1974 to promote the cultural life of the Dimasa of Cachar. It has also proposed to build a DimasaSanskriti Bhavan at Silchar which will be the centre for the promotion of Dimasa art and culture. It was due to the persistent endeavour of this Parishad that the Archaelogical Survey of India took necessary action for the preservation of the Bishnu Mandir of BorkholaBarohaliPukur in Bihara and the two Shibtilas of Hartikar and Sonai in Cachar. KarbiAnglong District Dimasa Association with its headquarter at Diphu was formed in 1975. It has a Dimasa cultural club at Diphu where meetings and cultural programmes are held to promote the cultural identity of the Dimasas.

Nikhil Hirimba Barman Samity, an organization of the Dimasas of Cachar put forward a political demand in 1980 for the reorganization of the Dimasa speaking areas of the North-east. This organisation believes in the concept of greater Dimasa nationality and opines that the existence of the Dimasa will be in danger unless all the Dimasa are brought within a single administrative unit. The members of the community claim that their demands are based on government documents, historical and geographical facts. They said that the southern part of Nowgong district including Howraghat, Jamunamukh, Dabaka, Lanka, Hojai, Namti, Jogijan and the area from Dimapur to Dhansiri should be included in the proposed administrative unit. They also threatened prolonged agitation in the event of the non-fulfilment of their demand. The organization, of course, did not take the path of agitation but this demand for reorganization of the Dimasa speaking areas has once again revived the urge for political and cultural supremacy among the Dimasa of Assam and in the event of any future reorganization of the north-east the Dimasa may renew their claim. The Dimasa leaders of N.C. Hills who demand the separation of the district from Assam, of course, have not yet raised any demand for the reorganization of the Dimasa speaking areas around N.C. Hills.

Fearon and Laitin (2003) have coded a list of 139 civil wars between 1945 and 2008 for and analyzed whether they were "sons of the soil" conflicts[9]. According to them Catholics in Northern Ireland see themselves as sons of the soil versus Protestant settlers, Serbs in Kosovo have the same view regarding Kosovar Albanians, Africans in South Africa vis-a-vis South African whites, or Abkhaz regarding Georgians (who migrated in Abhkazia mainly in the 1920s and 30s).

In India considerable attention has been paid to the "sons-of-the-soil" pressure groups in stateslike Karnataka, and has impacted the policies of the state government.The principal demand of all 'sons-of-the-soil' movements is governmental intervention—in the form of laws, regulations and administrativeorders—to provide jobs and admission to educational institutions to the members of indigenous groups. These interventions are often referred toas preferential policies. In India, generally, preferential policies are of two types. First, the policies areintended to impart special benefits and reservations to Scheduled Castes, Scheduled Tribes, and socially and economically backward classes inentry to educational institutions and in recruitment and promotion ingovernment services. They are also given reserved constituencies in State Legislative Assemblies. The second set of policies seeks to provide preferences to indigenous groups in a particular state as against the migrants from otherstates in employment.

However in Assam the character of the "son of the soil" movement differ in terms of the demand raised for homeland. In an article the general secretary of the PTCA wrote, "The Bodos are prescriptive citizens and the agriculture being the mainstay of their economy, their survival without the land is unthinkable" (Mittal and Sharma 1998: 300). There is also resentment about the intrusion of immigrants (mainly from Bangladesh) who occupied *patta* lands (Government waste land) which had been the traditional agricultural land for the Bodos as many of them practiced shift cultivation. The Bodos resent to the fact that they have been deprived of the provision provided in the Sixth Schedule and also in the Fifth Schedule[10]. Land alienation and belief of a lost ancestral homeland has been potent theme in the formulation of dissent in the Bodoland movement.

Contestations of the Bodo identity construct

The Bodoland movement not only enthused few politically inconspicuous communities to assert themselves for cultural and political suzerainty, but it also propelled some communities to assert themselves in response to their appropriation within the "greater Bodoland community". This refutation to accept the aegis of an umbrella identity is again a replication of the Bodolands themselves of their refusal to accept the "greater Assamese identity".

The kingdom that the Bodo leadership claims to be theirs, is the one known as the Kachari kingdom, which came to prominence as an organized administrative unit in the southern part of Assam in the late 17th century. However, this kingdom is claimed by the Dimasa-Kacharis. According to them the particular kingdom did not belong to the Bodo-Kacharis, rather it belonged to them, with its capital at Dimapur (now in Nagaland). The Bodoland leadership in response of this claim puts forward that the Dimasas are nothing but an offshoot of the greater Bodo stock. The Dimasa leadership is, however, unwilling to surrender the past 'glory' of the community to the Bodos. The cultural symbols that the Bodos appropriated to consolidate their specific identity has been also beset with problems. One such example is, in April 2001, a status of Daimaluo, the half mythical Dimasa hero of the medieval era, was set up in Kokrajhar as a symbol of Bodo might of the past. This act of the Bodo leadership came under severe attack from the Dimasas accusing the former of hijacking their national icon (Sharma 2007:13). Along with the Dimasas, the attempt to incorporate the Koch community under the aegis of the "greater Bodo stock" too fell short of agreement. The Bodo leadership tried to integrate the Koch community into the generic identity- 'the Bodos', by declaring that the Koches as an offshoot of the Bodo stock. On the basis of this consideration, the Bodo leadership supported the movement of the Koch people for Schedule Tribe (ST) status. When a relatively advanced Koch community was provisionally given the ST status in the mid 1990s (which was subsequently withdrawn), they took away an overwhelming share of the government jobs and seats in the educational institutions reserved for the STs. The new relationship of fraternity soon turned into one of competition. The response of other groups like the Sonowal-Kacharis and the Thengal-Kacharis were also not amicable to the project of identity building by the Bodos.

Besides, the refusal to accept the identity proposed by Bodolands, the various communities in contemporary Assam have been demanding to repeal the Bodoland Accord, as it is believed to have turned the Bodos hegemonic in the BTC. A repercussion of this was felt recently in July 2012 when the Bodos clashed with the immigrant Bangladeshi settled in BTC and ensued a pogrom, unmatched in recent history. About a hundred people lost their lives, several brutally wounded, villages set ablaze and thousands were displaced in a mere 30 days time. To rein in the deteriorating law and order conditions, the Union Home Ministry authorized Assam government to deploy as many as 116 companies of central armed police forcescomprising of 11,600 personnel. The central government grasping the magnitude of impairment announced a special assistance to the tune of Rs 300 crore; of which Rs 100 crore was for relief and rehabilitation, Rs 100 crore for development programmes in the affected areas and an additional fund of Rs 100 crore under Indira Awas Yojana for the affected areas.

However, what surfaced as a political quandary was the unprecedented responseto this violence in other parts of the country. The violence which had its epicentre mainly in three districts of Bodoland Territorial Area District - Chirang, Dhubri and Udalguri, propelled an unheard of cataclysm in the major cities of the country. In Mumbaitwo persons died and 46 were injured when a protest against Assam riots turned violent. Demonstrators torched vehicles, pelted stones, forcing the police to fire in the air and use batons to disperse the unruly mob. But what perhaps can be regarded as one of the drastic failure of the state in the recent times towards securing faith in the law among the citizens was the exodus of people from north-eastern states from Bangalore in the fear of retaliatory violence against them. The mass panic that spread virally through SMSes and social media led thousands to leave their jobs and studies and flee for life as the state in futility struggled to assure security to the people. Newspapers and television flashed news and visuals of hundreds of people waiting anxiously in the railway stations to make their journey of over 68 hours back home.

The fact that the violence in Assam is not merely a localized, isolated occurrence but has deeper rooted historical and political underpinning, have been laid open by these recent incidences. The specific violence is rather symptomatic of possibilities that have been persistent since a very long time and have not been translated in understanding the north-eastern region of the country in proper light. A revisit of the indices of the cause provides opportunities to unravel the issues that have clamored within the political and social fabric of north-east India.

Understanding the Bodo Identity Formation

The perception about the various identities existing in Assam by the common Assamese mind can be understood meaningfully by the words of Jnanpith award winning Assamese writer, Birendra Kumar Bhattacharyya, "The Assamese nationality is a heterogeneous community which includes tribal groups like the Rabhas, the Bodos, the Tiwas, the Mishings, the Karbis and the Dimasas. Compared to these members of this composite nationality, the Bengalis and others are newcomers to the land" (Bhattacharyya 1980:83)[11]. In another article in the same collection, another Assamese Muslim intellectual, Mohammad Taher, writes about the contribution of the Karbis, Mishings, Lalungs, Dimasas, Bodos and Kacharis towards building the foundation of Assamese culture "on which was superimposed the Aryan culture brought by the Hindu migrants in the past without giving rise to any social imbroglio. What gradually emerged in the process was certainly not a cross-breed of social systems, but a harmonious cultural entity, a colourful mosaic of diverse traditions and cultural traits, which was enriched further by fresh contributions in subsequent ages" (Taher 1980: 59). The various tribal groups, by and large, had expressed spirits of camaraderie with the Assamese nationality. Two evident instances when the various groups of Assam came together to meet common goal were- first, just prior to independence, the Cabinet Mission proposals on grouping brought all the indigenous people of undivided Assam together to resent upon the proposal of being gifted away to Pakistan. "The threat to the region's identity posed by Jinnah and the Muslim League became a common binding factor, even as the spectre of the autochthones being outnumbered by Muslim immigrants assumed added dimensions"(Misra 1999: 1267). Second instance was during the Assam movement on the issue of foreign nationals when the various groups came together to challenge the illegal immigrants.

The solidarity and unity of the of the various tribal group with the majority Assamese of Assam was tainted as disenchantment spread among the various group that the nascent Assam Government's attitude towards them is far from being impartial. As feeling of alienation and marginalization-politically and economically intensified, the Bodos (like the preceding disgruntled tribal groups) codified their cultural identity more and more.

Conclusion: In the Assam movement, the difficulty in identifying the citizens from the non-citizens amongst the population catapulted a process of employing the existing categories as a token of distinction. Ethnicity here became a metaphor to connote nationality. The ethnic underpinnings here were rooted in the colonial past when the formal category divide of the people took shape. Similarly, the ULFA for its framing of the "national" identity of the people north-east India adopted the available discursive perception about their identity and origin. The idea that the people of the region are distinct and different from rest of the country has been the rallying point of the ULFA for the demand of secession. This idea stems from the fact that the region is perceived as "exotic" and the people "alien". The colonial discourse of lending a fragmented notion about this region played its part in this imagination. The political entry point of the Bodos has been by dint of establishing a distinct identity more indigenous, more ancient than the Assamese. In formulating and consolidating this distinct identity, the Bodos have relied upon the discursive idea regarding their origin and cultural entity. These ideas about their identity, has stemmed from the much accentuated ethnic discourse of Assam.

Reference

1. http://www.asomganaparishad.in/swahid_list.htm (12.12.2008)a site maintained by the Assam Gana Parishad, the political party that was formed from AASU, gives the names of the 855 students who attained "martyrdom" during the Assam movement. The names include students belonging from Assamese, various "tribal" communities, native Muslim students.
2. http://www.asomganaparishad.in/movement.asp (13.12.2008) another site maintained by Assam Gana Parishad gives an account of the AASU's perception of the Assam movement.
3. Writing on the emergence and success of two reactionary political parties- the Purbanchalia Lok Parishad (PLP) and Assam Jatiyatabadi Dal (AJD), Boruah remarked on the divided situation of Assam as: "Both the PLP and AJD were floated before the Assembly elections in 1978. But neither of them could get a single candidate returned to the Assembly. Certain outstanding features of the

last Assembly elections of Assam were i) failure of Congress to secure a majority needed to form a post-emergency ministry, ii) emergence of the Janata as the ruling party and iii) the return of a leftist bloc of 24, with 11 members of the Communist Party of India (Marxist) in the Assembly of 126 members. With the Congress in political wilderness and Janata enfeeble by infighting, the reactionary forces of Assam pinned their hopes on the PLP and AJD. And backed by the reactionaries, the PLP and AJD started, almost from the beginning, a virulent attack on the left and democratic parties and organizations. Now, supported by AASU elements, their attack on the left and democratic parties and organizations continues unabated. Assam now is virtually under mass terrorism". (Boruah 1980:45).

4. The goal of the organization was to promote all round development of the community, the following were its objective:
   - Modification and simplification of social custom and rules.
   - Establishment of social integrity, equality and co-ordination.
   - To create interest for education and to help to spread it.
   - To draw attention towards health-care.
   - To educate members of the society to develop saving tendency in economic front.
   - To create interest in sports, music and crafts.
   - To create interest for trade and commerce.

5. National Democratic Front of Bodolandland (NDFB)
   United Liberation Front of Asom (ULFA)
   United Liberation Front of BarakValley (ULFBV)
   Adivasi Cobra Force (ACF)
   Dima Halim Daogah (DHD)
   Hmar People's Convention- Democracy (HPC-D)
   Kamtapur Liberation Organisation (KLO)
   Muslim United Liberation Tigers of Assam (MULTA)
   United People's Democratic Solidarity (UPDS)
   Black Widow (BW)
   All Adivasi National Liberation Army (AANLA)
   KarbiLongri North Cachar Hills Liberation Front (KLNLF)
   Adam Sena (AS)
   Adivasi Security Force (ASF)
   All Assam Adivasi Suraksha Samiti (AAASS)
   BarakValley Youth Liberation Front (BVYLF)
   Bodoland Liberation Tigers (BLT)
   Gorkha Tiger Force (GTF)
   Harkat-ul-Jehad
   Harkat-ul-Mujahideen
   Islamic Liberation Army of Assam (ILAA)

Islamic Sevak Sangh (ISS)
Islamic United Reformation Protest of India (IURPI)
Karbi National Volunteers (KNV)
Karbi People's Front (KPF)
Koch-Rajbongshi Liberation Organisation (KRLO)
Muslim Liberation Army (MLA)
Muslim Security Council of Assam (MSCA)
Muslim Security Force (MSF)
Muslim Tiger Force (MTF)
Muslim United Liberation Front of Assam (MULFA)
Muslim Volunteer Force (MVF)
People's United Liberation Front (PULF)
Rabha National Security Force (RNSF)
Revolutionary Muslim Commandos (RMC)
Tiwa National Revolutionary Force (TNRF)
United Liberation Front of BarakValley United Liberation Militia of Assam (ULMA)
United Muslim Liberation Front of Assam (UMLFA)
(http://www.satp.org/satporgtp/countries/india/states/assam/terrorist_outfits/index.html)

6. Please see Annexure I
7. However Baruah (1999: 115-143) notes that the power of the Assam movement rested in the fact that it projected itself to be inclusionary. Its popular slogan *Minorities are not Foreigners, AGP for all, all for AGP* did succeed in gaining popularity to the political parties in regions dominated by tribals (Lakhimpur, Sonitpur, Darrang districts) and Bengali Muslims (Nowgaon, Barpeta).
8. In the last 22 years, five tribunals had been set up under this act in the districts bordering Bangladesh from January 1983. They registered 423,021 cases, dealt with 65,000 cases and have disposed of 23,420 cases (Editorial, The Sentinel, December16, 2004) and have till January 2005 declared 12,424 persons illegal migrants. Only 1,538 of them have been deported (Staff Reporter, The Sentinel, July 13, 2005.)
9. They defined sons of soil conflict as "civil war involves an insurgent band fighting on behalf of an ethnic minority on the periphery of a state dominated by another ethnic group; against the state's military or paramilitary formations,and/or members of the majority group who have settled as farmers in the minority group's declared home area; and involves either land conflict with migrants from the dominant group or conflict over profits and control of fuel or mineral resources in the minority's home area".
10. This Sixth Schedule provision in the Constitution of India pertains to the administration of tribal areas in the states of Assam, Meghalaya, Tripura and Mizoram which allows constituting autonomous district and autonomous regions like the tribal blocks and belts for the tribal groups.

The Fifth Schedule of the Constitution also made some provisions for the protection of excluded areas of the British period.

11. This article titled "The Assamese Mind" was published in the collection of essays by some of Assam's leading intellectual-*Assam and the Assamese Mind,* brought out by Asom Sahitya Sabha at the helm of the Assam Movement.

Chapter - 3

Windings of the Ethnic Discourse

The ethnic attribute surfaces as the most impending character in the popular imaginations about the tensions in Assam. Assam, and the entire north-eastern region of India, is believed to be crisscrossed with ethnically variant sections of people, different not only from rest of the country but also among themselves. The tensions that arise in this space are considered to be innate result of existence of ethnic diversity. Any study of the conflicts inevitably inaugurates with the idea that the region is ethnically striking and the tensions are essentially because of the presence of ethnically distinct groups. The perception that the ethnic character of the region is pre-given has coloured almost all the enquiries into the region's issues and has obstructed their lucid understanding and eventual resolution. Studies from the standpoints of Political Science, History, Anthropology; so also Government documents and policies, media reports and literary and romantic descriptions of the region consistently underscores the ethnic character of the region. Eventually, what has arose as most momentous is the fact that the people of Assam themselves, in due course of time, have began to objectify themselves on the idea of ethnicity such that no other mode of identity formation is viable other than ethnic identity. Demands raised at various points of time did not subscribed to ethnic interest at its inception. However they ultimately percolated into the ambit of ethnic politics. The issue of presence of illegal immigrants in the Assam movement, question of underdevelopment in the ULFA and the malady of inequity raised in the Bodoland movement are not essentially "ethnic" problems, however in the course of their executions, they were packaged in ethnic overtones and were finally were labelled as ethnic assertions. This chapter proposes that it is because of the presence of pervasive ethnic discourse that issues raised in Assam are caught in the imbroglio of ethnic politics. The discourse is discordant, ubiquitous; generic identity, even if are attempted, fail to sustain itself. The chapter traces the epistemology roots of this discourse and establishes that it emerged during the colonial period. The chapter argues that the perpetuation of the colonial knowledge renders the imagination of the region as ethnically fragmented.

History of Assam's Ethnic Discord

In order to critically assess the tensions of contemporary Assam, it is benefiting to briefly assess Assam's first challenge after the Independence- the Naga Hill district's demand for independent state[1]. The dwellers of the Naga Hill districts are believed to have maintained a love-hate relationship with the medieval rulers of Assam- the Ahoms and had trade relationship with the Brahmaputra valley since centuries[2]. After the British annexed the Naga Hills, because of administrative difficulties, it was declared as "excluded area". In doing so, it severed the trade links and age old cultural interaction with the plain of the Brahmaputra valley. As a result the Naga Hills remained untouched by the nationalist freedom struggle of India (Chaube 1973:72; Misra 161-2:1988). At the eve of Independence the Nagas were psychologically not prepared to join the Indian nation (Misra 1998: 115) and give up their independent status. As India moved towards freedom from the British, the Naga National Council (NNC) called upon the Nagas to prepare for self-determination[3]. It appeared from the NNC's early statements that it did not intend to cut ties with India and willing to opt for some form of regional autonomy. The NNC demanded setting up of an "Interim Government" of the Nagas for a period of ten years, after which they would be free to decide their future. The Advisory Committee of Aboriginal Tribes (ACAT) refused to recommend this scheme to the Constituent Assembly, which resulted in deadlock. As the extremist wing within the NNC gained momentum with Angami Zapo Phizo being elected as President in 1949, it rejected the provisions of the Sixth Schedule and held a plebiscite on the question of Naga independence. Phizo took this opportunity of visiting the remotest Naga villages and winning over the support of the traditional Naga chiefs to form traditional tribal council in independent Nagaland against joining the India Union. Not being able to control the ever increasing popularity of the NNC, the Centre headed by Nehru decided to crack down on the NNC by 1953. This ensued a prolonged sanguinary arm conflict. *The Assam Disturbed Areas Act, 1955*, was promulgated in January 1956 and responsibility for law and order in Naga Hills was handed over to the armed forces. As the armed forces moved into the Naga Hills and hostilities intensified, a moderate section within the NNC expressed itself in favour of a negotiated settlement of the Naga issue. This led to a split in the NNC leadership. As the action by the security forces continued, the Indian government went ahead with the scheme to create the Naga Hills Tuensang Area, comprising the Naga Hills and the Tuensang Division of the North East Frontier Agency (NEFA). The State of Nagaland was formed in December 1963. In 1975, a leading section of the NNC signed the Shillong Accord under the provisions of which it laid down arms, it became evident that the Indian nation state was gaining in appeal. The Shillong Accord was rejected both by Phizo and by a section of the NNC led by MuivahThangkhul. Muivah's group broke away from the NNC and formed the National Socialist Council of Nagaland (NSCN). The NSCN issued its manifesto in 1980, in which it declared the NNC to be a spent force which had become "treacherous and reactionary", and declared its commitment to a sovereign independent Nagaland which would be socialist and Christian in character (Misra 1998: 120). The continuing tension between the Indian state and Nagaland can be traced to this genealogy.

If we consider the classical definition of "ethnicity" as markers, such as language, religion, race etc, ceasing to be mere means of social distinctions but becoming the basis of political identity and claim to a specific role in the political process or power, then the Naga experience eludes that it is the historical disjunction with the nation rather than the ethnic pride itself that is the cause of the strain. The Nagas in no part of the history emotionally and politically identified with the Indian nation. A study of the contemporary assertions also reveals that it is not ethnicity *per se* which causes the assertions. Distinctive and specific political developments provide the stimulus for the population of people to assert themselves. However why the assertions adorn ethnic contours in their process of demand calls for a close analysis. The study of the cases of Assam movement, ULFA and Bodoland movement provide an opportunity to understand the conundrum that plagues the society and politics of contemporary Assam. The three movements arouse with different agenda, representing different section of Assam's population and seeking varied remedy for their resentment. However they eventually adapted the process and ideology that let them get categorized as ethnic assertions.

Failure to Secure a "Generic" Identity

It is noteworthy that the three movements at their inception had attempted to consolidate generic identities. Though the appeal of the three movements was to different mass bases, yet there was an urge to form an expansive identity overarching a number of ethnic groups. The attempt was then, not at securing specific ethnic interest but at achieving a broad goal for the people of Assam.

As the movements proceeded, the leaders of the movements were caught in the rhetoric of identity and strive to form a generic mass base failed in all the three instances. What resulted at the end of the three movements was delineation and sharpening of the self identity of the initiators, against a particular “other”. Furthermore, this catapulted series of similar assertions from other groups. The Assam movement initiated with a call to all the people of Assam who were citizens of India, to stand united against the economic and demographic threat posed by unchecked immigration. The ULFA called upon the *Axombaxi* (dwellers of Assam) irrespective of their citizenship status to retort against the persistent marginalization. The Bodoland movement appealed to the numerable scattered tribal groups in the call to redress the inequity meted out to them within the state.

However in the course of the assertion, the identities got narrowed down. The Assam movement ended up as caste Hindu Assamese speaking population’s chauvinism against the non-Assamese, the ULFA boiled down to Assamese against the Indian state and the Bodoland movement decocted into the Tibeto- Burman speaking Indo-Mongoloid racial affiliated Bodo-Kachari group’s interest against the Assamese population.

The progression of degeneration of the generic identity can be traced as follows:

“Indigenous Population” and the Assam Movement

The popular song *Juye Pura Tiraxee*[4]composed by the cultural icon of Assam late Bhupen Hazarika, glorifies the sacrifices of the youths of Assam who laid down their lives during the Assam movement for the cause of “motherland”. Hazarika laments the demise of a “brother”, meticulously mentioning surnames such as Rongpi, Pegu, Gogoi, Basumatary, Rahim, Kurmi, Joseph, Khetri, Tiwari. These surnames connotes to the various section of Assam’s population: Rabha, Ahom, Bodo, Assamese Muslim, Assamese Christian, Tiwa, Nepali and North Indian respectively living in Assam. This song catches the imagination of the Assam movement at its inception when the various communities living in Assam came forward to consolidate a generic identity under the student leadership. Along with the Assamese students many students from other communities worked hand in hand to pressurize the government to “detect disenfranchise and deport” the illegal migrants who, according to them, was the greatest obstacle in the prosperity of the indigenous people.

Three areas that have been marked out in the previous chapter where the eventual ethnicization of the Assam movement took place were the elections, emergence of identity based organization and the Assam Accord. In the three spaces identities got distinguished from the one another and the generic identity propounded by the Assam movement and the preceding romantic idea of greater Assamese nationality disintegrated. What emerged sharply against all the other identities was the identity of the Assamese. The idea of greater Assamese nationality came to be challenged and it propelled the debate, first time in the socio-political history of Assam, on pining down- who is an Assamese. As the various indigenous communities refused to identify themselves with the Assamese identity, who they accused of having migrated to Assam themselves from other parts of the country, it became imperative for the Assamese to establish their distinct identity—connected to the land of Assam and different from the recently arrived Bengalis.

In the complex situation of inability to identity the Bengali speaking Bangladeshis from the Bengali speaking West Bengal origin Bengalis, the two terms *bahiragota* (outsider) and *bidexhi* (foreigner) came to be used interchangeably and were often conflated. The locale of the Assamese was, then, an identity that is in opposition to the Bengali. The long history of the Assamese's struggle against the hegemony of the Bengali under the British rule was conformed to, while framing the Assamese identity. The struggles against a series of events starting from placing Assam under the Bengal Presidency in 1826; replacement of Bengali and termination of Assamese from the school and colleges of Assam in 1837; partition of Bengal and formation of 'East Bengal and Assam' in 1905 and inclusion of Assam in Group C (to be included in East Pakistan along with Bengali dominated Cachar and Sylhet) during the Partition were some of the historical milestone that the Assamese recalled in forming their national identity in relation to Assam. Infact the British in Assam were referred to as*Boga Bongal*[5]. The figure of the Bengali for the Assamese became a crucial determinant for self identity. Bongal for the Assamese was someone who does not belong to Assam, are intruders and who threatens to marginalize them socially and politically.

"Inhabitants of Assam" and the United Liberation Front of Assam (ULFA)

ULFA's appeal was to all sections of the people living in Assam in the call for independence and to redress the injustice meted out to them by the central Government at New Delhi. In their document on who can join ULFA, it was a clear proposition that anyone irrespective of their prior membership to any ethnic group, who commit themselves to fight for Assam's liberation can join and become an ULFA member[6]. The ULFA went to the extent to call the Bangladeshi settlers neo-Assamese who have adopted the "language and culture" of the Assamese and identify Assam as their homeland. The list of ULFA's top cadres shows that there is fair participation of different sections of the population of Assam[7], though it is believed to be dominated by descendents of Ahom dynasty who had ruled Assam in the medieval times and lost their supremacy to the British colonizers.

The challenge to the generic identity proposed by the ULFA came in the form of various tribal identities who rebuffed their call for independence on the basis that it is they themselves who are the rightful masters of the land and not the "artificial" Assamese dominating the ULFA, hence any call on behalf of Assam is null and void.

Many believe that ULFA is the culmination of now-defunct LachitSena, which led the anti-Bengali agitations in the 1960s and 70s. The LachitSena was named after LachitBorphukan, the17th century commander in the Ahom kingdom[8]. Even today the people of Assam take pride in the fact that while the rest of India was conquered by the Mughals, it was the gallantry of the Ahom kings in general and heroism of LachitBorphukan in particular that the Mughals could never bring Assam in its domain. The ULFA considers LachitBorphukan as the symbol of Assamese free spirit and the Indian State as the invader. ULFA's commander-in-chief Paresh Baruah called the ULFA stir as the 18th war of independence, referring to the 17 wars fought against the invaders by LachitBorphukan[9]. LachitBorphukan was appropriated as national hero by the ULFA. For the ULFA, the battle of Saraighat was between "Assam and Bharat" (in the sense that at that time the Mughals had already dominated most of India)[10]. ULFA considers the Yandaboo Treaty between the Burmese and the British colonizers as the point which sealed Assam's glorious independence. It then transferred to the hands of "India" and the colonization continued.

The identity of the Assamese, as propounded by the ULFA, is against the Indian identity. Assamese in this regards is not a component of the Indian identity but an identity of resistance and a complete identity in itself.

"Tribal Identities" and the Bodoland Movement

The political demand by the Bodos for homeland-"Udayachal" was first raised under the aegis of the umbrella body of tribal people of Assam—Plains Tribal Council of Assam (PTCA) in the 1960s. PTCA included membership of various other tribal communities, like the Rabha, Rajbonshi, Dimasa, Mising, Tiwa and so on. However, till the movement reached the 1980s it became customary for almost all the tribal groups within the PTCA to demand exclusive homeland for themselves and lay claim to a particular territory on the basis that their ancestors had once ruled that space. The Koch-Rajbonshi started agitating for a separate Kamatapur state incorporating 11 districts in the Brahmaputra valley and 6 districts in the North Bengal region. The proposed Nagalim by the Nationalist Socialist Council of Nagaland incorporates large tracts of land which are natural habitats of some of the "indigenous" tribes of Assam like the Karbis, the Dimasa-Kacharis etc. Nagalim also includes considerable area of Manipur and Arunachal Pradesh. Along with these, the Karbis and the Khasi-Knars in Assam Meghalaya border have been engaged in several conflicts regarding exclusive rights over certain territory. Likewise, the Karbi and Dimasa in Karbi Anglong district of Assam are involved in hostile conflicts over land and rights[11]. The generic tribal identity did not sustain as each of the tribal groups constituted their own separate identity groups. The Bodoland movement then finally gave up the demand for "Udayachal" and raised the demand for separate Bodo homeland—the Bodolandland on the north bank of Brahmaputra. CurrentlyBodolandis an autonomous area dominated by the Bodoland population and includes the Bodolandland Territorial Area Districts (BTAD) administered by the Bodoland Territorial Council (BTC). The territory came into existence under the BTC Accord of 2003. BTA Dincludes the districts of Kokrajhar, Baksa, Chirang and Udalguri within the state of Assam. At present the capital of BTAD is Kokrajhar.

The Bodo community identifies itself as Indo-Mongoloid ethnic group of Tibeto-Burman language family and the rulers of Assam in the ancient times. The present territory that serves as Bodoland, the Bodo contends, was the kingdom of their ancestors in the epical era.

Conclusion

There was an attempt in the three instances to form a broad generic identity. However, this over arching identity failed to sustain itself and it soon fragmented into narrower ethnic identities, conforming to the ethnic discourse of Assam that it is a land "inhabited by diverse ethnic groups". The ethnic discourse of Assam therefore calls for a closer examination to see what the edifices are that builds it and makes it vastly overwhelming. The emergence of ethnic categories can be effectively traced back to the history, to the practice, started by the British administrators that translated into concretization of the ethnic identities. The identification and categorization of people was put in practice in three interrelated ways—Census and Cartography, Anthropological Studies and Administrative Policies and Acts.

Reference

1. The Naga Hill district was formed in 1866 with Samaguting as its headquarter. Even after the district headquarter was shifted to Kohima, the Naga Hill district covered only central Nagaland and did not include the Naga inhabited areas of neighbouring regions. Naga scholars of today blame the British of deliberately dividing their land into Naga Hill proper and parts of Assam, Manipur and Burma. (Misra 1998: 114).
2. In fact the various tribes even today communicate with each other by a pidgin Assamese language, the Nagamese. Even now the proceedings of Nagaland state Legislature and broadcast of the Nagaland radio is conducted in Nagamese because it is understood by all the sub-tribes.
3. The NNC was formed in 1946, it originated from Naga District Tribal Council (NDTC) and claimed to represent the various Naga tribes.
4. https://www.facebook.com/video/video. php?v =2082944588902 & oid = 16588174013268.
5. It literally meant White Foreigners or White Intruders *Bongal* was a derogatory word for foreigners and invaders in Assam under Ahom rule and it still is used.
6. Qualification for membership

   Clause 1:- Must be a permanent resident Assam. However, the volunteers from any other countries will be recognised conditionally.

   Clause-2:- Must has the firm determination to wage armed struggle until the successful conclusion of national liberation struggle.

   Clause-3:- Must have the mental ability. Membership may be provided to the physically handicapped regarding their integrity.

   Clause-4:- Must have maintained secrecy.

   Clause-5:- Must submit totally to the constitution of the party for the interest of the emancipation of Assam.

   Clause-6:- Must have the age above 18 years old. May be change with respect to time.

   Clause-7:- Must be disqualified any person, addicted to porno book-magazine,cinema and ordinary songs.

   Clause-8: - Mustn't take any intoxicating material.

Clause-9:- Must be disqualified for membership; anybody involved in the anti-social activities.

Clause-10:- Must disqualified for membership, anybody with Indian sentiment or spies of enemy side etc. however, if anybody submit himself totally to the constitution of the party or his severs all relations with other organisation, may be qualified for the membership through observation.

Clause-11:- Every member of the party must be ready for any task and he/she must be whole-time worker.

Clause-12:- Must comply with the responsibility of any appointment at any place heartily and without protest after receiving the membership.

Clause-13:- Irrespective of male or female, anybody will be illegible to be the member of the party.

(From ULFA's official website http://www.oocities.org/capitolhill/congress/7434/ulfa.htm).

7. http://en.wikipedia.org/wiki/List_of_top_ULFA_leaders.

8. LachitBarphukan (1612-1671) was the general of Ahom king Chakradhvaj Singha. The Mughal emperor Auranzeb in order to annex Assam to his empire sent a contingent of Army of ten thousand soldiers under general Ram Singha. Hearing this news Lachit ordered for fortification near Amingaon and gave the task to his maternal uncle. But Lachit found his uncle negligent in his duties and so beheaded his uncle saying: "My maternal uncle cannot be greater than my country". Under Lachit's direct supervision the fortification was completed hurriedly. Because of the fortification the Ahoms could give a heroic resistance against the invading Mughals in the battle of Saraighat near Pandu in 1671. The Mughals were beaten both at waters and the land. In this way Lachit saved Assam (Bhattacharjee 1993).

9. http://syednazakat.wordpress.com/2011/07/23/lone-ranger/.

   In fact an enquiry into the personal lives of the ULFA leaders forefronts that many of them had been influenced by LachitBorphukan's tales of heroism and his commitment for the cause of Assam. Another popular ULFA cadre KabiranjanSaikia (alias SwadhinataPhukan) who was central publicity secretary of ULFA also had been greatly influenced by Lachit. In his collection of poems (which ranged from the poems he had been writing since fifth standard) published posthumously, he expressed immense reverence for Lachit and his love for motherland. Saikia died of bullet shots by Indian Army in 2000.

   (http://www.telegraphindia.com/1111205/jsp/northeast/story 14840370. jsp #.UO qzaKznbKs).

10. http://akousaraighat.wordpress.com/

11. The hostility between the Meiteis and the Nagas and the Nagas and the Kukis in the state of Manipur are also result of space- centric politics.

Chapter - 4

Probing the Ethnic in Assam's Ethnic Discourse

Assam has been historically considered "anthropologist's delight" and an "administrator's dilemma"because of its demographic landscape. The category divide of the people have, of late, pronounced vehemently in the socio-political milieu. Sanjib Baruah (1999) refers to the recent ethnicization of identities and identity categories of the people of Assam as follows:

> In Assam's complex ethnic and political landscape the category "ethnic Assamese" can define a category of people as a somewhat more likely target of suspicion as possible sympathizers and fellow travelers of the Assamese insurgents. The "ethnic Assamese" can be distinguished from Assam's many "immigrant" communities and the "tribal" communities —the latter two, in recent years, less likely to be sympathizers with Assamese subnationalism. The category therefore manages to distinguish, in terms of stereotypical phenotypes, a particular group of people in a way that seems to be related to the logic of surveillance and social control in Assam. (Baruah 1999: xvii).

The emergence of these categories, however, can be traced back to the history, to the time when the people were identified and categorized based on the perceived idea of their origin. It was this practice, started by the British administrators that translated into concretization of the ethnic identities. The identification and categorization of people was put in practice in three interrelated ways—Census and Cartography, Anthropological Studies and Administrative Policies and Acts.

The ethnic discourse of Assam is constituted by the extensive writings about the inhabitants. Their origin, the route of immigration and time of arrival in Assam, their racial and cultural affiliation, historical allegiance are, without doubt, features of the colonial establishment. Though Assam has a history of writing and maintaining records even before the advent of the British, in the form of *Buranjis*, the chronicles of the Ahom dynasty, the study and detailing of the people and categorizing them based on their analysis created an unprecedented paradigm of identifying the people of Assam.

With the acquisition of Diwani of Bengal the East India Company came in direct contact with the medieval kingdoms of Jaintia, Cachar and Assam as well as the tribal communities of their adjoining hills. These sparsely populated territories did not yet have enough economic worth or surplus-revenue yielding potentiality to attract the attention of the British annexationists. They had therefore been left undisturbed until the Burmese invasion (1817-24) of Assam and the Cachar plains. This brought an end to the policy of indifference. The Burmese were finally forced to surrender under the treaty of Yandaboo in 1826. During the following one and a half decade, the kingdoms of Jaintia, Cachar and Assam along with their dependencies and all the petty independent tribal kingdoms of the Khasi hills were annexed. The Colonial province of Assam, by 1874, was a large administrative area with the annexation of Naga Hills in 1826, Jaintia, Garo and Khasi Hills by 1835 and the Lushai Hills in 1895 into British India. The North Cachar Hills were organized into separate administrative units, after their subjugation was complete in 1854. Annexation of parts of the Naga Hills and the Garo Hills were complete by 1889 and 1898 respectively, though the British could enjoy only loose political control over them. The boundaries of the British power in north-east India were always moving and were always in flux. Nevertheless the British province that came to be known as Assam was more or less shaped in 1873[1].

I have mentioned in the previous chapter that two key aspects of the colonial political geography of Assam, which profoundly affected its cultural dynamics, were: the segregation of plain and the hills, and the notion that Assam is an extension of Bengal[2]. Together with these Assam's late nineteenth century economic revolution[3] brought an inflow of people to Assam from various parts of the country to meet the newly emerged demand of labourers. Colonial officials actively encouraged immigration into Assam. Labourers in a large scale were brought in from present day Jharkhand, Chhattisgarh, Orissa, West Bengal and Andhra Pradesh to work in the gardens and fields. This economic transformation brought in a sea change in the demography of Assam. Together with this, the radical policies introduced were a sharp break from the past. At one hand the interconnection between the people of the hills and of the plains or valleys were curtailed and at the same time a new category of people, the "immigrants", was created. C.S. Mullan, a British colonial official responsible for the census report on 1931, had predicted that, "immigration was likely to alter permanently the whole future of Assam and to destroy more surely than the Burmese invasion of 1820, the whole structure of Assamese culture and civilization." In another thirty years Mullan predicted, it was not improbable that "Sibsagar district will be the only part of Assam in which the Assamese will find itself at home."[4]This juncture hence saw the emergence of the binary opposite categories: the indigenous and the immigrants; the plain people and the hill people; the tribal and the non-tribal and the hill tribal and the plain tribal. These categories have existed and dominate the social, political and economic life of Assam till date.

Bernard Cohn *Colonialism and its Forms of Knowledge* (1996) brings to the fore that colonialism was much more than a temporary overpowering of the home administration. But its appendages grow much deeper and the power it acquires is through the knowledge it generates about the colonized people. Knowledge about the people provides the colonial machineries the power to rule them. Nicholas B. Dirks in the opening remarks of Cohn's book describes the cultural project of control by the British in India as follows:

> Colonial conquest was not just the result of the power of superior arms, military organization, political power, or economic wealth—as important as these things were.... Colonialism was itself a cultural project of control. Colonial knowledge both enabled conquest and was produced by it; in certain important ways, knowledge was what colonialism was all about. Cultural forms in societies newly classified as "traditional" were reconstructed and transformed by and through this knowledge, which created new categories and oppositions between colonizers and colonized, Europeans and Asian, modern and traditional, West and East. Ruling India through delineation and reconstitution of systematic grammars for vernacular languages, representing India through the mastery and display of archaeological memories and religious texts, Britain set in motion transformations every bit as powerful as the better-known consequences of military and economic imperialism. (Cohn 1996: ix)

Cohn's work deals extensively with the "Investigative modality" of the British policy makers. "Investigative modalities", in Cohn's usage, were made official through the production of usable knowledge in the form of published reports, statistical returns, official proceedings, administrative histories, and legal codes. All of these Cohn treats as "texts" that can be deconstructed in relation to the way in which they were written as part of specific colonial projects. In his outline, Cohn lists the following types of modalities: historiography, observation and travel, survey, enumeration, museology, and surveillance.

Colonial state in India in the backdrop of its "civilizing mission"[5] also began to introduce some of the major instruments of control of populations and resources tried out in Europe, with suitable modification for colonial adaptation. Simultaneously the colonial administrations inducted cognitive and statistical projects of modern rule. The three crucial ways in which the people of Assam were made the subjects of British colonial knowledge were through:

Data Gathering Process

The data gathering and enumeration of land and population was processed through questioning and inferring about Indian life; family, religion, language, caste, occupation, marriage, literacy etc. This was a moment when practically all the major aspects of the social and cultural life was questioned and explained. This process, introduced as a part of administrative machinery, lead to objectification and crystallization of many facets of life. The information was ordered in tables and was made referential. These data were utilized in policy formulation and administrative procedures.

The first census gathering of Assam was conducted in 1881. The population was divided into three categories: Tribes, Hindus and Musalmans. The tribes and the Hindus were described and enumerated as follows:

> Chapter VI: Castes and Tribes.
>
> [Note—The Chapter on Castes in the Brahmaputra Valley has been drawn up by Mr. E. Stack, Director of Agriculture; the note on the Kacharis (para 118) has been contributed by the kindness of the Rev. Mr. EndleofTezpur and that on the Mikirs (para 132) is from the pen of Mr. C.J. Dyull, Secretary to the Chief Commissioner to all of whom the thanks of the Chief Commissioner are due. No data whatever have been furnished on which to write an account of the Surma valley.]

107. Division of Races in the Assam Valley: I. Bodo—The preceding sections, more particularly those which treat of language and religion, will have conveyed some notion of the extraordinary mixture of races which we find in the Assam valley, and of the interesting consequences thence arising. Taking race distinction as a test, the population of the valley may be broadly divided into four classes. Of the non-Aryans races the oldest inhabitants and much the more numerous are those upon whom Mr. Brian Hodgson has conferred the generic name of Bodo, being the title given to themselves by the most numerous branch of the race, namely the Kacharis. The nature covers a large variety of tribes, among these are included the Garos, who belong, not to the valley itself, but to the highlands which limit it on its south-western side. In the valley itself the names and numbers of the various branches of the Bodo, as returned by the census of 1881, stand as follows; they have been roughly classified according to their designation connoted immunity from, or contact with, the influence of the Hindu religion.

I. – uninfluenced by Hinduism

Name	Number
Kachari	265,418
Mech	57,885
Lalung	46,677
Hajong	3,689
Garo (plains)	23,373
Total	396,442

II.—In process of conversion

Rabha	56,285
Madhahi	13,149
Mahalia	6,198
Sarania	4,718
Totila	2,539
Total	82,889

III.—Wholly converted

Chutiya	59,163
Koch and Rajbanshi	336,739
Total	295,902
Grand Total	875,233

108. II. Shan Tribes—The second class of tribes are those of Shan origin, shown in the census under the three heads of Ahom, Khamti, and Shan. These are comparatively recent settlers. The Ahom came into the valley about the date of Magna Carta, and ruled over portions, and finally over nearly the whole of it, until the end of the eighteenth century. The Khamtis may possibly have come in small numbers with the Ahoms, from whom at that early period they were perhaps not very clearly distinguinshed, but their most important immigration is of quite recent date. The Shan returned in the census are probably the Aitonias, and Aitonias and Phakials seem to have been included alos under Khamtis, from whom they differ but little. The grand difference between these tribes and the Ahoms is that they have converted to Buddhism, while the Ahomshave been converted to Hinduism. The number of the Shan race within the inner line of frontier appears as follows:

Ahom	179,283
Khamti	2,883
Shan	275
Total	182,441

This enumeration, however, takes no account of settlements between the inner and the outer line.

Daphlas	549
Miris	25,636
Abors	821
Total	27,006

109. III. Tribes of the mountains east of Bhutan—Next comes the race inhabiting the mountains which form the northern frontier of Eastern or Upper Assam. The race has no generic name. preceding eastward from the frontier of Bhutan, those branches of which are settled in the valley are known to the Assamese as Akas, Daphlas, Miris and Abors. We know practically nothing about their history or their ethnological affinities. Their settlements in the Assam valley are shown in the present census as having a population of 27,006, divided as follows:

Abor and Miri villages beyond the inner line have not been counted. There are apparently no settlements of the Akas in the plains.

110. IV. Hindus—The fourth and the last class consist of those who, whatever their origin, are by common consent counted Hindus. Deducting the Mahalias and adding the Mataks, the number of this

> class appears as 857,450, whereof the most numerous castes are Kalita (241,589), Kewat or Kaibarttha (105,317), Dom (96,779), Brahmin or Ganak (86,174), and Katani or Jugi (81,931). The separation of Hindus as an ethnological class is open to the objection that it includes a large number who are not Aryans. The Doms, for example, are a numerous body of origin certainly not Aryan. Again there are 22,052 Bhumij tea-coolies from Central India, who are certainly not Aryans, and probably not Hindu even by religion. For general purpose, however the classification is exact enough, as distinguishing the non-Aryans of the Assam valley from those who, as a mark of superiority call themselves Aryans. (*Report on The Census of Assam for 1881*).

S.R. Maheshwari's work *The Census Administration Under the Raj and After* (1996) gives a detailed account of the aspect of life that was sought to quantified by the British administration. According to her work India has a long history of census. It was primarily employed for the purpose of taxation. Kautilya'sArthasastra[1], written around 321-296 B.C. laid stress on census taking as a measure of state policy for the purpose of taxation. Census is discussed comprehensively in his chapter thirty-five dealing with the duty of the revenue collector. While defining his functions, Kautilya writes, "He shall also keep an account of the number of young and old men that reside in each house, their history (Charitra), occupation (ajiva), income (aya) and expenditure (Vyaya). They (spies specially deputed by him) shall also find out the causes of emigration and immigration of persons of migratory habit, the arrival and departure of men and women of condemnable (anarthya) character, as well as the movements of (foreign) spies" (Shamasastry 1929: 159).

But it is only under the British that the use of the term "Census" for population count and record of all the important aspect of the life was put in place. Writing about the commencement of Census in India, Maheshwari writes:

> The British came to India for trade, but stayed to rule. The transition passed through three broad phases. The trading role commenced when Queen Elizabeth I granted the Charter to the East India Company in 1600, and continued undiluted till 1765. In that year, in addition to the trade, the company began to perform the ruler's role as well. The trading concerns came to an end in 1833 when the British commercial role was terminated and it emerged as India's ruler. In 1857, after Indians unsuccessfully revolted against the

British rule, direct control of the British crown was established all over India. The East India Company was wound up after an existence of 357 years.

Among the first concern of Great Britain in the role of direct ruler of India, was to find out its population. The government in India was asked in London in July 1856 to organize a census, but the census could not be held on account of the armed uprising in 1857. The matter was taken up in 1860 with the return of peace. (Maheshwari 1996: 26).

The 1931 census sought information on sixteen items. These were:

1. Name
2. Religion and Sect
3. Male or Female
4. Married, Unmarried or Widowed
5. Age
6. Race, Tribe or Caste
7. Earner or dependent
8. Principal occupation
9. Subsidiary occupation
10. Industry in which employed
11. Birth district (or country)
12. Mother tongue
13. Other languages in common use
14. Whether literate (i.e. able to write and read a letter)
15. Whether able to read and write English
16. Insane, totally blind, deaf, mute or leper (*Census of India*: 1935)

While the 1941 census gathered information on further aspects of life:

1. Name
2. Sex
3. Race, Tribe or Caste
4. Religion
5. Married, Unmarried, Widowed or Divorced
6. Age
7. No. of children born to a married woman

8. Her age at birth of first child
9. Are you wholly or partly dependent on anyone else
10. If so, means of livelihood of persons on whom dependent
11. Do you employ (a) paid assistant (b) members of household
12. Are you in employment now
13. (Only to those who reply in negative to question 12)
    Are you in search of employment?
    To those who reply in affirmative the further question will be put- How long have you been in search of it?
14. Means of livelihood in order of importance
15. (Only to be asked in regard to means of livelihood of a person shown as partly dependent against or any subsidiary means of livelihood returned by other person against question 14) Does this mean of livelihood exist throughout the year? If not for what part of the year?
16. If you are employed by someone else what is his business?
17. Were you born in this district? If not then in what district?
18. Mother tongue?
19. Other Indian language in common use
20. Can you both read and write? If so, what script do you write? Can you read?
21. How far have you read? Give any examination passed?
22. Are you literate in English?[2]

Along with the enumeration and categorization of the people, the boundary of Assam was constantly drawn and redrawn during the colonial rule. The present turmoil in Assam of identities demanding territories exclusively for themselves are in many ways result of the whim of the colonial rulers to assign identities to a particular territory.

Colonial writer G. Dunbar describes the Abor-Mishmi inhabited region of Assam in the following words:

> It would be difficult to find more tremendous inhabited country than the home of the Abors and their neighbours. A close succession of thickly wooded mountains, their sides as steep as the roof or the walls of a house, rise higher and higher northwards to the main Snowy Range. Upto the furthest limits of the Indian monsoon these highlands are drenched under very nearly the most torrential rainfall

> in the world... One of the greatest rivers of Asia thunders in its deepest gorges on the long journey from Tibet, through a labyrinth of mountains echoing with streams, down to the wide expanse of the Assam valley and out into the Bay of Bengal. The razor edged foot-hills are covered with dense sub-tropical forest, where orchids grow on the branches above and the thick undergrowth is infested with leeches... Midway between the foot-hills and the main Snowy Range there is a narrow zone of open valleys, where flourishing villages are set amidst their fields. This is the heart of the tribal country. It is beyond the influence of Assam with its Indian and western forms of Civilization and it is too far south to be affected by the religious ideas and customs of Tibet. (Gunbar 1938:230-231).

The colonial rulers imagined the land of Assam to be segregated exclusively into dwelling places of different communities. Bodhisattva Kar (2009) provides a description of the urgency of the British colonial rulers to define the territories in Assam. Narrating Assam's first chief commissioner Richard Keatinge's dismay of not finding the boundaries well marked, Kar writes:

> Much to his chagrin, the first chief commissioner discovered that in most places the minimum prerequisite did not exist in a readily identifiable shape. 'The Naga Hill District had been constituted in 1867, but its boundaries had not been formally settled (Robb 1997:257). Apart from a few miles in the west, the boundaries of Lakhimpur, theoretically the largest district in British India, were 'wholly undefined and unknown'. The boundaries of the Sibsagar district have never been defined. While Bivar and Williamson had just laid down the Khasi-Garo boundary in 1873, the Khasi-Kamrup boundary was not yet defined. Even after the successful war in 1864, border disputes with the Deb Raja did not stop. Kelso's 1849-50 demarcation between Goalpara and Kamrup was found to be faulty, and this was a source of tension with the estate of Bijni. In 1872, Beckett had defined the boundaries between Goalpara and Garo Hills, but Goalpara's boundary wit Rangpur was still left undecided. (Kar 2009: 51).

After Assam became a colonial province—a chief commissionership, the boundaries of the province was altered to suit the administrative exigencies. Sanjib Baruah (1999: 28) writes that the primary goal of making Assam into a new administrative entity was to find an inexpensive and effective way to administer the area; considerations of historical continuity or cultural contiguity were not in the minds of colonial officials.

Studying the People

Assam and the entire north-east India has a long tradition of anthropological research. Right from the second quarter of the nineteenth century the British explorers, soldiers, tea-planters took great interest in the culture of local people and prepare notes based on their impressions. The roots of anthropological research in this region may thus be tracked back to more than more than two hundred years ago from today. The social anthropological research had an early start in the region as compared to many regions elsewhere in India. This could be related to the production of sixteen detailed monographs under the auspice of an honorary director of ethnography of Government of Assam. Hodson's work on Meiteis and published in 1908; Plafair published his book on the Garos in 1909; a book on the Lushai-Kuki clans by Shakespeare was published in 1912; Gurdon's book on the Khasi was published in 1914. One of the earliest accounts on the people of Assam is Francis Hamilton's *An account of Assam: with Some Notices Concerning the Neighbouring Territories.* It wasfirst compiled in 1807-1814, writes that:

> The principle caste and tribes in Asam are as follows:
>
> The Rarhi Brahmans of Bengal, as I have before said, have obtained the spiritual guidance of the king and principal officers of the court, and it is probably through their influence that two men of the same caste have procured the lucrative farm of the trade with Bengal. The spiritual guide and officiating priest of the king (Guru and Purohit) are men of great reputation for learning.
>
> There are Brahmans called Assamese. They are Vaidikas of Kanyakubja, and one of them told me that they were introduced from that place by Viswa Singha, the Koch Raja; but that having penetrated into Assam they no longer intermarried with those who remained in the western parts of Kamrup, as they could not mutually be informed how far each party had reserved its purity. Before their arrival there were learned men among the Kolitas, who were Gurus for all the people.
>
> Many KamrupiVaidika Brahmans are now settled in Asam, and it is said that among them there are many persons learned in Hindu science. Very few among either the Vaidikas of Asam or Kamrup worship the Saktis or female destructive spirits. They are chiefly of

the sect of Vishnu. They have a few academics (Chauvaris) where the grammar called the Ratnamala, law and metaphysics are taught, and some Pandits are skilled in astrology and magic. The grand study with the Mahajons, or spiritual guides, is the Sri Bhagwat.

Some of the Vaidikas in this country have degraded themselves, have become Varna, and instruct the impure tribes, a meanness to which none of those in Bengal have submitted.

The persons called Man Singha's Brahmans are pretty numerous, and are employed in all low offices, totally unconnected with religion.

The Deo-dhaings, descended from the religious guide of Khuntai, may now amount to thirty men, besides women and children. Their chief is called Deo-dhaing Boruya, and has the charge of the god Chung, of his worship, and of the royal insignia, such as the sword Hyangdang, and the sacred feathers. The Deo-dhaings possess a learning and language peculiar to themselves; and keep them a profound secret; but they have in many points adopted the worship pf Vishnu. They are still highly respected.

In the eastern part of the present dominions of Asam, beyond Koliyabar, and exclusive of the Kampos, Miri, and Dophlas, the most numerous class of inhabitants are the Ahams, or governing nation. Those legitimately descended from the companions of Khuntai still retain all the principal offices of state. They may be considered as the nobility, and are said to be now reduced to twenty-six families, two Danggoriyas, one Duyara, one Dihingga, one Lahon one Sondike, and twenty Hatimuriyas. Of these last five families are attached to each of the Danggoriyas, and ten to BarapatraGohaing, who is descended of Khuntai. The reminder of the nation is by some alleged to owe its origin to the illegitimate issue of these families; but, as I have before mentioned, many of them are probably descended from the soldiers and servants who accompanied the princes; but since the introduction of caste the Ahams confine their marriages to their own tribe. The whole have now adopted the language of Bengal, as their colloquial dialect, and have also relinquished the use of beef; but about a fourth part have yet no other priests than the Deodhaings. The remaining three-fourths have adopted the religion of the Hindus, chiefly as taught by the followers of Madhava Acharya.

> In the parts east from Koliyabar the tribe next most numerous is called Chutiya, and is divided into two classes, called Hindu and Aham. The former have abandoned many of their impure customs, and have received degraded (Varna) Brahmans as their spiritual guides. The latter wallow in their impurity, and adhere to the Deodhaings.
>
> West from Koliyabar, the two most numerous tribes, and nearly equal in strength are the Kolitas and Koch. (Hamilton 1940).

On similar note, British explorer L.A. Waddell (1901) writes about the people of Assam as follows:

> Zoologically this tract stands at the junction of the 'Indo-Chinese', 'Indo-Malayan' and 'Indian', sub-regions of the 'Oriental region' of naturalists. Its tribes represent racial elements from all these three. In trying to trace out these elements, history does not help us much.
>
> The race-wars which raged in this area in ancient times have left little evidence beyond those vestiges which survive in the names of rivers and certain places. This was doubtless owing to the wildness and illiterateness of the tribes concerned, for Assam has the misfortune (or fortune?) not to possess anything worthy of the name of ancient history. What history there is relates to the more modern waves of invasion which have swept up and down the rich central valley…
>
> [S]ince then the Hinduising of the tribes along the central river has steadily progressed, till now those tribes of the valley who pose as Hindus, especially the *Ahoms*, *Koch* and *Kachari* are scarcely to be distinguished by a casual observer from *Bengalis* in dress, manner and language, except for their lighter colour and Mongoloid eyes. Now however that they have fallen to the rank of a caste within the Hindu system, comparatively little inter-mixture seems now to be going on, although previously there doubtless must have been some leavening with Indian blood. These tribes then appear to be a mixed progeny of the various Indo-Chinese, and to a more or less extent also of the Himalayan Mongoloids who swept into the fertile valley wave after wave; and in the flux and reflux of invasion within this ethnological backwater they appear to have undergone considerable intermixture; but they now emerge tending to become petrified into hard and fast castes.
>
> On the other hand, the wilder tribes who have clung to the mountains have doubtless retained their racial purity more intact; but

even amongst these there must be some impurity of type by intermixture with adjoining tribes owing to their inveterate practice of raiding and carrying off marriageable girls from the plains and from adjoining tribes. (Waddell 1901: 9-11).

The 1931 census report on Assam gives a description of the people after the enumeration as follows:

Assam

The easternmost part of northern India separated from Bhutan by the Himalayan range and from Upper Burma by the Patkoi Mountains, and connected with the plain of Bengal on the north-west, is known as Assam (from Ahom, the Burmese conqueror of the land). It is a land consisting mostly of mountains, with two fertile plains separated by Khasi-Jaintia hills. From the purely anthropological standpoint there is no part of India which is more interesting than Assam. Situated as it is, between the Eastern Himalayas, Southern Tibet, China, Burma and Bengal, its population has been derived from all these sources. From the former three it has received the bulk of its population, while Burma supplied it with its Ruling dynasty from 1228 A.D. till the advent of the British in 1887. Besides these, the rich fertile valleys of the land have invited Hindu immigrants North-Eastern India who carried the Hindu civilization and social orzanization into Assam at a very early date. The latter have formed the upper classes, with various degrees of intermixture, while the bulk of the population has remained since the days of Hiuen Tsang (7th century) "Indo-Chinese" in the main. The nature of the topography of the country has kept the larger portion of the hill tribes in extreme isolation, with all their primitive habits and institutions almost intact.

The metric date available on the people of Assam consist of (1) the measurements of Waddell[3] on the different hill tribes, (2) on the Naga tribes by Hutton, and (3) the Khasis by the present writer, besides accounts of several series of skulls.

Col. Waddell measured 580 individuals belonging to 21 Assamese and 3 Foreign tribes, but as most of these series consist of a small number of individuals, the Co-efficients of racial Likeness were calculated on 3 Assamese and one Sikkimese tribes only, as shown in the following table.

Assam and Sikkim Tribes

Tribes	*Crude C.R.L.*	*Reduced C.R.L.*
Mande (Garo) and Lepcha	18.06	51.47
Lepcha (Rong) and Khasia	10.40	20.99
Khasia and Bodo (Kachari)	3.21	6.74
Bodo and Lepcha	8.13	23.57
Mande and Khasia	10.89	22.76
Mande and Bodo	3.69	10.89

It will be noticed from these figures that the lowest Co-efficient is found between the khasia and the Kachari. The value of the C.R.L. between the Mande and the Bodo is also close, showing that these three tribes have a common racial substratum. With the Lepcha however none of the Assam tribes seems to bear any relationship.

Of the Assamese proper, of the Brahmaputra Valley, we have no metric data exceptimg 6 Kolitas measured by Waddell. In the absence of reliable measurement, it is impossible to determine how far they are racially allied to the neighbouring people of Bengal and Behar, though the inhabitants of the Eastern Surma Valley being composed to later immigrants from Eastern Bengal, are probably still closely related to them.

The tribes living along the hills on the Eastern frontiers are disclosed by Hutton's measurements of the Angami Naga[4], and Turner's[5] 'Studies of Chin Lushai skull', are in the main dolichocephalic in the shape and proportions of the head, but containing a small element of brachycephalic type allied to the Burmese. An examination of the large series of the Naga crania recovered by the Dewar Expedition from the Triangular Area in Upper Burma,[6] also confirmed this conclusion of the dolichocephalic character of the Naga head, but showed at the same time the presence of a definite Negrito strain. This is in agreement with Hutton's[7] discovery of frizzly haired men among the Angami Nagas.

Around the same time, the American Baptist missionaries undertook the work of reform in Assam. The writings of the missionaries also reflect similar ideas like the British writers. American Christian missionary Rev. P.H Moore (1887) writes about the people of Assam as follows:

The valley of the Brahmaputra is believed to have been colonized by Aryans at a very early period. Perhaps, as early as the eighth century of our era, these Aryans were overcome by the Chutias, a horde who pressed into the valley from the north-east. They, however did not wholly destroy or expel the Aryans, but gradually adopted their religion and amalgamated with them. These in turn was overcome by the Kochis, who entered from the west in the twelfth century, and established themselves in the lower part of the valley, but did not press on to its eastern end.

The Ahoms, a tribe of Shan origin, whose depredations extended over several hundred years, entering the head of the valley in force in the thirteenth century overcame the remnant of the former dynasty left by the Koch invasion. These Ahoms, or Asams, multiplied and grew more and more powerful, pressing down further and further into the valley, until they came into collision with the Mussulman invaders from the west.

These Ahom kings were the last native dynasty in Assam, and from them, the province takes its name. For a long period, they had fierce conflicts with the Muhammadans, who were trying to annex the valley to Bengal. But they finally successfully foiled these invasions, and maintained their sway till 1810.

They are said to have adopted Hinduism about the middle of the seventh century. Though successful in war they succumbed to the enervating influences of their surroundings. Intestine strife and anarchy prevailed. At length the Burmans were called in as arbitrators. They saw their oppourtunity and in ten years' time were masters of the valley. Their atrocities are still matters of common traditions. So barbarous was their rule, that the whole districts were depopulated.

The British occupied Assam in 1824 as an incident of their war with the Burmese, and at the conclusion of that war in 1826, it was ceded to them by treaty.

The British occupancy and development of the valley has been steadily carried forward since that date. (Moore 1887: 3-5)

The writing of the missionary was evidently influenced by the census enumeration of the British colonial rule:

"There is no distinct Assamese nationality." Under the heading "Prevailing Languages" the Report on the Administration of the Province of Assam for 1885-86 gives forty distinct languages and dialects, some of which are known to include other dialects not mentioned in the Report. This variety of language is a fair index of the mixed ethnic elements in the population of the plains of Assam. Take an Aryan substratum, mingle with a Mongolian element from the north; then with this mixture a Dravidian element from the west; add to this an element whose quality and quantity are both unknown; once more mingle with this a strong element from the Shan race; allow many centuries for the process of commingling; give now a sprinkling of Burmese; keep in mind that each one of these elements is preserved in every degree of change from absolute purity to the most thorough adulteration; take into account on the one hand a fluctuating immigration not hitherto mentioned, and on the other the influence of the tribes on the hill sides that have preserved their aboriginals qualities in various degrees of purity, and you have the people of the plains of Assam. Is not the typical Assamese a nondescript? And yet there is a prevailing type of features, described as Indo-Chinese which, in our eyes, is fairer than either the pure Indian or Chinese. The Assam Census Report of 1881 divides the people according to language into 3 classes:

(1) 3,881,775 permanent inhabitants, speaking the Aryan languages as follows: Bengali, 2,425,878; Assamese, 1,361,359; Urdu, 94,538. These are the bulk of the people of the plains of the Brahmaputra and Surma valleys.

(2) 882,307 speaking non-Aryan languages. Twenty different languages are enumerated under this head, and of those speaking them the most numerous classes are the following—Kacharis, 263,186; Khasis, 157,699; Garos, 112,248, and Mikirs 77,765. Although about two-thirds of these 882,307 are enumerated as in the plain districts, they are generally speaking the inhabitants of the hills surrounding the plains of Assam.

(3) 18,284 temporary settlers, mostly in the plains, speaking twelve different languages, and besides these 1,624 speaking a European language, and 5,130, whose language is not specified. These figures indicate how heterogeneous is the population.

The ethnical relations of several of the hill tribes are as yet undetermined. They are divided according to language into seven groups. Several of them show strong Mongolian features.

The following are names of the leading tribes: Bhutanese, Akas, Daphlas, Miris, Abors (several tribes), Kamptis, Singphos, Mishmis (several tribes), Nagas (several tribes), Mikirs, Kukis,

> Kacharis, Khasis and Jaintias, Garos, and further to the south Manipuris and Lushais. (Moore 1887:5-6)

The Anthropological Studies conducted among the population of Assam categorized them into diverse racial and linguistic stock. These categories are still referred to while discussing the people of Assam.

Administrative Mechanism

I have discussed in my previous chapter that the two policies of the British colonial rule in Assam whose impacts can be felt even today are: Considering Assam as an extension of Bengal and segregation of the Hills from the Plains. These two policies, stemmed from the British perception of peoplehood of the region coupled with administrative exigency have marked the beginning of evocation of recurring ethnic categories.

Basudev Dutta-Ray's (1978) work provides a description of the criteria of selection of individuals into the government jobs and positions during the British colonial rule. Here the choice was among the Assamese, the tribals and the Bengali settlers.

> In 1903, appointment to public services in Assam was restricted to residents and natives of Assam. The rule laying down a residential qualification for appointments in public service including secretariat service was contained in Rule 537 of the Assam Executive Manual. This rule was in substance based on resolution No. 9890-915G dated November 17, 1903 which provided that save with the previous sanction of the Chief Commissioner, appointments should be limited to the residents of Assam. It did not exclude persons who came to Assam and had made their home permanently in it. The rule restricted appointment to member of families of natives or domiciled in Assam.
>
> It was by no means the Government's intention to treat men, who had come from outside and settled in Assam as foreigners. A native of Assam must be taken to mean a person of whatever origin, who had his permanent residence or owned land or houses in Assam and would stay in Assam after superannuation.
>
> A person who was not a native of Assam was deemed to be domiciled in the province only when he had become the owner of a house or land in Assam and had already lived in that homestead for a period of ten years and intended to live until he died...

It appears that the Assam Government's communal table was based on distinction of race or nationality except in the case of Muslims. The communities recognized for proportionate representation in appointments were: (i) Assamese, (ii) Muslims, (iii) Bengali Hindus of Sylhet and Cachar, (iv) Ahoms, (v) Khasis, (vi) Domiciled Bengali other than those of Sylhet and Cachar. The direct object of Assam Governement's orders was to secure that these communities received the minimum number of appointments, calculated on the basis of their populations provided qualified candidates were available... In the Eastern Bengal and Assam Secretariat, it was very difficult to get Assamese clerks to go to Dacca and still greater difficulty in keeping them after they had joined the Secretariat and they often tried to get appointment in the Assam valley. The Secretariat, therefore, hardly got an I.A. passed Assamese on Rs. 50 per month and even if one was available, he would leave the Secretariat in no time.

In 1893, out of the total of 55 assistants in the Assam Secretariat only 7 were natives of the Assam Valley. Of them 1 had passed the Entrance and 2 F.A. examination. Of the Bengalis 10 had passed the Entrance and 1 the F.A. 1 was a B.A. and 1 was a B.L. Of the natives of Sylhet, a Bengali speaking district of Assam, 4 had passed the Entrance examination, 4 F.A. 1 was a B.A. and one was a M.A.

In the P.W.D Secretariat only 5 were Assamese out of total number of 16 Assistants. Of the Assamese 1 had passed the Entrance. Of the Bengali 3 had passed the Entrance. Of the others ne had passed the Entrance.

Total Strength	1,091
Assamese	422
Bengalis other than Sylhetis	298
Sylhetis	321
Native of Cachar (Bengali speaking district of Assam)	10
Others	40

Grand total of the Whole Province

The office as it stood in 1915, was transferable wholesale from Dacca to Shillong after the reformation of the province of Assam in 1912.

There were altogether 68 clerks in the Assam Secretariat of which the number of Assamese and Khasis was very small. The following statements show the Assamese element in the secretariats, civil as well as P.W.D.

Civil Secretariat

	Assamese	*Bengalis from Sylhet and Cachar*	*Other Bengalis*	*Khasis*	*Others*	*Total*
Permanent 78	14	23	25	10	6	
Temporary 15	5	5	-	5	-	

P.W.D. Secretariat

	Assamese	*Bengali from Sylhet and Cachar*	*Other Bengali*	*Khasis*	*Other*	*Total*
Permanent 26	6	6	7	4	3	26
Temporary 8	-	2	2	2	2	8

In 1934, the Government of India recommended the reservation of a certain percentage of direct appointments to redress communal inequalities. The Assam Government already fixed the percentage of appointments to which the Assamese were entitled to on population basis. No provincial Government services were exclusively reserved for the natives or domiciled people in Assam. But no appointment was ordinarily given to a man who was not a native of or domiciled in Assam. Special care was taken by the Assam Government to give Government jobs including Secretariat appointments to the children of the soil provided they possessed the necessary qualifications. (Datta Ray 1978:163-175).

The institution of the service sector jobs together with land policies, described in the previous chapter, installed an unprecedented competition for resources. This competition still colours the socio-political context of Assam.

Exploring the Present

The ethnic discourse of Assam that emerged from the macro facet of British colonial discourse had a pervadingimpact in the way that it colours the imagination about the region even on the present day. The popular, official and intellectual approaches towards the north-eastern part of India are loaded with the British colonial perspective about the land and its people. A cursory look at the writings- official, academic or popular of the post-colonial times exudes the continuation of the approach.

The unchanged fragmentary understanding about the region underlined by ethnic diversity has provided the precursor for the assertions in the region to take ethnic route. Writers belonging from and outside Assam, writing about the region, echo similar ideas about the ethnic divisions. Publications from Assam's premier literary organization *Assam Sahitya Sabha* has been buttressing the similar ideologue about the people and the land that Assam is a region crisscrossed by ethnic diversity.

> The Negritos came to India in the pre-historic time and moved as far as Assam. There are a few specimens of the aboriginal Negritos amongst the Nagas of Assam and the races and tribes living in the jungles of the Andaman and Nicobar Islands and South India. The Negritos discovered the use of bows and arrows. They collected their food and did not produce food themselves. A mode of tree worship practised by them was subsequently adopted by other races. Secondly, the Austric race also collected food like the Negritos but the latter discovered the method of cultivation by means of pointed instruments like hoes and spades. Another of the racial characteristics was their rearing of the elephants. The Khasi-Jaintias belong to the Mongoloid race though they speak Austric languages. The influence of the culture and civilization of the Austrics, described as Nisada and *savara* in the old Sanskrit literature is widespread in the hills and plains of Assam. Matriarchal system of society and the worship of Mother Goddess Kamakhya are also two of the contribution of the Austric race. Afterwards, the Mongoloid who conquered the Austrics may have adopted many of their customs and manners. The speakers of the Santali, Savara, Munda, Khasi and Kol languages are the surviving specimens of the Austrics. BanikantaKakati and Birinchi Kumar Barua have discussed about the contribution of the Austric race.
>
> The Mongoloid or Kirata race came to Assam at different times and through different routes. The Mongoloids were for sometime the ruling race in Assam, Manipur and Tripura and North Bengal and were the patrons of learning, religion, language, literature and culture of ancient Assam. The ruling princes of the Barman, Salastamba Pal, Ahom, Kachari, Chutia, Koch, Khasi, Jaintia, Manipuri, Tripuri and Nepalis are the crowning glory of the Kirata race. The various contributions of the Kiratas in the field of dance and song language, literature and culture are well marked. W.C. Smith has observed thirteen characteristics of the Kirata race. Of these, chewing of

betel-nuts, freedom in marriage, use of the handloom and cultivation in the old methods will always point out to a cultural fusion of the Kirata under-current in the development of the Assamese race. The Ahom rule and the Ahom contribution to Assamese culture are also some of the manifold contributions of the Mongoloid or the Kirata race. We have already discussed their influences on the Assamese language.

The cultural remains discovered in Harappa and Mohenjodaro amply prove the existence of a high order of civilization and culture owned by the Dravidians, a Mediterranean race that lived in India in the pre-Aryan times. It may not be possible to present a descriptive chronological account of the Dravidian habitation in Assam. But the Dravidian influences are clearly observable in many of its place-names. Scholars are of opinion that the institution of Siva worship is a Dravidian contribution. On the other hand the Kiratas were the adherents of the Saiva sect. it may so, that the Kiratas took over their Siva worship from the Dravidian. Worship of the Goddess Marai is also a religious institution of the Aryan Hindu fold. No wonder, the Dravidian worship of the serpent Goddess, Manchama, may have cast some influence in the *Marai* worship. BanikantaKakati found some influence of the Dravidian religion of worship on the vaishnava cult of Assam.

The Western race known as Bracycephls has come to India from the region of the Dinaric Alps, Armenia etc, prior to the Nordic Aryans and lost themselves in the Aryan society at a subsequent age. The Nordic Aryans, who lived in the Indus valley had come to Assam sufficiently early and lived in her fertile land. Their language came in contact with speakers of the Tibeto-Chinese (Tibeto-Burman and Tai-Ahom) and the Austric language there and developing under such environment, they evolved the Assamese language of the Pragjyotish-Kamrupi people which is Prakrit-Apabhramsa of the Aryan Sanskrit. Assam's language, literature, culture and national consciousness are growing under the leadership of the Aryan Hindus. Yet, the active co-operation of the Austric, Kirata and Dravidian races cannot be lost sight of. (Shastri and Bhattacharya 1958).

Writers belonging from outside Assam writing about the region propound the same views about the ethnic difference among the people:

The racial history of this easternmost portion of India is extremely complicated. A great number of races have invaded it from all directions. And there was an almost continuous migration of the tribes and people within the area which has not yet come to an end in present times.

The first inhabitants appear to have been Negrito race. The occurrence of curly or even kinky hair, in connection with a short stature and strikingly Papuan profile suggests, in the opinion of J.H. Hutton, the survival of some submerged Negrito strain.

Next came the Khasi and Sytengs (or Pnars), the Wars, Bhois or Lyngnams, tribes that now inhabit the recently formed state of Meghalaya. They numbered 314,161 in 1961. Linguistically these tribes belong to the Austro-Asiatic or Mon-Khmer group. The origin can thus be traced back to southern China. Through their language they form a link between the Munda tribes further west and the tribes in Indo-China. They also resemble them culturally; they have, for instance, stone monuments to their dead ancestors like the Mundas and Hos of Chota Nagpur and, on the other side, like the tribes of Indonesia. The Khasi and Syntengs are remarkable for their strong muscular development, especially of the leg. They are rather fair, often of ruddy complexion, but have flat round faces and epicanthic fold.

Linguistically, the aborigines of Nicobar Islands (13,993 in 1961), near the coast of Burma also belong to the Mon Khmer group. Needless to say, there are also tribes of Mon Khmer linguistic group in Burma, such as the Palaungs and the Was in upper Burma, as also the Mons or Talaings of Pegu.

> The Khasi and Syntengs are now separated from their tribal cousins in north-eastern central India through the Aryan speaking Hindu castes, mostly Bengalis but also people from northern India., who entered Assam in the beginning of the Christian era from the west and ever since continued to infiltrate and take possession of the fertile lowlands and river valleys. They brought Hindu culture and social organization. (Fuchs 1973).

The Census that is being conducted in India after the Independence has not altered the colonial model of data gathering. The process and categories follow the colonial administrative modality. The Census of 1961 (*Census of India* 1965) categorized the people of Assam as follows:

Garo Hills

In Garo Hills, there are 263,003 persons belonging to the category of schedule tribes. The main tribal communities and their numerical strength are as follows:

Name of Schedule Tribe	*Persons*	*Males*	*Females*
Dimasa (Kachari)	1,320	622	698
Garo	239,747	121,036	118,711
Hajong	21,597	11,274	10,323
Khasi and Jaintia	50	29	21
Kuki	2	1	1
Man (Tai-speaking)	253	136	117
Mikir	6	5	1
Mizo	18	9	9
Naga	10	9	1

There is no indigenous Scheduled Caste population in the district. The Schedule Caste with the highest population in the district is Namasudra (429). It appears that most of them are refugees from East Pakistan.

United Khasi and Jaintia Hills

In United Khasi and Jaintia Hills, there are 376 persons belonging to the category of scheduled tribes. The main tribal communities and their numerical strength are follows:

Name of Scheduled Tribes	*Persons*	*Males*	*Females*
Chakma	1		1
Dimasa (Kachari)	100	83	17
Garo	15,037	7,809	7,223
Hajong	1,055	601	454
Hmar	1,491	952	539
Khasi and Jaintia	351,981	172,794	179,187
Kuki	208	160	48
Lakker	1	-	1
Mikir	4,188	2,296	1,892
Mizo (Lusai)	1,158	310	348
Naga	938	728	210

In United Mikir and North Cachar Hills the most important tribal community is the Mikir, with total population of 116,387. The next important tribal population is the Dimasa (Kachari) with population of 67,284. The other tribal communities with total population of more than 1,000 are Naga (8,338), Kuki (7,150), Hmar (4,131), Khasi and Jaintia (3,931) and Garo (3,326).

Mizo Hills

The Mizo Hills, there are 2,61,014 person below to the category of schedule tribes. The main tribal communities and their numerical strength are as follows:

Name of the Scheduled Tribe	*Persons*	*Male*	*Female*
Chakma	19,337	9,967	9,370
Dimasa (Kachari)	14	5	9
Garo	12	11	1
Hmar	3,119	1,367	1,752
Khasi and Jaintia	193	103	90
Kuki	11,677	6,118	5,559
Lakher	8,790	4,150	4,640
Mikir	1	1	-
Mizo	213,261	104,939	108,322
Naga	23	13	10
Pawi	4,587	2,156	2,431

The data about the people of Assam according to the 2001 Census was as follows:

Statement-1: Population of Major STs, 2001 Census

Sl. No.	*Name of the Scheduled Tribe*	*Total Population*	*Proportion of the Total ST Population*
1.	All Scheduled Tribes	3,308,570	100%
2.	Boro	1,352,771	40.9
3.	Miri	587,310	17.8
4.	Mikir	353,513	10.7
5.	Rabha	277,517	8.4
6.	Kachari	235,881	7.1
7.	Lalung	170,622	5.2
8.	Dimasa	110,976	3.4
9.	Deori	41,161	1.2

(http://censusindia.gov.in/Tables_Published/SCST/dh_st_assam.pdf)[8]

Besides the Census of India, since the late 1950s several research organizations have emerged which are engaged in conducting research among the tribal and the non-tribal communities of Assam and in the other states of the north-eastern region of India. These are: (1) Anthropological Survey of India, (2) Tribal Research Institutes of Assam, Meghalaya, Arunachal, Mizoram and Nagaland, (3) Agro-Economic Research Centre of North-East India (Jorhat) etc.

Conclusion

The British administration initiated processes that consolidated into creating a knowledge base which in turn formed the basis of control and power of the British over the colonized masses. This created a discourse turning the masses into subjects of the knowledge and objectified their identity. This objectification led to the emergence of a discourse—the ethnic discourse which then permeated the socio-political milieu of the region. The all pervasive nature of this discourse made it difficult for any other form of identity to emerge. The tensions in the post-colonial times have taken up ethnic dimensions as the only mode of identity formation plausible in Assam is ethnic. The imagination of the region even in the post-colonial times and the government attitude of policy making have not significantly deviated, making it difficult to shed the ethnic mode of identity formation and assertions.

Reference

1. Gait (1905)
2. The Bengal Eastern Frontier Regulation of 1873 empowered the colonial government to prescribe an "Inner Line". The line was drawn along the foothills, and the people living beyond this line were supposedly left to manage their own affairs. The British considered most of the people living in the hills of Assam as "primitive tribes". They were kept in reservation-like territories called "backward" or "excluded" tracts. The colonial policy of drawing a hard boundary between the hills and the plains was a sharp break from the past. The perception that the peoples in the hills and the plains were distinct entities and enforcing policies for strict boundary maintenance instilled a new sense of peoplehood in the region.

   The second aspect of the colonial policy geography of Assam that had significant long-term implications for the cultural politics of Assam was the notion that Assam was an extension of Bengal. Throughout the entire colonial period, the British treated Assam as a land frontier for Bengal. Justifying a move to combine Assam and East Bengal into a single province, an official said that, since Bengal is very densely populated and Eastern Bengal is most densely populated part, it needs "room foe expansion" and it can expand only eastward. "Far from hindering national development," he said, "we are really giving it greater scope and enabling Bengal to absorb Assam" (Guha 1977).
3. Discovery of tea and petroleum, setting up of coal fields, timber production were some of the developments.
4. S.K. Sinha, "Report on Illegal Migration into Assam." Report submitted by the Governor of Assam to the President of India. November 8, 1998. http://www.satp.org/satporgtp/countries/india/states/assam/documens/papers/illegal_migration_in_assam.htm (accessed May 12, 1998).
5. An example of civilizing mission of the British administrators can be gathered from the following account of Major John Butler, Principal Assistant Agent to the Governor General North East Frontier of Assam, during his visit of Naga village: "There were forty boys assembled; we gave them presents of knives, beads, and scissors, and asked them whether they would learn to read Assamese, if a schoolmaster were appointed to teach them. They were highly pleased with

the presents, and declared they would most assuredly try to learn the Assamese language, if a schoolmaster was appointed. A schoolmaster was accordingly at once located in the village, and the Bible in Assamese and Bengalee, with other books, was supplied. In the course of a year, several boys learned the first rudiments of the language, and one has attained such proficiency as to be able to write an Assamese letter. Who shall say that the Bible will not be the means of changing the habits and ideas of these wild savages? The experiment is worthy of a trial; they have no caste or prejudices of creed to deter them from adopting Christianity; and, if successful in one instance, it cannot be deemed visionary to anticipate that the darkness and ignorance that now overshadow the land may be speedily dispelled, when our rule will prove a blessing to these benighted tribes, who would henceforth enjoy the fruit of their labours in peace and prosperity." (Butler: 1855:24).

6. R. Shamasastry. Kautilya's Arthasastra. Mysore. Wesleyan Press. 1929.
7. http://censusindia.gov.in/Data_Products/Library/Indian_perceptive_link/History_link/censushistory.htm.
8. Waddell, L. A.—The Tribes of the Brahmaputra Vlley, J.A.S.B., Volume LXIX, Part III, pages 1-127. Based on Waddell's measurement.
9. Hutton, J.H.—AngamiNagas, London 1921.
10. Turner, Sir William, — Trans. Of Royal Society Edinburgh, Volume XXXIX, Part III, pages 703-747.
11. Guha. B.S. and Basu, P.C. – Anthropological Bulletin of the Zoological Survey of India, No. I., page II, Calcutta 1929.
12. Hutton, J.H. – *Man in India*, Volume VII, pages 257-262, 1927.
13. Please see Annexure II.

Conclusion: The Discordant Discourse

Assam, so also the rest of north-east India, is a pulsating ground of ethnic manoeuvring. It remains to be seen what turns the recent land-swap deals between India and Bangladesh[1] and the "Framework Agreement"[2] between Central Government and Naga leaders take in the course of time. The context of thiswork is the continuing tensions in Assam, necessitating a proper understanding of their crux, which has not received proper focus as yet. The general practice of addressing the problem has been of inaugurating the issue describing the ethnic diversity, followed by examining it under the rubric of ethnic problem. The effort of the book was to question this very approach of explaining the problem. Ethnic diversity is not self-explanatory and ethnic tensionsare not instinctual; the analysis of the ethnic discourse reveals the complex underpinnings that constitute the innumerable tensions in Assam as ethnic. A recent work on Post colonial ethnic tensions in south-east Asia suggests that ethnic dissidence is a governance issue:

> Postcolonial states in South and Southeast Asia continue to be challenged by violent ethno-nationalist and secessionist insurgencies. These insurgencies usually exhibit complex causation and long and chequered histories. However, a key factor behind many of these insurgencies has been postcolonial states' desire to produce pulverised and uniform sense of national identity to coincide with artificial and arbitrary state boundaries, which seldom overlap with the real ethnic divisions on the ground. Influenced heavily by the modernisation school, which posits that multi-ethnic states cannot be both stable and democratic, post-colonial nation-building strategies in South and South-east Asia typically legitimised the over centralization of state power in an effort to safeguard territorial integrity and achieve political stability. This, in turn, often resulted in the neglect or ill treatment of ethnic minorities and the denial of minority ethnic nations' political rights, thereby producing an "ethnic backlash" in the form of ethno-nationalist and secessionist movements... Ethnic conflict in South and Southeast Asia is, therefore, in essence a

"governance problem" which today sits squarely at the centre of the rapid transformation that these regions and societies are experiencing. (Ganguly 2012: 1).

The attempt of this book has been to demonstrate the factors leading tothis 'governance problem'. The factor lays in the fact that Post colonial governance, so also Post colonial imaginationof Assam and other north-eastern states, has not been able to topple the colonial disposition.

Foucault's method of discourse analysis has helped us arrive at a conclusive understanding on the causations that comprise the tensions as ethnic. The need in Assam, so also other regions of the world comprised by diversified identities, is not to dwell and treat the heterogeneity in a fragmentary manner. But, provide necessary conditions for the discursive ideas to inspire self-confidence amongst the community and esteem for others. Exclusivist ethno-nationalistic theories and the corresponding political incentives do more harm than good for the peaceful co-existence. The work is a way towards understanding the nuances that inculcate conflicts and ruptures the amity of the nation.

The book had set to arrive at a meticulous understanding of the reasons as to why there has been a rise of ethnic conflicts in the contemporary world and had situated Assam as a location to understand the phenomenon. At the outset it had recognized that each conflict needs to be contextualized and understood in its totality in order to decipher the cause behind its acquiring ethnic dimension. The main contribution of the study, is the amassment and piecing together of the arbitrary empirical data regarding the framing of the ethnic question in the assertions. Using discourse analysis as enunciated by Foucault, the book seeks to maintain that the colonial ethnic discourse existentially plays a pivotal role in propelling the conflicts in Assam. Foucault describes the process of analyzing a discourse not only as an exercise of tracing the continuity that forms the discourse but also by taking into account the discontinuities. He says:

> And the great problem presented by such historical analyses is not how continuities are established, how a single pattern is formed and preserved, how for so many different, successive minds there is a single horizon, what mode of action and what substructure is implied by the interplay of transmissions, resumptions, disappearances, and repetitions, how the origin may extend its sway well beyond itself to that conclusion that is never given- the problem is no longer one of tradition, of tracing a line, but one of division, of limits; it is no longer one of lasting foundations, the rebuilding of foundations. What one

> is seeing, then, is the emergence of a whole field of history is trying to develop its own theory: how is one to specify the different concepts that enable us to conceive of discontinuity (threshold, rupture, break, mutation, transformation). (Foucault: 1972: 5).

The central hypothesis for the work has been that the colonial ethnic discourse, emerged as a micro discourse from the macro discourse of British colonialism, has gone about colouring the imagination of the region under study. The colonial period was a moment when all aspects of the life of the colonized masses were objectified turning them into subjects of the colonial power – knowledge combine. The book argues that it is the continuation of the discursive colonial knowledge in the form of narrative, interpersonal relationship and political and governmental policies that incite the particular trajectory of the assertions. The study makes out that a wide range of tensions have been clamped together under the rubric of ethnic problem and focuses on Assam in order to answer the question as to why the ethnic politics. It sustains: a) Assam is a region distinguished by its ethnic diversity and b) the demands raised by various quarters at different points of time had a single commonality amongst them—all rallied upon their ethnic exclusivity while placing their demands. The argument is that it has been an unwavering practice to imagine Assam, so also the entire north-eastern India, as a region crisscrossed by wide ranging ethnic diversity, which are different not only from rest of the country but also amongst themselves.

All the narrative about the region—governmental, sociological, political, anthropological, as also the literary and romantic description about the region stresses on the variance amongst the people. In such an academic and social context where categorization and their consequent politicization are regarded as self explanatory, it is pertinent to ask as to what constitutes these categories. Reviewing the existing literature on Assam, the book identifies a gap between the presumption that the ethnic diversity as pre-given and ethnicity as the most important tool of political mobilization in Assam. It is working on in this gap the book seeks to understand critically the underpinnings that empower ethnicity as the defining feature of socio-cultural and political expression in Assam. The book brings out that the diversity amongst the population is figuratively placed in order to express lack of homogeneity and naturalize hostility. The crucial argument is that the predicament lies not in the presence of diversity but in its discursive narration and representation. We maintain that the ethnic discourse in its present form had emerged during the colonial period as enabled by documenting and cataloguing of the population. In other words, the discursively constructed identity of the colonial times is a quandary that surfaces time and again in the post colonial situations.

The ethnic discourse of Assam has been analyzed by examining the three contemporary assertions in Assam termed as "ethnic"— the Assam movement (1979-1985), the United Liberation Front of Assam (1979-present) and the Bodoland movement (1987- present). Analyzing the six year long Assam movement which had started as a peaceful protest by the people of Assam against the alleged enfranchising of illegal immigrants by the government, we infer from the many debates both within the intelligentsia and the public sphere that any attempt to define an Assamese in Assam percolates to the discursive idea of identity that had emerged during the colonial period. The threat faced by the indigenous people from the "educated Hindu Bengalis", the "hardworking Bengali Muslims" and "the enterprising Marwaris" brought in by the colonial rulers to fulfill the new enterprises initiated by the empire infused a threat amongst the people against "outsiders". Assamese, in the Assam movement, were people living in Assam prior to the onrush of immigrants encouraged by the British rulers. The idea of "greater Assamese nationality" popularized during the Assam movement was sought to encompass the various tribal communities believed to be natural ancient inhabitants of Assam. However, the very idea of ethnic solidarity fragmented till the time the movement culminated with the signing of the Assam Accord, demonstrating that ethnic specificity is the sole defining feature of the socio-cultural and political context of Assam. The argument is that the disintegration of the "greater Assamese nationality" and ethnicization of identities occurred at three sites: the elections, emergence of identity based bodies and the Assam Accord. This study makes it explicit that the intimidating ethnic discourse in Assam preempts the possibility of any other form of identity formation. Besides, the culmination of the movement with the signing of the Assam Accord incited a fresh wave of identity consciousness among the various communities which in turn gave rise to a chain of ethnic upheavals.

The book affirms that ULFA too like the Assam movement sought to evoke a greater identity. The main difference between the two was on the question of identifying itself with the nation as Indians. For the Assam movement the nation was the supreme power to evoke and seek redemption whereas for the ULFA it was the complete rejection of the nation that generated its impetus. The centrality of the issue of Bangladeshi immigrants as the biggest deterring factor against Assam's prosperity shifted to the question of membership of Assam within the Indian nation, as its biggest cause of woe. ULFA gave a violent turn to the long nurtured theory of "Colonial Hinterland" to renounce the validity of the Indian nation to rule Assam and articulated an idea of Assam's population as a sovereign people; corresponding with its status of independence before the British arrived. The ULFA too like the Assam movement was not able to sustain its formulation of a greater identity for the people of Assam and soon it came to be regarded only as an extremist organization of "Upper Caste Assamese". The various communities rejected its demand for secession as for them ULFA was a group of "artificial Assamese" who did not possess the right to decide the future of Assam. ULFA, however, holds significance in the public and intellectual parlance of Assam as it, for the first time was able to show through the stress on economic exploitation that the Indian state had abdicated its responsibility of nation building. The argument is that ULFA provides a specific instance of locating what ethnicity connotes in the context. The "Citizen" Assamese of the Assam movement was a "non-Indian" in ULFA's formulation.

The study of the Bodoland movement (1987-present), a tribal uprising against the alleged hegemony of the Assamese, had consolidated and asserted themselve even before the Independence. Their uprising took a radical turn in the 1980s and reached its peak during the 1990s till the formation of the autonomous Bodoland Territorial Council (BTC) in 2003. The observation of the book is that the Bodos directly conformed to the pre-existing idea about their identity in the process of culling out an identity distinct and a plane more organic than the Assamese with respect to Assam, in two stages, a) Reversing assimilation and b) Eroding of the "greater Assamese nationality".

The "Sons of the Soil" theory propounded by the Assamese was dismissed by the Bodos who termed them as "artificial Assamese" settled in Assam from other parts of the country. The Assamese who were "citizens" in the Assam movement, "non-Indians" in the ULFA were projected as "non-indigenous" in the Bodoland movement. The Bodos in the course of their assertion and to strengthen their claim attempted to forge a consolidated tribal identity comprising of all the tribal groups, believed to be indigenous to Assam, under its fold. However, this consolidated tribal identity also failed to sustain itself and after the Bodoland movement there was a string of similar uprising from tribal groups like the Rabha, Tiwa, Rajbonshi etc demanding exclusive territory like the Bodos. The book explains that the ethnic discourse supplies the communities with the necessary precursor that enables them to articulate their distinctiveness, in a fractional pattern.

Cornell (2002) has argued that autonomy arrangements, by empowering ethnic elites with state like institutions that enhance their leadership capacities and ambitions, by generating greater economic viability of the autonomous territorial entity, and by increasing the prospects for partisan external support, may actually end up promoting a greater sense of separate ethnic identity amongst minority peoples and increase their motivation and capacity to seek secession and independence. Hence, the end result of autonomy arrangements may ironically be more or less conflict. The book suggests that impending ethnic tensions in Assam will not be solved by providing autonomy but a deeper acknowledgment of the disparate imagination of the region is required.

The main inference that we derive analyzing the three movements as well as other ongoing conflicts in Assam is that none of them initiated as ethnic conflict *per se* and the content of ethnicity never remained the same. Examining as to why and how in the three instances the attempts to constitute generic identities failed and the identities were reduced to specific ethnic units, the book explains—that while the presence and acknowledgment of diversity cannot be negated since earlier times, colonialism brought in a new dimension to the existing diversity; one of objectification of the colonized masses. Identities recognized in this form turned into subjects of colonial politics. Colonialism is much more than a temporary overpowering of the home administration. Its appendages grow much deeper and the power it acquires is through the knowledge it generates about the colonized people. Knowledge about the people provides the colonial machineries the power to rule them.

Analysing the modalities by which the British administration converted the masses into colonial subjects, and as to how the categorization and thus objectification of the people were done, the book locates three modalities – Census and Cartography, Anthropological Studies and Administrative Policies and Acts – that accomplished the crystallization of identities. We argue that the form of imagination the people of Assam, so also the entire north-eastern India, initiated by the British has not been altered even after the end of the colonial rule. The main argument is that the processes of categorization of the people, initiated in the colonial period consolidated into creating a knowledge base which formed the basis of control and power of the British. This created a discourse turning the masses into subjects of the knowledge and objectified their identity. This objectification led to the emergence of a discourse—the ethnic discourse which subsequently became the defining actor of the socio-political milieu of the region making it difficult for any other form of identity to emerge. The tensions in the post-colonial times have taken up ethnic dimensions as the only mode of identity formation possible in Assam is ethnic. The imagination of the region even in the post-colonial times and the government attitude of policy making have not altered making it difficult to shed the ethnic mode of identity formation and assertions.

We have tried to show, by tracing a continuum from the colonial times, that ethnic identity needs to be historicized in the framework of state processes and machinery. We have tried to show that it is important to re-read the movements in Assam in their historic specificity and interpret the plural trends that are emerging. We have tried to contextualize the debate on ethnicity by placing it in the historical context of colonialism and political strife in post-colonial Assam and thus produce a discursive field around the issue.

Following Benedict Anderson who writes, the long pre-colonial past in Southeast Asia, in which people were enumerated by the ruling authority and argues that the real innovation of the census-takers of the 1870s was, not the construction of ethnic-racial classifications, but rather in their systematic quantification, we can argue that Assam was also not devoid of population identification before the British colonial times. Just as he states that from 1850, the colonial states imposed an imagined grid that gradually sprouted institutions of bureaucratic governance that, in time gave real social life to the state's earlier fantasies, it is viable to argue that the Ahom monarchy that ruled Assam for six hundred years (1228-1826) in the medieval period had the unique system of writing *buranjis*, which only recorded the political events of the Ahom kingdom but also contain information about the neighbouring and foreign states, matrimonial relations, war and treaty, social customs etc., the names of various officers with the mention of their original tribe and clan, give details of foodstuff given to the foreign envoy, present to and from neighbouring countries and many such details[3]. As Anderson's observation, that the previously fluid indigenous categories hardened, like waffles, around the alien grid, and they maintain a brittle identity even when detached from it.

Unlike the colonial discourse which treats the identities as discreet and wide ranging, the impression that the *buranjis* give is that the Assamese culture was formed and developed into one entity absorbing numerous cultural elements of varied cultural traits. The ancient Kamrupa kingdom under the Ahom rule was on the roads to becoming Assam and people of various ethnic groups mingled together to emerge into one Assamese culture. Synbook was the dominant trait of that culture. The Ahoms had their own religion, culture, language, literature, script, dress and costumes and a distinct way of life which they brought with them. They brought with them some scriptures; they used to talk in Tai and used to discuss political matters in Tai even upto the seventeenth century; they followed a distinctive form of Buddhism mixed with Animism; they wore black clothes like the Buddhist Tai people of today; they performed *caklong*, the Ahom system of matrimonial rituals; they used their own personal definitive of Tai origin; they had no such prohibition or taboo regarding food as among the Hindus. But gradually, they adopted Hinduism and merged into one homogenous culture retaining a few original traditions like marriage, personal definitive. Worshipping of some traditional gods and goddesses got confined to the priestly clans like Mohan, Bailung and Deodhai.

Also, during this period Vaisnava saint Sankaradeva appeared on the scene who gave a form of Assamese culture contributing new and significant things combining pan-Indian trait of Indo-Aryan culture through his neo-Vaisnavite movement. The Vaisnava order founded by Sankaradeva flourished under the patronization of Koch and Ahom kings which enriched Assamese culture. The Ahoms adopted children and persons from different ethnic groups to their own fold and created a unique atmosphere of racial assimilation which enhanced the spirit of amity and integrity. Simultaneously Sankaradeva denounced casteism and called upon all the people to join his *bhakti* movement, which encouraged people of all the tribes to affiliate themselves into one social entity. As such, the *buranjis* projects that Assamese culture developed through mutual process of amity and cultural sharing and assimilation[4].

However, the possibility of absolute refrains from coaxing and coercion by the Ahom rulers in enforcing social and cultural attributes cannot be ruled out. Nevertheless, the treatment of the diversity by the Ahom rulers, as the *buranjis* establish, was that of integration and not exclusion. The British ethnic discourse when juxtaposed with the *buranjis* underscores that whereas the *buranjis* fostered multicultural existence, the colonial discourse positioned the diversity in a manner that facilitated disjunction which was subsequently replicated in the political and social ambit enforced by the British rule. We agree with what Sumit Guha expresses as the crystallization of this "culture" was the highlight of the imperial rule and has been inherited by independent India. (Guha 2003)

The main arguments of the present study are—the different tensions in Assam arose for varied reasons: Assam movement was an attempt of the people of Assam to secure political and economic privilege against the onslaught of unchecked immigration, the ULFA was reciprocatory or a counter campaign against the lack of social integration of the people of Assam with rest of India and the Bodoland movement was an attempt of the indigenous people to safeguard their rights over the land and resources. Likewise, the sporadic tensions erupting in Assam have their discreet rationale. The reason why they get engulfed ethnic bearings is because the prevalent conditionality facilitates no other, but, only ethnic vocabulary of expression in the case of Assam. This vocabulary, the book argues, have been derived from the colonial lexicon, which is still being replicated by the post-colonial India. The book seeks to affirm that the tensions of contemporary world call for an abounding epistemological understanding instead of the current practice of unreflectively categorizing them under "ethnic tensions".

Reference

1. The India-Bangladesh enclaves were the enclaves along the Bangladesh-India border, in Bangladesh and the Indian states of West Bengal, Tripura, Assam and Meghalaya. The original deal between the two nations was signed in 1974, The Indira Gandhi -Sheikh Mujib Land Boundary agreement. Both countries agreed to exchange the enclaves of land. India even agreed to forgo compensation for land that would be transferred to Bangladesh. there are 111 Indian enclaves in Bangladesh spread over 17,000 acres and 51 Bangladesh enclaves in India spread over 7,110 acres. The decision to approve the Constitution (119th Amendment Bill), 2013, on the land boundary agreement was taken at a cabinet meeting chaired by Prime Minister Narendra Modi. A revised version of the agreement was adopted by the two countries on 7 May 2015, when the Parliament of India passed the 100th Amendment to the Indian Constitution. India is expected to lose 40 sq. km under the agreement. But the move is expected to finally resolves a procedural complication. Modi, during the rally in Assam where he promised to enforce the agreement, said that it will end illegal migration from Bangladesh into India, " Believe in my word that land swapping deal will be done for a permanent solution to this problem of Assam," Modi said handing over of land (to Bangladesh) will be done only to ensure security of people of Assam and the border and not for "any harm" to the state. A joint census in 2010 found 51,549 people residing in these enclaves: 37,334 in Indian enclaves within Bangladesh and 14,215 in Bangladeshi enclaves within India. The land swap is largely viewed as procedural, as most of the people within the enclaves would prefer staying in

present location and shifting of people across borders is expected to be minimal. (http://indianexpress.com/article/india/india-others/explained-land-swap-in-offing/) retrieved 25 October 2015.

2. On 3rd August 2015 leaders from the Nationalist Socialist Council of Nagalim (NSCN) (Isak-Muivah) (IM) and Government of India representatives met in New Delhi. The details of the meeting are yet to be written, yet the "Framework Agreement" is raising large anxiety over its socio-politico implications. (Kikon 2015:10).

3. The *buranji*, is a genre of writing, a distinct form of literature, is an outstanding contribution of the Ahoms, a branch of the great Tai race, who founded the Ahom kingdom in the Brahmaputra valley and ruled over the country for long six hundred years (1228-1826). The tradition of Buranji writing and its preservation was brought by them along with their migration from Mao-lung, a Tai kingdom of upper Burma; earlier to that from Mung-ri-Mung-ram, a territory of Chinese province, Yunnan. Even though linguistically they belong to the Siamese Chinese family, in their new settlement in Assam, they adopted Assamese as their working language which was not effected by series of foreigners' invasion during long six hundred years. The Ahom enriched Assamese literature with their solid contribution of buranjis as compiled by the royal historiographer and other elite nobles. The Sattras, a centre of Vaisnava culture and religion also preserve their historical accounts systematically and regularly. (Gogoi 1986:ix).

   Some well know *buranjis* are: Assam *Buranji*, Asamar, Padya *Buranji* (*Buranji* of Assam in verse) Ahom *Buranji*, Changrung Phukanar *Buranji* (Architect and public work), Deodhai Asam *Buranji* (compilation of old chronicles which contains details about political relations of the Ahoms with Chutiya, Burmese, Kacharis, Jayantiyas).

   Padshah *Buranji* (Buranji containing relationship of Ahom with the Moghuls), Purani Assam Buranji (ancient Assam Buranji), Satasari Assam Buranji (gives an account of the Ahom dynasty from the time of king Kamaleswar Singha to king Purandar Singha), Tungkhungia Buranji (account of Tungkhungia dynasty of Ahom sovereign), Tripura *Buranji* (account of neighbouring kingdom Tripura).

4. Medieval historian of Assam Lila Gogoi writes about the mention and interaction of diversity in the *buranji* as such, "It is evident from the sources of *buranjis* that the Ahom subdued the Morans and the Barans and the Barahis and established the capital at Charaideu where the Barahis worshipped their god. They appointed immediately some Morans and Barahis to assist the Ahoms in administration and they married girls from both the tribes. They also came into contact with two other local tribes the Kacharis and the Chutiyas. In course of time their kingdoms were merged into Ahom kingdom. People were allowed to settle in the Ahom jurisdiction and they were also provided with royal responsibilities. The artisans captured in the Chutiya kingdom were employed under the Ahom administration and provided due status in *khels* and *mela.* Suhungmung, the Dihinguya Raja (1497-1539) expanded the boundary of his kingdom from the Patkai ranges to the river Karatoya on the west. He had a conflict with the Bhuyans and later on annexed the principalities adopting number of cultural elements from the Bhuyans". (Gogoi 1986: 246) .

Annexures

Annexure - I

ASSAM ACCORD, 1985

1. Government have all along been most anxious to find a satisfactory solution to the problem of foreigners in Assam. The All Assam Students Union (AASU) and the All Assam Gana Sangram Parished (AAGSP) have also expressed their keenness to find such a solution.
2. The AASU through their Memorandum dated 2 nd February 1980 presented to the late Prime Minister Smt. Indira Gandhi, conveyed their profound sense of apprehensions regarding the continuing influx of foreign nationals into Assam and the fear about adverse effects upon the political, social, culture and economic life of the State.
3. Being fully alive to the genuine apprehensions of the people of Assam, the then Prime Minister initiated the dialogue with the AASU/ AAGSP. Subsequently, talks were held at the Prime Minister's and Home Minister's level during the period 1980-83. Several rounds of informal talks were held during 1984. Formal discussions were resumed in March, 1985.
4. Keeping all aspects of the problem including constitutional and legal provisions, international agreements, national commitments and humanitarian considerations, it has been decided to proceed as follows:

Foreigners Issue

5.1 For purposes of detection and deletion of foreigners, 1.1.1966 shall be the base data and year.

5.2 All persons who come to Assam prior to 1.1.1966, including those amongst them whose names appeared on the electoral rolls used in 1967 elections shall be regularised.

5.3 Foreigners who came to Assam after 1.1.1966 (inclusive) and upto 24th March, 1971 shall be detected in accordance with the provisions of the Foreigners Act, 1946 and the Foreigners (Tribunals) Order 1964.

5.4 Names of foreigners so detected will be deleted from the electoral rolls in force. Such persons will be required to register themselves before the Registration Officers of the respective districts in accordance with the provisions of the Registration of Foreigners Act, 1939 and the Registration of Foreigners Rules, 1939.

5.5 For this purpose, Government of India will undertake suitable strengthening of the government machinery.

5.6 On the expiry of a period of ten years following the date of detection, the names of all such persons which have been deleted from the electoral rools shall be restored.

5.7 All persons who were expelled earlier, but have since reentered illegally into Assam shall be expelled.

5.8 Foreigners who came to Assam on or after March 25, 1971 shall continue to be detected, deleted and practical steps shall be taken to expel such foreigners.

5.9 The Government will give due consideration to certain difficulties expressed by the AASU/AAGSP regarding the implementation of the Illegal Migrants (Determination by Tribunals) Act, 1983.

Safeguards and Economic Development

6. Constitutional, legislative and administrative safeguards, as may be appropriate shall be provided to protect, preserve and promote the culture, social, linguistic identity and heritage of the Assamese people.

7. The Government take this opportunity to renew their commitment for the speedy all round economic development of Assam, so as to improve the standard of living of the people. Special emphasis will be placed on education and science and technology through establishment of national institutions.

Other Issues

8.1 The Government will arrange for the issue of citizenship certificates in future only by the authorities of the Central Government.

8.2 Specific complaints that may be made by the AASU/AAGSP about irregular issuance of Indian Citizenship Certificates (ICC) will be looked into.

9. The international border shall be made secure against future infiltration by erection of physical barriers like walls, barbed wire fencing and other obstacles at appropriate places. Patrolling by security forces on land and rivering routes all along the international border shall be adequately intensified. In order to further strengthen the security arrangements, to prevent effectively future infiltration, an adequate number of check posts shall be set up.

9.2 Besides the arrangements mentioned above and keeping in view security considerations, a road all along the international border shall be constructed as to facilitate patrolling by security forces. Land between border and the road would be kept free of human habitation, wherever possible. Riverine patrolling along the international border would be intensified. All effective measures would be adopted to prevent infiltrators crossing or attempting to cross the international border.

10. It will be ensured that relevant laws for prevention of encroachment of government lands in tribal belts and blocks are strictly enforced and unauthorized encroachers evicted as laid down under such laws.

11. It will be ensured that the relevant law restricting acquisition of immovable property by foreigners in Assam is strictly enforced.

12. It will be ensured that Birth and Death Registers are duly maintained.

Restoration of Normalcy

13. The All Assam Students Union (AASU) and the all Assam Gana Sangram Parishad (AAGSP) call off the agitation, assure full co-operation and dedicate themselves towards the development of the country.

14. The Central and the State Government have agreed to:

    Review with sympathy and withdraw cases of disciplinary action taken against employees in the context of the agitation and to ensure that there is no victimization;

    Frame a scheme for ex-gratia payment to next of kin of those who were killed in the course of the agitation;

    Give sympathetic consideration to proposal for relaxation of upper age limit for employment in public services in Assam, having regard to exceptional situation that prevailed in holding of academic and competitive examinations, etc., in the context of agitation in Assam;

Undertake review of detention cases, if any, as well as cases against persons charged with criminal offences in connection with the agitation, except those charged with commission of heinous offences;

Consider withdrawal of the prohibitory orders/ notifications in force, if any.

15. The Ministry of Home Affairs will be the nodal Ministry for the implementation of the above.

Signed/-

(P.K. Mahanta)
President
All Assam Students Union

Signed/-

(R.D. Pradhan)
Home Secretary
Govt. of India

Signed/-

(B.K. Phukan)
General Secretary
All Assam Students Union

Signed/-

(Smt. P.P. Trivedi)
Chief Secretary
Govt. of India

Signed/-

(Biraj Sharma)
Convenor
All Assam Gana Sangram Parishad

In the presence of

Signed/-

(Rajiv Gandhi)
Prime Minister of India

Date : 15 th August, 1985

Place: New Delhi

Election Commission will be requested to ensure preparation of fair electoral rolls.

Time for submission of claims and objections will be extended by 30 days, subject to this being consistent with the Election rules.

The Election Commission will be requested to send Central Observers.

Signed/-

Home Secretary

Oil refinery will be established in Assam.

Central Government will render full assistance to the State Government in their efforts to re-open:

Ashok Paper Mill.

Jute Mills

I.I.T. will be set-up in Assam.

(http://cdpsindia.org/assam_accord.asp)

Annexure - II

The questionnaires since the inception of Census in India to the recent years are as follows. The categories for inferring affiliation to ethnicity have remained continuous.

1872: House Register

1. Number of houses, whether terraced, tiled or thatched
2. Name of Males
3. Agc
4. Religion
5. Caste or Class
6. Race or Nationality or Country of Birth
7. Occupation
8. Youths upto age 20 attending school, college or under private tuition
9. Able to read and write
10. Name or Designation of Females
11. Age
12. Religion
13. Caste or Class
14. Race or Nationality or Country of Birth

15. Youths upto age 20 attending school, college or under private tuition
16. Able to read and write
17. Remarks showing number of males and females, blind, deaf, dumb, insane, idiots or lepers

1881: Census Schedule

1. Serial No. of each inmate
2. Name
3. Condition i.e. whether married, unmarried, widow or widower
4. Sex
5. Age last birthday
6. Religion
7. Religion
8. Caste, if Hindu, sect, if of other religion
9. Mother tongue
10. Place of birth
11. Occupation of men; also of boys and females who may do work
12. Education
    i. Under instruction
    ii. Not under instruction but able to read and write
    iii. Not under instruction and not able to read and write
13. Infirmities
    i. Unsound mind
    ii. Deaf-mutes from birth
    iii. Blind
    iv. Lepers

1891: Census Schedule

1. Serial no. and name
2. Main religion
3. Sect of religion
4. Caste or race-Main caste & c
5. Sub-division of caste or race
6. Male or female
7. Age
8. Married, single, or widowed

9. Parent tongue
10. Birth district or country
11. Occupation or means of subsistence
12. Learning, Knowing, Illiterate
13. Foreign language known (if any)
14. If any, be blind, insane, deaf-mute or a leper, enter the infirmity below

1901: Census Schedule

1. House number
2. Serial number
3. Name
4. Religion
5. Male or female
6. Married, Unmarried or widowed
7. Age
8. Caste of Hindus & Jains, Tribe, or race of others
9. Occupation or means of subsistence of actual workers: Principal
10. Occupation or means of subsistence of actual workers: Subsidiary
11. Means of subsistence of dependants on actual workers
12. Birth place
13. Language ordinarily used
14. Literate or Illiterate
15. Know or does not know English
16. Insane, deaf-mute from birth, totally blind or leper

1911: Census Schedule

1. Census number painted on the house
2. Serial number of persons enumerated
3. Name
4. Religion (and sect of Christians)
5. Male or Female
6. Married, Unmarried or Widowed
7. Age completed last birthday
8. Caste of Hindu and Jains, tribe or race of those of other religions
9. Occupation or means of subsistence of actual workers : Principal Occupation
10. Occupation or means of subsistence of actual workers : Subsidiary Occupation, if any
11. If dependant, principal occupation or means of subsistence of actual worker on whom dependent

12. District, Province or Country in which born
13. Language ordinarily spoken in the household
14. Literate or Illiterate
15. Whether literate in English
16. If the person be insane or totally blind or suffering from corrosive leprosy or both deaf and dumb from birth, enter as such here

1921: Census Schedule

1. House No.
2. Serial number of person
3. Name
4. Religion
5. Male or Female
6. Married, Unmarried or Widowed
7. Age
8. Caste, Tribe or Race
9. Occupation or means of subsistence of actual workers : Principal
10. Occupation or means of subsistence of actual workers : Subsidiary
11. For dependants, the occupation of the worker by whom supported
12. Birth district
13. Language ordinarily used
14. Literate or Illiterate
15. Whether literate in English
16. Insane, totally blind, leper or deaf-mute

1931: Census Schedule

1. Serial No. of house or tenement
2. Serial No. of person
3. Name
4. Religion and Sect
5. Male or Female (enter M or F)
6. Married, Unmarried, or Widowed (enter Divorced persons as widowed)
7. Age (in years to nearest birthday)
8. Race, Tribe or Caste
9. Earner or dependant
10. Principal occupation (this will be blank for dependant)
11. Subsidiary occupation (occupation of dependants may be given)
12. Industry in which employed (for organized employees only)
13. Birth district (or country)
14. Mother tongue

15. Other language in common use
16. Whether literate (i.e., able to write and read a letter)
17. Whether able to read and write English
18. Insane, totally blind, deaf-mute or leper

1941: Individual Slip

1. Name
2. Sex
3. Race, Tribe or Caste
4. Religion
5. Married, unmarried, widowed or divorced
6. Age
7. Number of children born to a married woman and number surviving
8. Her age at birth of first child
9. Are you wholly or partly dependent on any one else?
10. If so, means of livelihood of person on whom dependent
11. Do you employ
    (a) paid assistants
    (b) members of household?
    If so, how many?
12. Are you in employment now?
    (Only to those who reply in the negative to question 12)
13. Are you in search of employment?
    (To those who reply in the affirmative the further question will be put)
    How long have you been in search of it?
14. Means of livelihood in order of importance
15. (Only to be asked in regard to means of livelihood of a person shown as partly dependent against question 9 or any subsidiary means of livelihood returned by other persons against question 14).
    Does this mean of livelihood exist throughout the year?
    If not, for what part of the year?
16. If you are employed by some one else, what is his business?
17. Were you born in this district? If not, in what district
18. Mother tongue
19. Other Indian languages in common use
20. Can you both read and write? If so, what script do you write?
    Can you only read?
21. How far have you read? Give any examination passed.
22. Are you literate in English?

1951: Individual Slip

1. Name and relationship to the head of the household
2. Nationality, Religion and Special Group
   Part (a) Nationality
   Part (b) Religion
   Part (c) Special Groups
3. Civil condition
4. Age
5. Birth place
6. Displaced persons
7. Mother tongue
8. Bilingualism
9. Economic Status
   Part one: Dependency
   Part two: Employment
10. Principal means of livelihood
11. Secondary means of livelihood
12. Literacy and Education
13. ....(Optional to State Government)*
14. Sex

Note: (a) Name of States: Assam, Manipur & Tripura; Bihar; Bombay,

   a. Saurashtra & Kutch; Madhya Pradesh; Vindhya Pradesh; Mysore;
   b. Orissa; Punjab, PEPSU, Bilaspur, Delhi & Himachal Pradesh;
   c. Rajasthan & Ajmer; Uttar Pradesh; West Bengal & Sikkim;
   d. Hyderabad; Travancore-Cochin

(b) NATURE OF QUESTION NO. 13 OF 1951 CENSUS
   e. (OPTIONAL)

1. Indigenous Persons:
   (a) Are you an indigenous person of Assam?
   (b) If so, state in the nearest bigha,
      (i) the land you own;
      (ii) the land you have rented in cash or in kind from others
2. Fertility
3. Unemployment
4. Number of children born to a married woman and age at birth of the first child
5. Unemployment
6. Unemployment

7. Area of land owned and cultivated by the household
8. Are you unemployed since 9th Feb. 1951? If so, give reason
9. Infirmities
10. Unemployment
11. Do you cultivate land for which you pay rent? If so,
    (a) how much do you cultivate yourself and or through hired labourers; and
    (b) how much do you cultivate through bargadars, bhagdar or adhiyars?
12. Are you unemployed and in search of employment? If so, since when?
13. Duration of marriage and size of family
    (a) Completed years of married life
    (b) Age of mother at first maternity
    (c) Number of children born
    (d) Number now alive

1961: Individual Slip

1. (a) Name
   (b) Relationship to Head
2. Age last birthday
3. Marital Status
4. (a) Birth place
   (b) Born R/U
   (c) Duration of residence, if born elsewhere
5. (a) Nationality
   (b) Religion
   (c) S.C./S.T.
6. Literacy & Education
7. (a) Mother tongue
   (b) Any other language(s)
8. Working as Cultivator
9. Working as Agricultural Labourer
10. Working at Household Industry
    (a) Nature of work
    (b) Nature of Household Industry
    (c) If Employee

11. Doing work other than 8, 9 or 10
    - (a) Nature of work
    - (b) Nature of Industry, Profession, Trade and Service
    - (c) Class of worker
    - (d) Name of Establishment
12. Activity, if not working
13. Sex

1971: Individual Slip

1. Name
2. Relationship to head
3. Sex
4. Age
5. Marital Status
6. For currently married women only
    - (a) Age at marriage
    - (b) Any child born in the last one year
7. BIRTH PLACE
    - (a) Place of birth
    - (b) Rural/Urban
    - (c) District
    - (d) State/Country
8. LAST RESIDENCE
    - (a) Place of last residence
    - (b) Rural/Urban
    - (c) District
    - (d) State/Country
9. Duration of Residence at the village or town of enumeration
10. Religion
11. S.C. or S.T.
12. Literacy (L or O)
13. Educational level
14. Mother tongue
15. Other languages

16. MAIN ACTIVITY
    - (a) Broad category
        - (i) Worker (C, AL, HHI, OW)
        - (ii) Non-worker (H, S, T, R, D, B, I, O)
    - (b) Place of work (Name of Village/Town)
    - (c) Name of Establishment
    - (d) Nature of Industry, Trade, Profession or Service
    - (e) Description of Work
    - (f) Class of worker
17. SECONDARY WORK
    - (a) Broad Category (C, AL, HHI, OW)
    - (b) Place of work (Name of Village/Town)
    - (c) Name of Establishment
    - (d) Nature of Industry, Trade, Profession or Service
    - (e) Description of Work
    - (f) Class of Worker

(http://censusindia.gov.in/Data_Products/Library/Indian _perceptive _link/Census_Questionaires_link/questions.htm).

Bibliography

"Assam: Towards a Consensus". *Economic and Political Weekly*. Editorial Issue. Vol. 37, No. 41. October 12, 2002. pg. 4173

"Consultation Findings". *Religion and Society*. Vol. 9, No. 4. Bangalore. Christian Institute for the Study of Religion and Society. 2011. pg. 80.

"Divide Assam Fifty-Fifty". All Bodo Students' Union. Kokrajhar, Assam. August 23, 1987.

Abdi, S.N.M. "India, Burma Rebels Work on Breakaway Plan". *Illustrated Weekly of India*, Supplement. December 15-16, 1990. pg. 1.

Acharyya, N.N. *Assam and Neighbouring States Historical Documents*. New Delhi. Omsons Publications. 1983.

___. *The History of Medieval Assam: From the Thirteenth to the Seventeenth Century*. New Delhi. Omsons. 1992.

Ahmed, Abu Nasar, Joydeep Baruah and Bhuyan Ratna. *Election Politics in Assam: Issues, Trends and People's Mandate*. New Delhi. Akansha Publishing House. 2006.

Akhup, Alex. *Identities and their Struggles in North East*. New Delhi. Adivaani. 2015.

Aloysius, G. *Nationalism without a Nation in India*. Delhi. Oxford University Press. 1998.

Anderson, Benedict. *Imagined Community Reflection on the Origin and the Spread of Nationalism*. New York. Verso. 1991.

Appadurai, Arjun. *Modernity at Large: Cultural Dimensions of Globalization*. New Delhi. Oxford University Press. 1997.

Asad, Talal. *The Kababish Arabs*. London. C. Hurst. 1970

Assam Accord. Memorandum of Settlement. August 15, 1985.

Barkakati, S. *Tribes of Assam*. New Delhi. National Book Trust. 1969.

Barkataki, S.N. *Tribal Folktales of Assam (Hills)*. Gauhati. Publication Board. 1970.

Barpujari, H.K. (ed.) *The Comprehensive History of Assam*. Vol. 1. Ancient Period. Guwahati. Publication Board Assam. 1990.

Barpujari, H.K. *Assam: In the Days of the Company 1826-1858*. Gauhati. Lawyer's Book Stall. 1963.

___. *Political History of Assam*. Guwahati. Government of Assam. 1977.

Barth, Fredrik. *Ethnic Groups and Boundaries*. Boston. Little, Brown, and Co.1969

Barua, Birinchi Kumar. *A Cultural History of Assam*. Gauhati. Lawyer's Book Stall. 1969.

Barua, Hem. *The Red River and the Blue Hills*. Guwahati. Lawyer's Book Stall. 1954.

Barua, Rai Sahib Golap Chandra. *Ahom-Buranji*. Guwahati. Spectrum Publication. 1985.

Barua, Sandhya. "Language Problem in Assam". *Social Scientist*. Vol. 6, No. 12. July 1978. pp. 66-74.

Baruah, Apurba K. "Middle Class Hegemony and the National Question in Assam". Sangma, Milton (ed.). *Essays on North-East India*. New Delhi. Indus Publishing House. 1994.

Baruah, S.L. *A Comprehensive History of Assam*. Guwahati. Munshiram Manoharlal Publishers. 1985.

Baruah, Sanjib. "The State and Separatist Militancy in Assam: Winning a Battle and Losing the War". *Asian Survey*. Vol. 34, No. 10. October 1994. pp. 863-877.

___. *India Against Itself: Assam and the Politics of Nationality*. New Delhi. Oxford University Press. 1999.

___. "The Rise and Decline of a Separatist Insurgency: Contentious Politics in Assam". Ganguly, Rajat (ed.). *Autonomy and Ethnic Conflict in South and South-East Asia*. New York. Routledge. 2012.

Basu, Amrita; Kohli, Atul. *Community Conflicts and the State in India*. New Delhi. Oxford University Press. 1998.

Basu, Durga Das. *Constitutional Law of India*. New Delhi. Printice Hall. 1998.

Basu, Nirmal Kumar. *Assam in the Ahom Age 1228-1826*. Calcutta. Sanskrit Pustak Bhandar.1970.

Bhabha, Homi. K (ed.). *Nation and Narration*. New York. Routledge. 1990.

Bhadra, R.K. and Bhadra, Mita. *Ethnicity, Movement and Social Structure Contested Cultural Identity*. Jaipur. Rawat Publication. 2007.

Bhargava, Rajeev, Amiya Kumar Bagchi, Sudarshan R (eds.). *Multi-culturalism,Liberalism and Democracy*. New Delhi. Oxford University Press. 1999.

Bhattacharjee, Arun. *Assam in Indian Independence*. New Delhi. Mittal Publications. 1993.

Bhattacharjee, Chandana. *Ethnicity and Autonomy Movement: Case of Bodo Kacharis of Assam*. New Delhi. Vikas Publishing House Pvt. Ltd. 1996.

Bhattacharyya, Birendra Kumar. "The Assamese Mind". Saikia, Nagen (ed). *Assam and the Assamese Mind*. Jorhat. Assam Sahitya Sabha. 1980.

Bhaumik, Subir. *Troubled Periphery Crisis of India's North East*. New Delhi. Sage Publication. 2009.

Bhuyan, Arun Chandra and De, Sibopada. *Political History of Assam*. Guwahati. Publication Board of Assam. 1999.

Bhuyan, S.K. (ed.). *An Account of Assam Compiled by Francis Hamilton in 1807-1814*. Gauhati. Department of Historical and Antiquarian Studies. 1963.

Bidwai, Praful. "ULFA: Assam's Irrational Syndrome". *Sunday Times of India*. December 23, 1990.

Bonacich, E. "A Theory of Ethnic Antagonism: The Spilt Labor Market". *American Sociology Review*. Vol. 37. 1972. pp. 547-549.

Bora, Shiela. *Student Revolution in Assam 1917-1947*. New Delhi. Mittal Publication. 1992.

Borbora, Arup. *Comprehensive Note on Armed Conflict in Assam (India) and Political Resolution through Peace Process*. OHCR, UNOG Geneva. 9th Session, Human Rights Council. September8-26, 2008.

Bordoloi, B.N. *The Dimasa Kacharis of Assam*. Guwahati. Tribal Research Institute. 1984.

Boruah, Kaustavmoni. "Foreigners" in Assam and Assamese Middle Class". *Social Scientist*. Vol. 8, No. 11. June 1980. pp. 44-57.

Brass, Paul R. *Ethnicity and Nationalism: Theory and Comparison*. New Delhi. Sage Publication. 1991.

Brass, Paul R. *The Politics of India since Independence*. New Delhi. Cambridge University Press. 1990.

Buchanan, Francis Hamilton. *An Account of Assam*. Government of Assam Department of Historical and Antiquarian Studies. Gauhati. 1963.

Butler, Major John. *Travels and Adventures in the Province of Assam.* Delhi. Vivek publishing company.First published 1855. Reprinted 1978.

Calhoun, Craig. "Nationalism and Ethnicity." *Annual Review of Sociology.* Vol. 19. 1993. pp. 211-239.

Census of India 1931. Vol 1- India. Part 3. Ethnographical. Simla. Government of India Press. 1935.

Census of India, 1961. Volume 15, Part 10. Office of the Registrar General Publisher. Manager of Publications. 1965.

Chakrabarty, Dipesh. "Modernity and Ethnicity in India: A History for the Present". *Economic and Political Weekly.* Vol. 30, No. 52. December 30, 1995. pp. 3373-3380.

Chakrabarty, Saroj. "How Dr. B.C. Roy Solved the 1960 Assam Crisis". *Sunday.* July 12, 1981.

Chakrabarty, Saroj. *The Upheaval Years in North-East India, 1960-1983.* Calcutta. 1984.

Chakraborty, Amalendu Kishore. "The Quest for Identity: The Tribal Solidarity Movement in North-East India 1947-69". Kolkata. The Asiatic Society. 2004.

Chakravarti, B. "Cultural History of the North-East India (Assam)". *The Himalayan People and Culture Series.* Volume V. Calcutta. Self Employment Bureau Publications. 2000.

Charles, Hirschman. "The Meaning and Measurement of Ethnicity in Malaysia: An Analysis of census Classifications." *The Journal of Asian Studies.* Vol. 46. No. 3. 1987. pp. 555-582.

Chandra, Bipan. *India after Independence.* New Delhi. Viking. 1999.

Chandra, Sudhir. "Regional Consciousness in 19th Century India: A Preliminary Note". *Economic and Political Weekly.* Vol. 17. No. 32. August 7, 1982. pp. 1278-1284.

Chapman, Malcolm (ed.). *History and Ethnicity.* London. Routledge. 1989.

Chatterjee, Partha (ed.). *State and Politics In India.* New Delhi. Oxford University Press. 1997.

Chatterjee, Partha.*The Omnibus, Comprises Nationalist Thought And TheColonial World; The Nation and Its, Fragments and Possible India.* New Delhi. Oxford University Press. 1999.

Chatterji, Suniti Kumar. *The Place of Assam in the History and Civilization of India.*Gauhati. Gauhati University. 1955.

Chaube, S. *Hill Politics of North-East India*. New Delhi. Orient Longman. 1973.

Chaudhury, S. "Assam: Genesis of the Present Ethnic Crisis". *Janata*. Bombay. January 27, 1991.

Chhabra, K.M.L. *Assam Challenge*. New Delhi. Konark Publishers Pvt. Ltd. 1992.

Chottopadhyay, Dilip Kumar. *History of the Assamese Movement since 1947*. Guwahati. Minerva Associate Publications. 1988.

Choudhuri, Sujit. "Election Commission and the Assam Accord". *Economic and Political Weekly*. Vol. 20, No. 49. December 7, 1985. pp. 2146-2147.

Choudhury, Srimati Bijaya Laxmi Brohmo. *Bodo (Kacharis) at a Glance*. Bongaigaon. Modern Offset Printers. 1993.

Cohen, Abner. *The Politics of Elite Culture*. University of California Press. Berkeley. 1981.

Cohn, Bernard. *Colonialism and its Forms of Knowledge the British in India*. New Jersey. Princeton University Press. 1996.

___. "The Census, Social Structure and Objectification in South Asia". *An Anthropologist among the Historians and Other Essays*. Delhi. Oxford University Press. 1987.

Colson, Elizabeth. "Contemporary Tribes and the Development of Nationalism". June, Helm (ed.) *Essays on the Problem of the Tribe*. Seattle. University of Washington Press. 1968.

Corbridge, Stuart. "Hindu Nationalism and the Mythologies of Governance in Modern India". Smith, Graham (ed). *Federalism: the Multiethnic Challenge*. London, New York. Longman. 1995.

Cornell, Svante E. "Autonomy as a Source of Conflict: Caucasian Conflicts in Theoretical Perspective." *World Politics*. Vol. 54, No, 2 (January). 2002. pp. 245-76.

Cronin, Richard Paul. *British Policy and Administration in Bengal, 1905-1912: Partition and the New Province of Eastern Bengal and Assam*. Calcutta. Firma KLM Private Ltd. 1977.

Das, B.M. *The People of Assam*. New Delhi. Gian Publishing House. 1987.

Das, Farida Ahmed and Barua Indira. *Communities of North-East India: an Anthropological Perspective*. New Delhi. Mittal Publications. 1996.

Das, Gautam. *Insurgencies in North-East India: Moving Towards Resolution*. New Delhi. Pentagon Press. 2013.

Das, N.K. *Ethnic Identity Ethnicity and Social Stratification in North-East India*. Inter- India Publications. New Delhi. 1989.

Dasgupta, Anindita. "Civilians and Localization of Conflicts in Assam". *Economic and Political Weekly*. Vol. 36, No. 1. October 2, 2004. pp. 59-65.

Dasgupta, Jyotindra. "Ethnicity, Democracy, and Development in India: Assam in a General Perspective". Atul Kohli (ed.). *India's Democracy*. New Delhi. Orient Longman. 1991.

Dass, Susanta Krishna. "Immigration and Demographic Transformation of Assam, 1891-1981". *Economic and Political Weekly*. Special Article. Vol. 15, No. 19 May 10, 1980. pp. 850-859.

Data, P.S. *Ethnic Movements in Poly Cultural Assam*. New Delhi. Har-Anand Publications in Association with Vikas Publishing House Pvt. Ltd. 1990.

Data-Ray, Basudeb. *Assam Secretariat 1874-1947. An Administrative History of North-East India*. Calcutta. K. P. Bagchi and Company. 1978.

Datta, P.S. (ed.) *Ethnic Movement in Poly-Cultural Assam*. New Delhi. Vikas. 1990.

De Vos, George A and Romanucci-Ross, Lola (eds.). *Ethnic Identity: Cultural Continuities and Change*. Chicago. The University of Chicago Press. 1982.

Despres, L. "Towards a Theory of Ethnic Phenomenon". Despres, L. (ed.). *Ethnicity and Resource Competition*. The Hague. Mouton Publishers. 1975.

Deutsch, K. *Nationalism and Social Communication*. Cambridge. MIT Press. 1953.

Devi, Lakshmi Devi. *Ahom-Tribal Relation (A Political Study)*. Guwahati. Lawyer's Book Stall. 1968.

Dhareshwar, Vivek. "Valorizing the Present". *Cultural Dynamism*. Vol. 10, No. 2. 1998.

Dirks, Nicholas B. "Caste of Mind". *Representations*. Special Issue: Imperial Fantasies and Postcolonial Histories. No. 37. 1992. pp. 56-78

___. *Castes of Mind: Colonialism and the Making of Modern India*. New Delhi. Permanent Black. 2001.

___. *The Hollow Crown: Ethnohistory of an Indian Kingdom*. Cambridge. Cambridge University Press. 1987.

Dommen, Arthur J. "Separatist Tendencies in Eastern India". *Asian Survey*. Vol. 7, No. 10. October 1967. pp. 726-739.

Dreyfuss, H; Rabinow, P and Foucault, M. *Michel Foucault. Beyond structuralism and hermeneutics* (2nd edition). Chicago. University of Chicago Press.

Dubey, S.M. (ed.) *Assamese Society in the Early British Period A Sociological Study*. Delhi. Concept Publishing Company. 1978.

Dunbar, G. *Other Men's Lives*. London. 1938. pp. 230-231.

Dutta, K.N. *Landmarks of Freedom Struggle in Assam*. Guwahati. Lawyers Book Stall. 1969.

Edward Albert Gait. *A History of Assam*. Calcutta. Thacker, Spink& Co.1926.

Eller, Jack and Coughlan. "The Poverty of Primordialism: The Demystification of Ethnic Attachments". *Ethnic and Racial Studies*. Vol. 16, No. 2. 1993.

Encyclopedia Britannica. Volume 21. Macropaedia. 15thedition. Encyclopedia Britannica Inc. Chicago. 1990.

Endle, Sidney. *The Kachari*. London. MacMillan and Co., Ltd. 1911.

Engineer, Asagharali. *Communal riots in Post-Independence India*. Hyderabad. Sangam Press. 1984.

Eriksen, Thomas. *Ethnicity and Nationalism*. London. Pluto Press. 1993.

Fearon James D. and David D. Laitin. "Ethnicity, Insurgency, and Civil War". *American Political Science Review*. Vol. 97, No. 1. 2003. pp. 75-90.

Fernandes, Walter. "IMDT Act and Immigration in North-Eastern India". *Economic and Political Weekly*. Vol. 40, No. 30. 2005. pp. 3237-3240.

Fishman, Joshua A. *Language and Ethnicity in Minority Sociolinguistic Perspective*. Clevedon: Multilingual Matters Ltd. 1989.

Foucault, Michel. *The Archaeology of Knowledge and the Discourse of Language*. Smith, A.M. Sheridan (Trans.). New York. Pantheon Books. 1972.

___. "Politics and the Study of Discourse". Burchell Graham, Gordon, Colin and Miller Peter (eds.). *The Foucault Effect: Studies in Governmentality. Chicago. University of Chicago Press. 1991. pp. 53-72.*

Fuchs, Stephen. *The Aboriginal Tribes of India*. New Delhi. Macmillan India. 1973.

Gait, Edward. *A History of Assam*. Guwahati. LBS Publications. 2005. (first published 1905).

Ganguly, Rajat. *Autonomy and Ethnic Conflict in South and South-East Asia.* New York. Routledge. 2012.

Gans, Chaims. *The Limits of Nationalism*. Cambridge. Cambridge University Press. 2003.

Gellner, Ernest. *Nations and Nationalism.* Ithaca, New York. Cornell University Press. 1983.

___. "Scale and Nation". *Philos. Soc. Sci.* Vol 3. 1973. pp. 1-17.

George, Sudhir Jacob. "The Bodo Movement in Assam: Unrest to Accord". *Asian Survey*. Vol.34, No. 10. October 1994. pg. 880.

Ghai, Yash (ed.). *Autonomy and Ethnicity Negotiating Competing Claims in Multi-ethnic States*. Cambridge United Kingdom. Cambridge University Press. 2000.

Glazer, N. and D. Moyniban. (eds.). *Ethnicity: Theory and Experience.* Cambridge. Harvard University Press. 1975.

Glazer, Nathan; Moynihan, Daniel Patrick and Schelling Corinne Saposs (eds.). *Ethnicity: Theory and Experience*. Cambridge. Harvard University Press. 1975.

Gogoi, Lila. *The Buranjis Historical Literature of Assam (A Critical Survey).* Guwahati. Omsons Publications. 1986.

Gogoi, Padmeshwar. *The Tai and the Tai Kingdoms with a Fuller Treatment of the Tai-Ahom Kingdom in the Brahmaputra Valley*. Guwahati. Lawyer's Book Stall. 1968.

Gogoi, Troilukya. *Reservation Policy and OBC Movement in Assam*. Kolkata. Maulana Abdul Kalam Azad Institute of Asian Studies. 2005.

Gohain, Hiren. "Bodo Stir in Perspective". *Economic and Political Weekly.* Vol. 24, No.25. 1989. pp. 1377- 1379.

___. "Extremist Challenge and Indian State: The Case of Assam". *Economic and Political Weekly*. August 3, 1996. Vol. 31, No. 31. pp. 2066-2068.

Gohain, Hiren. "Little Nationalism Turned Chauvinist a Comment". *Economic and Political Weekly*. Vol. 16, No. 9. February 28, 1981. pp. 339-340.

___. "Origins of the Assamese Middle Class". *Social Scientist*. Vol. 2, No. 1. Aug 1973. pp. 11-26.

Gopalkrishnan, R. *Assam Land and People*. New Delhi. Omsons Publication. 2000.

Gordon, Colin (ed.). Foucault, Michel. *Power/Knowledge: Selected Interviews and Other Writings 1972-1977.* New York. Pantheon. 1980. pp. 78-108.

Goswami, Atul. "Assam's Industrial Development Urgency of New Direction". *Economic and Political Weekly*. Vol. 16, No. 21. May 23, 1981. pp. 953-956.

Goswami, Praphulladatta. *Ballads and Tales of Assam A Study of the Folklore of Assam*. Gauhati. Department of Publication University of Gauhati. 1960.

Government of Assam Employment Review Committee Report on Some aspects of Employment, Welfare Activities and Economic Development vis-a-vis Tea Industry in Assam,1991. Guwahati. Government of Assam. 1991.

Greetz, Clifford. "The Integrative Revolution". *Old Societies and New States.* New York. Free Press. 1963.

Guha, Amalendu. "Little Nationalism Turned Chauvinist, Assam's Anti-foreigner Upsurge, 1979-1980". *Economic and Political Weekly*. Special Number. Vol. 15, No. 41-43. October 1980. pp. 1699, 1701, 1703, 1705-1707, 1709-1711, 1713, 1715, 1717, 1719-1720.

___. *Medieval and Early Colonial Assam: Society and Polity*. Calcutta. K.P. Bagchi and Company. 1991.

___. *Planter-Raj to Swaraj: Freedom Struggle and Electoral Politics in Assam, 1826-1947*. New Delhi. People's Publishing House. 1977.

Guha, B.S. and P.C. Basu. *Anthropological Bulletin of the Zoological Survey of India*, No. I. Calcutta 1929. pg. II.

Guha, Sumit. "The Politics of Identity and Enumeration in India c. 1600-1990". *Comparative Studies in Society and History*. Vol.15, No. 1. January 2003. pp. 148-167.

Gupta, Shekhar. *Assam: A Valley Divided.* Delhi. Vikas Publishing House. 1984.

Hall, Stuart. "The New Ethnicities". J. Donald and A. Rattansi (eds.). *Race, Culture andDifference*. London. Sage. 1992. pp. 441-449.

Hamilton, Francis. *An account of Assam: with Some Notices Concerning the Neighbouring Territories. First compiled in 1807-1814*. Gauhati. Govt. of Assam in the Dept. of Historical and Antiquarian Studies, NarayaniHandiqui Historical Institute. 1940.

Handelman, Don. "The Organisation of Ethnicity". *Ethnic Groups*. Vol. 1. 1977.pp. 187-200.

Hannan, M.T. "The Dynamics of Ethnic Boundaries in Modern States". J.W. Meyer and M.T. Hannan (eds.). *National Development and the World System.* Chicago. University of Chicago Press. 1979.

Hardgrave, Robert and Stanley Kochanek. *India: Government and Politics in a Developing Nation.* San Diego: Harcourt Brace Jovanovich. 1986.

Hastings, James (ed.). *Encyclopaedia of Religion and Ethics.* Vol. 2. New York. Charles Scribner's Sons. 1922.

Hazarika, Bijay Bhushan. *Political Life in Assam during the Nineteenth Century.* Delhi. Gian Publication House. 1987.

Hechter, M. *Internal Colonialism: The Celtic Fringe in British National Development 1536-1966.* Berkeley. University California Press. 1975.

History of Failure of Central Govt. and State Govt. to Implement the Assam Accord. Guwahati. All Assam Students Union. (no date available).

Hluna, John V. *History and Ethnic Identity formation in North East India.* New Delhi. Concept Publishing Co. 2013.

Hockings, Paul (ed.).*Encyclopedia of World Cultures.* Volume III. Boston. G.K. Hall and Company. 1992.

Horowitz, D. "Ethnic Identity". Glazer, N. and Moyniban, D. (eds.). *Ethnicity: Theory and Experience.* Cambridge. Harvard University Press. 1975.

Hunter, Brian (ed.) *The Statesman's Year Book.* 128th ed. 1991-92. Martin's Press. New York. 1991.

Hussain, Imdad. *The Guwahati Declaration and the Road to Peace in Assam.* New Delhi. Akansha Publications. 2005.

Hussain, Monirul. "Tribal Movement for Autonomous state in Assam". *Economic and Political Weekly.* Vol. 22, No. 32. August 8, 1987. pp. 1329-1332.

___. *The Assam Movement: Class, Ideology and Identity.* Delhi. Manak Publications. 1993.

Hutchinson, John and Anthony D Smith (eds.). *Nationalism.* New York. Oxford University Press. 1994.

Hutchinson, John and Anthony D Smith. *Ethnicity.* New York. Oxford University Press. 1996.

Hutchinson, John. *Modern Nationalism.* London. Fontana Press. 1994.

Hutton, J.H. "Assam and the Pacific". *Man in India.* Volume VII. 1927. pp. 257-262.

___. *AngamiNagas: With Some Notes on the Neighbouring Tribes*. London. MacMillan and Co. 1921.

___. Some Astronomical Beliefs in Assam. *Folklore Transaction of Folklore Society*. Vol. 36, No. 2. June 1925. pp.113-131.

Imperial Gazetteer of India: Provincial Series-Eastern Bengal and Assam. New Delhi. Usha Publications. 1989.

Joshi, Mahesh. *Assam: the Indian Conflict*. New Delhi. Prachi. 1981.

Kakati, S.C. *Discovery of Assam*. Gauhati. The Author. 1954.

Kakoti, B.K. *Assamese, Its Formation and Development*. Guwahati. Lawyers book Stall. 1972.

Kamath, M.V. "Neglected Assam". *The Illustrated Weekly of India*. January20-26, 1980. pg. 9.

Kamrupee. "AGP Facing Multiple Challenges". *Economic and Political Weekly*. November 18, 1989. Vol. 24, No. 46. pp. 2533-2534.

Kar, Bodhisattva. "When was the Postcolonial? A History of Policing Impossible Line". Baruah, Sanjib (ed.) *Beyond Counter-Insurgency Breaking the Impasse in Northeast India*. New Delhi. Oxford University Press. 2009.

Kikon, Dolly. "What is Unique about Naga History". *Economic and Political Weekly*. Vol. 1. No. 35. 29 August 2015. Pp. 10-13.

Kosambi, D.D. *The Culture and Civilization of Ancient India*. New Delhi. Vikash Publishing House. 1970.

Kurien, Prema A. *Kaleidoscopic Ethnicity: International Migration and the Reconstruction of Community Identities in India*. New Delhi. Oxford University Press. 2002.

Kymlicka, Will and Wayne Norman (Eds.). *Citizenship in Diverse Societies*. Oxford. Oxford University Press. 2000.

Light, I.H. *Ethnic Enterprise in America*. Berkeley. University California Press. 1972.

Mahanta, Nani Gopal. "Assam: Politics of Peace-Making". *Economic and Political Weekly*. Vol. 40, No. 1. January 1-7, 2005. pp. 25-27.

Mahanta, Prafulla Kumar. *The Tussle between the Citizens and Foreigners in Assam*. New Delhi. Vikas Publishing House. 1986.

Maheswari, Shriram. *The Census Administration under the British Raj and After*. New Delhi. Concept Publishing Company. 1996.

Majumdar, R.C, A.K Majumdar and D.K Ghose (eds.). *The History and Culture of the Indian People*. Vol. 9. British Paramountcy and Indian Renaissance. Bombay. Bharatiya Vidya Bhaban. 1970.

Mallick, Ross. *Development, Ethnicity and Human Rights in South Asia.* New Delhi. Sage Publication. 1998.

Mamdani, Mahmood. *When Victims Become Killers: Colonialism, Nativism, and the Genocide in Rwanda.* New Jersey. Princeton University Press. 2001.

Manju Singh. *Assam. Politics of Migration & Quest for Identity.* Jaipur. Anita Publication. 1990.

Manor, James. "Ethnicity' and Politics in India". *International Affairs (Royal Institute of International Affairs 1944-).* Vol. 72, No. 3. Ethnicity and International Relations. 1996. pp. 459-475.

Marvah, Ved. *Uncivil Wars: Pathology of Terrorism in India.* New Delhi. Harper Collins Publisher. 1997.

Miles, Moffatt A.J. *Report on the Province of Assam.* Gauhati. Publication Board, Assam. 1984. (first published 1854).

Misra, Madhu Sudan. *Politics of Regionalism in India with Special Reference to Punjab.* New Delhi. Deep and Deep Publications. 1998.

Misra, Sanghamitra. *Becoming a Borderland: The Politics of Space and Identity in Colonial Northeastern India.* New Delhi. Routledge Chapman & Hall. 2011.

Misra, Tilottama and Misra, Udayon. "Movements for Autonomy in India's North- East". Sathyamurthy, T.V. (ed.). *Region, Religion, Caste, Gender and Culture in Contemporary India.* Vol. 3. New Delhi. Oxford University Press. 1998. pp. 107-144.

Misra, Tilottoma. "Assam: A Colonial Hinterland". *Economic and Political Weekly.* Vol 15, No. 32. August 1980. pp. 1357-1359, 1361-1364.

Misra, Tilottoma. *Literature and Society in Assam: A Study of the Assamese Renaissance.* Guwahati. Omsons. 1987.

Misra, Udayaon. "The Transformation of Assamese Identity: A Historical Survey". *H.K. Barpujari Endowment Lecture (4).* Shillong. The North East India History Association. 2001.

___. "All Assam Students' Union: Crisis of Identity". *Economic and Political Weekly.* Vol. 22, No. 13. March 28, 1987. pp. 535-536.

___. "Immigration and Identity Transformation in Assam." *Economic and Political Weekly.* 22-28 May, 1999. Vol. 34, No. 2. pp. 1264-1271.

___. "No Tears for the Liberators". *Economic and Political Weekly.* Vol. 28, No. 32/33. August 7-14, 1993. pp. 1635-1636.

___. "Roll Call of the Dead". *Economic and Political Weekly*. 14-20. Vol. 37, No. 37. September 14, 2002.pp. 3781-3785.

___. "Set for Confrontation". *Economic and Political Weekly*. Vol. 14, No. 49. December 8, 1979. pp. 1993-1994.

___. "Sub-national Challenges to Indian State: An Assamese Perspective". *Economic and Political Weekly*. May 13, 2000. Vol. 35, No. 20. pp. 1727-1730.

___. *The Periphery Strikes Back: Challenges to the Nation-State in Assam and Nagaland.* Shimla. Indian Institute of Advanced Study. 2000.

___. *The Transformation of Assamese Identity: A Historical Survey*. Shillong. The North East India History Association. 2001.

Mitra, Subrata K. "The Rational Politics of Cultural Nationalism: Subnational Movements of South Asia in Comparative Perspective". *British Journal of Political Science.* Vol. 25, No. 1. Jan 1995. pp. 57-77.

Mittal, A.C. and Sharma, J.B. *Tribal movement, Politics, and Religion in India.* New Delhi. Radha Publications. 1998.

Mittra, Rathin and Barun Das Gupta (ed.). *A Common Perspective for North-East India*. Pannalal Das Gupta. Navana Printing Works. 1967.

Moffatt, Mills A.J. *Report on the Province of Assam (1854).* Guwahati Publication Board. Assam. 1984.

Mohanty, Manoranjan, Mukherji, Partha N and OlleTornquist. *People's Rights:Social Movements and the States in the Third World*. New Delhi, Sage Publication. 1998.

Molla, M.K.V. *(The) New Province of Eastern Bengal and Assam, 1905-1911.* Bangladesh. The Institute of Bangladesh Studies. 1981.

Mondal, Anshuman A. *Nationalism and Post-Colonial Identity: Culture and Ideology in India and Egypt*. London. Routledge. 2003.

Moore, Rev. P.H. "General View of Assam". *The Assam Mission of the American Baptist Missionary Union: papers and discussions of the jubilee conference held in Nowgong, December 18-29, 1886 (1887).* Guwahati. Spectrum Publications. 1992.

Mukherjee, Dilip. "Assam Reorganization". *Asian Survey*. Vol. 9, No. 4. April 1969. pp. 297-311.

Nag, Sajal. *Roots of Ethnic Conflict: Nationality Question in North East India*. New Delhi. Manohar. 1990.

Nagel, Joane. "Constructing Ethnicity: Creating and Recreating Ethnic Identity and Culture". Social *Problems*. Vol. 41, No. 1. Special Issues on Immigration, Race and Ethnicity in America. February 1994. pp. 152-176.

Nairn, T. *The Break-Up of Britain*. London. New Left Books. 1977.

Narzary, Cbaran. *The Bodos: Their Plight and Aspiration*. 1976. (no other information available).

Narzi, Bhaben. *Bodo-Kacharir Samaj Aru Sanskriti* (Assamese). Guwahati. Bina Library. 1985.

Nath, R.M. *The Back-ground of Assamese Culture*. Gauhati. Datta Baruah and Co. 1948.

Neog, Maheswar. *Anandaram Dhekiyal Phukan*. New Delhi. 1980.

Newcomer, Peter. "The Nuer are Dinka". *Man*. Vol 7, No. 1. 1972. pp. 5-11.

Novati Giampaolo Calchi. "Postcolonial State versus Ethnicity: A Reassessment of Decolonization in Africa". *Latin American Perspectives*. Vol. 23, No. 2. Ethnicity and class in Latin America. 1996. pp. 130-138.

Olzak, Susan. "Contemporary Ethnic Mobilization". *Annual Review of Sociology*. Vol. 9. 1983. pp. 355-374.

Omvedt, Gail. "Little Nationalism Turned Chauvinist A Comment". *Economic and Political Weekly*. March 28, 1981. Vol. 16, No. 13. pp. 589-590.

Oommen, T. K. *Citizenship, Nationality and Ethnicity: Reconciling Competing Identities*. Cambridge. Polity Press. 1997.

Osborne, Peter and Stella Sandford (eds.). *Philosophies of Race and Ethnicity*. London. Continuum. 2000.

Pakem, B. *Nationality, Ethnicity and Cultural Identity in North-East India*. Guwahati. Omsons Publications. 1990.

Palanithurai G. and Thandavan R. *Ethnic Movement in India*. Delhi. Kanishka Publishing House. 2003.

Pandey, Onkareshwar. "ISI and New Wave of Islamic Militancy in the NE". *Dialogue*. Vol. 3, No.3. March 2002.

Phukan, Niranjan. "Decline of ULFA". *Economic and Political Weekly*. Vol. 28, No. 38. September 18, 1993. pp. 2014.

Prabhakara, M.S. "Changing Face of ULFA". *Hindu*. January 17, 1993. pg. 9.

___. "Rebels Acquiring Legitimacy". *The Hindu*. Chennai. March 9, 1990.

Prakash, Gyan (ed.). *After Colonialism: Imperial Histories and Post-*

Colonial Displacements. New Jersey. Princeton University Press. 1994.

Pulloppillil, Thomas and Aluckal, Jacob. *The Bodos: Children of Bhullumbutter*. Guwahati. Spectrum Publications. 1997.

Puri, B.N. *Studies in Early History and administration in Assam*. Gauhati. Department of Publication Gauhati University. 1968.

Rafiabadi, Hamid Naseem. *Assam from Agitation to Accord*. New Delhi. Genuine Publications & Media. 1988.

Ranger, Terence (Ed.). *The Invention of Tradition*. Cambridge. Cambridge University Press. 1983.

Reid, Robert. *History of the Frontier Areas Bordering on Assam from 1883-1941*. Shillong. Assam Government Press. 1942.

Report on the Census of Assam for 1881. Calcutta. Office of the Superintendent of Government Printing. India. 1882.

Richards, Audrey. *The Multicultural State of East Africa*. Montreal: McGrill. Queens University Press. 1969.

Risley, Herbert and Crooke, William. *The People of India*. New Delhi. Asian Educational Service. 1915.

Robb, Peter. "The Colonial State and Constructions of Indian Identity: An Example of the Northeast Frontier in the 1880s." *Modern Asian Studies*. Vol. 31, No. 2. 1997.

Rokkan, S. *Citizens, Elections, and Parties*. New York. Rand McNally. 1970.

Rothschild, J. *Ethnopolitics: A Conceptual Framework*. New York. Columbia University Press. 1981.

Roy, David. *The Frontiers of North-East India*.Shillong. R.K. Press. 1947.

Said, Edward W. *Orientalism*. New York. Vintage Books. 1978.

Saikia, Nagen (ed.). *Assam and Assamese Mind*. Jorhat. 1980.

Sathyamurthy, T.V. (ed.). *Region, Religion, Caste, Gender and Culture in Contemporary India*. New Delhi. Oxford University Press. 1996.

Schermerhorn, Richard. *Comparative Ethnic Relations*. New York. Random House Inc. 1978.

Sen, Sipra. *Tribes and Castes of Assam: Anthropology and Sociology*. New Delhi. Gyan Publishing House. 1999.

Sengupta, Sarthak (ed.). *Peoples of North East India*. New Delhi. Gyan Publishing House. 1996.

Shamasastry, R. *Kautilya'sArthasastra*. Mysore. Wesleyan Press. 1929.

Sharma Hanjabam, Shukhdeba and Roy Burman J.J. *Social Dynamics in Contemporary North East India*. New Delhi. Concept Publishing Co. 2013.

Sharma, K.M. "The Assam Question- A Historical Perspective". *Economic and Political Weekly*. Vol. 15, No. 31. 2 August 1980. pp. 1321-1324.

Sharma, Chandan Kumar. *AxhomiyaKun? EkRajnoitik Samajtatwik Abalukan*. Guwahati. Span Publication. 2006.

Sharma, Chandan Kumar. "Genealogy Contested: Oral Discourse and Bodo Identity Construction." M.D.Muthukumaraswamy. (ed.). *Folklore as Discourse*. Chennai. National Folklore Support Centre. 2007.

___. "The Bodo Movement A Preliminary Enquiry into the Role of the Middle Class and the State." Phukon, Girin (ed.). *Political dynamics of North East India: essays in honour of professor Barrister Pakem*. New Delhi. South Asian Publishers. 2000.

Sharma, Kalpana. "The Killing Fields." *Times of India*, Sunday Review. June 10, 1990.

Sharma, Manorama. *Social and Economic Change in Assam: Middle Class Hegemony*. Delhi. Ajanta Publications. 1990.

Sharma, Suresh. *Tribal Identity and the Modern World*. New Delhi. Sage Publications. 1994.

Shashi, S.S. *Encyclopedia of Indian Tribes*. New Delhi. Anmol Publications. 1994.

Shastri, Biswanarayan and Promod Chandra Bhattacharya. *This is Assam*. Jorhat. Asam Sahitya Sabha. 1958.

Shils, Edward. "Primordial, Personal, Sacred and Civil Ties". *British Journal of Sociology*. 7. 1957. pp. II3-45.

Shimray, U. "Socio-Political Unrest in the Region Called North- East India". *Economic and Political Weekly*. 16-20. October 16, 2004. Vol. 39, No. 42. pp. 4637-4643.

Shourie, Arun. "Assam Elections: Come What May". *IndiaToday*. May 15, 1983.

Sillitoe K. and P.H. White. "Ethnic Group and the British Census: The Search for a Question." *Journal of the Royal Statistical Society. Series A. (Statistic in Society)*. Vol. 155, No. 1. 1992. pp. 141-163.

Singh, B.P. "North- East India: Demography, Culture and Identity Crisis." *Modern Asian Studies*. Vol. 21, No. 2. 1987. pp. 257-282.

Singh, Bhawani. *Politics of Alienation in Assam*. Delhi. Ajanta Publications. 1984.

Singh, K.S. *People of India*. New Delhi. Oxford University press. 1992.

Smith, A.D. *The Ethnic Revival*. Cambridge. Cambridge University Press. 1981.

___. *The Origins of Nation*. Oxford. Blackwell. 1986.

Srikant, H. "Militancy and Identity Politics in Assam". *Economic and Political Weekly*. November 18-24, 2000. pp. 4117-4119, 4121-4124.

Stavenhagen, Rodolfo. *Ethnic-Conflict and the Nation-State. Great Britain*. United Nations Research Institute of Social Development. 1996.

Stone, John and Dennis, Rutledge. *Race and Ethnicity Comparative and Theoretical Approaches*. Blackwell Publishing. Berlin. 2003.

Sturtevant, William. "Creek into Seminole." in Leacock, Eleanor B and Lurie, Nancy O (eds.) *NorthAmerican Indian in Historical Perspective*. New York, Random House. 1971.

Sujata, Bose and Ayesha Jalal. *Nationalism, Democracy and Development: State and Politics in India*. New Delhi. Oxford University Press. 1998.

Sword, Victor Hugo. *Baptists in Assam: A Century of Missionary Service 1836-1936*. Guwahati. Spectrum Publications. 1992.

Taher, Mohammad. "Pride of Being an Assamese". Saikia, Nagen (ed.). *Assam and the Assamese Mind*. Jorhat. Assam Sahitya Sabha. 1980.

Taylor, Charles and Amy Gutmann. *Multiculturalism: Examining the Politics of Recognition. Princeton*. Princeton University Press. 1994.

The Constitution of India. Article 342. New Delhi. Government of India. 1950.

Verghese, B.G. *India's Northeast Resurgent Ethnicity, Insurgency, Governance, Development*. New Delhi. Konark Publishers. 1996.

Visaria, Pravin and Leela Visaria, "India's population: Second and growing," *Population Bulletin*. Vol. 36, No. 4. October 1981.

Vos George de and Romanucci-Ross. *Ethnic Identity*. Chicago. University of Chicago Press. 1982.

Waddell, L.A. *The Tribes of the Brahmaputra Valley A Contribution on their Physical Types and Affinities*. Delhi. Sanskaran Prakashak. 1975. (First published in 1901).

Wallang, D.N.S. *Collection of Articles*. Shillong. (No other information available.)

Weber, Max. "Ethnic Groups". G. Roth and C. Wittich (eds.). *Economy and Society*. Los Angeles. University of California Press. 1978.

Weiner, Myron. "The Political Demography of Assam's Anti- Immigrant Movement". *Population and Development Review*. Vol. 9, No. 2. June 1983. pp. 279-292.

___. *Sons of the Soil: Migration and Ethnic Conflict in India*. Princeton. Princeton University Press. 1978.

Weiner, Myron. *When Migrants Succeed and Natives Fail*. Center for International Studies. Massachusetts Institute of Technology. Cambridge, Massachusetts. 1975.

Wright, Susan. "The Politicization of Culture". *Anthropology Today*. Vol. 14, No. 1. February 1998.

Yancey, W., E. Ericksen and R. Juliani. "Emergent Ethnicity: A Review and Reformulation". *American Sociology Review*. Vol 41. 1976. pp. 391-403.

Yinger, J. Milton. *Annual Review of Sociology*, Vol. 11. 1985.pp. 151-180.

- Akhup, Alex. "Identities and their Struggles in North East". New Delhi. Adivaani. 2015.
- Das, Gautam. "Insurgencies in North-East India: Moving Towards Resolution". New Delhi. Pentagon Press. 2013.
- Sharma Hanjabam, Shukhdeba and Roy Burman J.J. "Social Dynamics in Contemporary North East India". New Delhi. Concept Publishing Co. 2013.
- Misra, Sanghamitra. "Becoming a Borderland: The Politics of Space and Identity in Colonial Northeastern India". New Delhi. Routledge Chapman & Hall. 2011.
- Hluna, John V. "History and Ethnic Identity formation in North East India". New Delhi. Concept Publishing Co. 2013.

Index

O

P

Q

R